"Part of every pastor's faith-walk is wrestling with cultural issues that conflict with the clear teaching of Scripture. Ken Parker addresses some of the most difficult issues of this kind in the context of life in the United States. As you read *Elephants in the Church*, you learn quickly from a compassionate, reasonable, and sensible pastor that it is okay to struggle and doubt, so long as you embrace a biblical ethic.

"Dr. Parker walks readers through the process of making informed biblical choices on a full array of issues. To read this book is to learn from one who has wrestled with the hard questions while standing firm on a biblical foundation."

Dr. John Yeats
Executive Director, Missouri Baptist Convention
Recording Secretary, Southern Baptist Convention

"As a member of First Baptist Church (Kearney), I had the privilege of hearing Dr. Parker bring God's Word to life as he preached these messages. Rarely do sermons alone move the discipleship and obedience needle as much as the *Elephants in the Church* series. This is a must-read book for those questioning how to navigate contemporary cultural issues with absolute biblical clarity."

Dr. Rodney A. Harrison, President
Baptist Homes & Healthcare Ministries
Jefferson City, Missouri

"Few pastors know their congregation better than Ken Parker knows his. I have preached in his pulpit several times. His people know him, love him, and trust him. They have learned he speaks to them where they really are. Ken knows what the elephants in the room are. He has something to say worth hearing."

Dr. John Marshall, Retired Pastor
Second Baptist Church
Springfield, Missouri

"Many pastors have a tendency to turn a blind eye or a deaf ear to the current and critical issues in the church that desperately need to be addressed. Dr. Ken Parker would not be one of those who are muted. In his latest book, *Elephants in the Church*, Dr. Parker powerfully and prophetically takes those issues on with insight and application. You will be edified and enriched by reading *Elephants in the Church*."

Dr. Steve Dighton, Pastor Emeritus
Lenexa Baptist Church
Lenexa, Kansas

"Having followed Dr. Parker's ministry for many years, I was glad to see him address the important subjects of this book. The church needs sound instruction, and Dr. Parker provides it with honesty and tact. He combines theological insight with practical information to aid Christians in thinking about modern challenges. This book will be a useful resource and a helpful tool for individual or group study."

Jon Duncan, Attorney
Chairman, First Baptist Church of Kearney Pastor Search Committee

"*Elephants in the Church* by Dr. Ken Parker offers insight into many of the issues we face today. Using his extensive background in pastoring a congregation for many years and serving as a professor at Midwestern Baptist Theological Seminary, Dr. Parker's book is more like a conversation with a friend as he gives background lessons on a variety of topics and includes personal illustrations that make this book an enriching read. Using historical background and thoughtful analysis, he ends each chapter with thought-provoking encouragement. Who doesn't need readable, relatable theology? I highly recommend Dr. Parker's book for a class study or for an individual who just wants to learn more about the 'elephants' we all encounter."

Patricia Kern, CFRE
Kearney, Missouri

———

"In a time when there is a lack of biblically sound discipleship materials, I am pleased to recommend *Elephants in the Church*. Dr. Parker has put together a treasure trove of information that addresses contemporary topics that need a careful biblical response. Whether you are a mature disciple or a young believer, this work is an indispensable resource that can be used in one-on-one discipleship or in group Bible studies. I can't wait to utilize this resource with university students at Hannibal-LaGrange University!"

Dr. Anthony W. Allen, President
Hannibal-LaGrange University

———

"This is a book about good news! Dr. Parker asks and answers questions about important contemporary issues from an unapologetically biblical perspective. He speaks the truth and brings a refreshing clarity about our faith, articulating in a winsome manner what we believe and why it matters. This book is a great resource for all who have a desire to more effectively engage contemporary culture from a biblical worldview."

Dr. Keith Ross, President
Missouri Baptist University
St. Louis, Missouri

"Dr. Parker has produced an inestimable work with this contribution. We rarely find the skillful approach with which he blends depth of theological truth with the wisdom of a practitioner in popular writings for the church. While the selected topics are diverse, they represent some of the most crucial issues facing the community of faith today. His subtle use of humor makes the work a pleasure to read. I commend this book to anyone engaged in the work of the gospel. It will be a help to the Kingdom for generations to come."

Dr. Thomas Willoughby, Assistant Professor of Christian Studies
North Greenville University
Tigersville, South Carolina

"Dr. Ken Parker has produced a timely, frank, and readable love letter to Christians in this book. His earnest efforts to rightly divide God's Word — wherever that takes us — is balanced with pastoral love and self-deprecating humor. The issues Ken addresses are crucial, and often controversial, but he provides us with a clear biblical perspective in refreshingly contemporary language."

Rob Phillips, Director, Ministry Support & Apologetics
Missouri Baptist Convention

ELEPHANTS IN THE ~~ROOM~~ CHURCH

WHAT THE BIBLE SAYS ABOUT 14 CONTEMPORARY ISSUES

KEN PARKER

high street press

Acknowledgments:

Executive editor: Dr. John Yeats
Editor: Rob Phillips
Cover design and graphics: Leah England
Layout: Brianna Boes
Production management: Leah England
Kindle production: Brianna Boes
Proofreading: Nancy Phillips, Christie Dowell

High Street Press is the publishing arm of the Missouri Baptist Convention (MBC) and exists because of the generous support of Missouri Baptists through the Cooperative Program. To learn more about the MBC and the way its nearly 1,800 affiliated churches cooperate voluntarily for the sake of the gospel, visit mobaptist.org.

DEDICATION

To the grandest grandchildren a man could ever have:
Ryann Kay, Hudson James, and Jack Andrew Parker

But from eternity to eternity
the Lord's faithful love is toward those who fear him,
and his righteousness toward the grandchildren
of those who keep his covenant,
who remember to observe his precepts.
Psalm 103:17-18 (CSB)

CONTENTS

FOREWORD

Ministry in the 21st century is not for the faint of heart. Our generation, and those who minister to it, daily encounter a rapidly changing culture marked by increasing secularization and hostility to biblical truth.

Indeed, issues such as human sexuality, gender, marriage, and a host of other flashpoints have been rapidly redefined before our very eyes. Such issues that were once socially settled based upon the clear teaching of Scripture are now up for reimagination and renegotiation in the culture and, unfortunately, often in the church as well.

Additionally, issues that have confronted the church for many decades remain before local congregations. Questions such as: Why trust the Bible? What's wrong with gambling? And, of course, the never-ending struggle for the sanctity of human life remains front and center.

What is more, the church continues to grapple with issues like social media and its impact on how we interact with one another, the growing acceptance of alcohol and legalized marijuana, and the pressing issues of racism and sexism.

All of this is to say, those who care about the church of the Lord Jesus Christ and who want to be faithful as they serve within it, need wise and faithful ministers to whom they can look. I'm thankful that Dr. Ken Parker is one such minister and that he is willing to impart his wisdom to the reader through *Elephants in the Church: What the Bible Says About 14 Contemporary Issues*.

And it is urgently important that we have this resource. For one of the more demoralizing aspects of local church ministry is the realization that worldly ideas, sooner or later, will most likely show up within the local church. It's simply impossible to preach, no matter how long the sermon, a world's worth of influence out of your people in Sunday morning worship. But, to be clear, that is exactly what the minister is called to do. We are called to faithfully exposit God's Word and bring it to bear in the lives of our people.

Yet, as we do that we will find ourselves again and again and again needing to speak to pressing issues of concern. Speaking to these issues with biblical clarity, personal courage, and Christian grace is a delicate balance to maintain. But Dr. Parker does just that, both in the context of this book and throughout his broader life in ministry.

In fact, Dr. Parker has become well known in the state of Missouri and beyond as just such a pastor. He is not only faithful to his congregation, but he is a faithful encourager to other ministers — and other Christians — as they seek to be faithful to the Lord's call on their lives.

To that end, Dr. Parker has authored this book. Whether you are a new believer with legitimate questions, an established believer who is seeking to be better equipped to give a defense for the hope that is within you, or a young minister seeking to lead your church through these knotty matters, I heartily commend this book, and the author who penned it, to you.

Jason K. Allen, Ph.D.
President
Midwestern Baptist Theological Seminary

INTRODUCTION

I did some really stupid and sinful stuff when I was younger. Now that I've got that off my chest ... can we talk? I still fight to keep from doing stupid and sinful stuff. I tell you this so you'll know that what you're about to read are not the words of someone who thinks he's "speaking from Sinai." It was, and is, reading and then applying the truth of the Bible that keeps me from being a whole lot worse. So, I'm grateful to point all of us to some of what the Bible records.

One of my first interactions with the Bible took place when my mother taught me my first memory verse. I was about three years old. It was Genesis 1:27. Back then, most of us used the King James Version: *"So God created man in his own image, in the image of God created he him; male and female created he them."* I think I memorized the verse for a sticker, or a popsicle, or some little prize we were to receive in Sunday School. Who gives kids popsicles before noon, anyway?

My mother had a different agenda. Unbeknownst to me, she was countering much of what I would be taught in school related to my own origin. I didn't just *evolve*; I was *created*! And that's an important distinction. With that one verse, she reinforced God's gift of gender. I was created a male. With that one verse, she taught me there is a God in charge of the universe, and I should yield myself to him. With that one verse, she introduced me to the reality that I am an image-bearer of God.

While I didn't understand it at the time, that one act of Christian parenting — having me memorize a key verse — became foundational to my life as a follower of Jesus. And it's foundational to the book you hold. While I preached a series of sermons for more than a year on cultural hot topics, fourteen messages were chosen for this book. The impetus for the sermon series (and now for the book) was to offer Christians a readily accessible guide to understand and defend a biblical worldview as it intersects with a lot of unbiblical ideology prevalent in the culture (think 1 Pet. 3:15).

I owe a tremendous debt of gratitude to a lot of people who have invested in my life. So, I'd like to think of this as some small labor of love in their honor. Space is too limited to list them all. Certainly, I want to thank my parents, Kin and Betty Parker (in heaven now), and my wife, Lori, who has supported me in too many ways to number; my sons, who taught me patience (that's a joke ... kind of); my daughter-in-law, who made it possible for me to have the title "Grandpa;" my sisters, who always encourage their "little brother;" the churches I've served; my staff; the wonderful First Baptist Church of Kearney family; the schools I've attended; the students and colleagues at the seminary where I teach; and countless friends.

So, I write as one desiring to pass along tidbits of wisdom I've been fortunate enough to have picked up along the way. I'm a pastor and a professor, so I write from that angle. But please don't miss the fact that I'm writing as a father and a grandfather, as well. The names of the children to whom this book is dedicated are names I carry on my heart day in and day out. I want them to learn the truths of the Christian faith. I want them to "buck the system" of an "anything goes" culture. And if I can play some small role in helping with that, I've fulfilled a large percentage of my life's purpose.

I want to say a special word of thanks to Dr. John Yeats for getting the wheels turning for this project in the first place. Thanks to Rob Phillips, my editor, for the countless ways he's helped with this. And I want to thank some of my other faith heroes, as well. Some of them are still here; some of them are in that "great cloud of witnesses." I'm grateful for men of God who have believed the Word and had the courage to proclaim it: Rev. Kenneth Hall (my childhood pastor); Dr. Dale Prince (the first pastor with whom I served); Rev. Bucky Phillips, who taught me to be myself while living for Jesus; and powerful Christian communicators like Dr. Adrian Rogers, Dr. Steve Brown, Dr. Fred Luter, Dr. Jason Allen, Dr. Alistair Begg, and, of course, my own father, who surrendered his life to Jesus at fifty-three years of age and spent the rest of his years making up for lost time.

So, pull up a chair, get a cup of coffee, and let's tackle some elephants together ...

Dr. Kenneth J. Parker
The Pastor's Study
First Baptist Church
Kearney, Missouri

WHY TRUST THE BIBLE?

IF YOU BELIEVE IN JESUS, WHY WOULDN'T YOU BELIEVE WHAT HE BELIEVED?

I'm a sucker for sentimental poetry. I like sentimental poems and sad songs. There's a great old poem about the Scripture that I love. The author is anonymous, which is probably best. It's called *The Precious Bible* and it reads:

> *Though the cover is worn*
> *And the pages are torn,*
> *And though places bear traces of tears,*
> *Yet more precious than gold*
> *Is the Book, worn and old,*
> *That can shatter and scatter my fears.*
>
> *When I prayerfully look*
> *In the precious old Book,*
> *Many pleasures and treasures I see;*
> *Many tokens of love*
> *From the Father above,*
> *Who is nearest and dearest to me.*

This old Book is my guide,
'Tis a friend by my side,
It will lighten and brighten my way;
And each promise I find
Soothes and gladdens my mind
As I read it and heed it today.[1]

I love that! I especially love the last line: "As I read it and heed it today." I know a lot of Christians who own lots of Bibles. They say great things to defend the Bible. They make a big deal about making sure people know they believe the Bible. They get angry when anyone denigrates the Bible. They even say things they *think* are in the Bible that really aren't. They do all kinds of things except actually *read* the Bible and *heed* the Bible. And frankly, that doesn't make a whole lot of sense to me.

I'm concerned about biblical illiteracy, not just in the world, but more critically within the church. I'm further concerned that a lot of believers aren't well-versed enough in Christian doctrine to offer a ready defense for the Bible's teaching. I think it's important that we do what we can to understand the Bible.

A lot of people think the Bible is some sort of mystery reserved only for pastors. Not so! Thankfully, not so! Just as there are rules to interpret Shakespeare, much more importantly there are rules of biblical interpretation.

With the advent of *angry atheism* in our country, a lot of atheists try to argue rather than converse (and Christians are sometimes guilty of this, too, by the way). But they try to stump Christians about the Bible. They say things like, "You actually believe that? Don't you know that was written by men?" And unless Christians have thought it through or been trained to talk about how the Bible actually came to be, they sometimes act as if they're blown away. Well, of course the Bible was written by people!

Sometimes people point out what they believe to be inaccuracies or contradictions in the Bible. I don't get rattled about that at all. You shouldn't, either. There are good explanations for these challenges.

And for the record, don't worry about defending God. I know Peter reminds us to offer a defense for the hope that we have (1 Pet. 3:15), but you don't have to go to bat for God. He's been stepping up to the plate long before you and I came on the scene.

When people say things like, "If God really existed and really loved people, then why ... (you fill in the blank)?" You don't have to defend God. His thoughts and his ways are higher than ours. Look at what God said about his own thoughts through Isaiah the prophet:

> *For my thoughts are not your thoughts, neither are your ways my ways, declares the LORD. For as the heavens are higher than the earth, so are my ways higher than your ways and my thoughts than your thoughts (Isa. 55:8-9).*

But we ought to be able to converse about the Bible. We ought to know why we believe what we say we believe. We ought to have some understanding of how we received the Bible in the first place, as well as why it plays a prominent role in our lives.

Let's look at a passage in the Gospel of Luke to continue this conversation:

> *As they were talking about these things, Jesus himself stood among them, and said to them, "Peace to you!" But they were startled and frightened and thought they saw a spirit. And he said to them, "Why are you troubled, and why do doubts arise in your hearts? See my hands and my feet, that it is I myself. Touch me, and see. For a spirit does not have flesh and bones as you see that I have." And when he had said this, he showed them his hands and his feet. And while they still disbelieved for joy and were marveling, he said to them, "Have you anything here to eat?" They gave him a piece of broiled fish, and he took it and ate before them.*
>
> *Then he said to them, "These are my words that I spoke to you while I was still with you, that everything written about me in the Law of Moses and the Prophets and the Psalms must be fulfilled." Then he opened their minds to understand the Scriptures, and said to them, "Thus it is written, that the Christ should suffer and on the third day rise from the dead, and*

that repentance for the forgiveness of sins should be proclaimed in his name to all nations, beginning from Jerusalem. You are witnesses of these things. And behold, I am sending the promise of my Father upon you. But stay in the city until you are clothed with power from on high" (Luke 24:36-49).

Most often, when I talk about my belief in the Bible — or preach or write about it — I appeal to 2 Timothy 3:16, where Paul reminds us that *"All Scripture is breathed out by God ..."* I love that we can read that verse. But there are other places in Scripture we can go to be assured that the Bible is, in fact, the Word of God, and therefore, trustworthy. So, let me start with Jesus.

I TRUST THE BIBLE BECAUSE OF JESUS' WORDS

And he said to them, "These are my words that I spoke to you while I was still with you, that everything written about me in the Law of Moses and the Prophets and the Psalms must be fulfilled" (Luke 24:44).

In everything you note about the Bible, please see that it contains the words of Jesus. Let me clarify. The context here is Jesus talking with his disciples post-resurrection. In fact, he is about to be taken up to heaven. When Jesus refers to *"my words,"* he's talking about what he has said regarding his death and resurrection. So, the Bible has recorded these words of Jesus.

Throughout the Gospel accounts, we're privileged to read the words of Jesus, which we know to be the very words of God. Remember, Jesus *is* God; he is God in the flesh. So whatever Jesus says is the Word of God, and in fact everything in the Bible is the Word of God. So just to be clear, the Bible doesn't just *contain* the Word of God; the Bible *is* the Word of God.

What Moses records about creation in Genesis is the Word of God, and what Jesus says about his return in Matthew's Gospel is the Word of God. In order for something to be the Word of God, it doesn't have to be printed in red in the New Testament. The Old Testament is just as much the Word of God as are the words of Jesus in the New Testament.

If you get that, and if you believe that, it saves you a lot of grief in terms of understanding truth. The Old Testament most certainly points to Jesus, and the New Testament shows the fulfillment of the Old Testament's prophecies about Jesus, but they are equally the Word of God. At least Jesus thought so. And if you believe Jesus, you should believe what he believed, right?

Consider the Scripture Jesus learned as a child. It wasn't Romans or Revelation; it was the Old Testament. That's obvious, or should be, because the New Testament had not yet been written.

But then Jesus says in Luke 24 that *"everything written about me in the Law of Moses and the Prophets and the Psalms must be fulfilled."* The Law of Moses, the Prophets, and the Psalms simply represent the three major divisions of the Hebrew Bible. Jesus is doing for the disciples what he had done for the two on the road to Emmaus (Luke 24:13-35); he is explaining the Scriptures to them.

The point is this: Jesus explains the Scriptures because he believes them to be the Word of God. I believe in the verbal plenary inspiration of Scripture. By *verbal*, I mean every word is inspired, and by *plenary*, I mean all parts — not some — are fully authoritative. One of the most convincing arguments for my belief is the fact that Jesus regarded his Bible as such. Jesus constantly appeals to the Scriptures as authoritative. How often he says to his detractors, *"Have you not read?"* or *"It is written,"* or *"Search the Scriptures ..."*

Consider John 5:39. Speaking to the Jews, Jesus says, *"You search the Scriptures because you think that in them you have eternal life; and it is they that bear witness about me ..."* Jesus reminds them that the Scriptures, as the written Word of God, point to him as the Living Word of God.

I TRUST THE BIBLE BECAUSE JESUS TRUSTED THE BIBLE

Look at this again:

> *And he said to them, "These are my words that I spoke to you while I was still with you, that everything written about me in the Law of Moses and the Prophets and the Psalms must be fulfilled"* (Luke 24:44).

We've seen already what Jesus believed. He believed in the Hebrew Scriptures, the Old Testament, as the Word of God. That was his Bible. His words to that effect cause me to also believe the Bible. If Jesus is God, and I believe he is, then whatever he says about anything — including Scripture — is right. I believe because Jesus believed.

Do you know why I believe what I do about creation — that is, why I believe God created everything in six days, and on the seventh day he rested, just as the Book of Genesis records? Because that's what Jesus believed!

I have a friend who is somewhat troubled because each time I mention gay marriage, I say "so-called gay marriage." He says that's demeaning. I suppose some people could see it that way. Do you know why I say it that way? Because there's no such thing as gay marriage in the sight of God. It really is only "so-called." I'm not out to be offensive, but the truth is that Christians who truly accept Scripture recognize marriage is only a man/woman arrangement. That's it. There's no such thing as gay marriage in the eyes of God.

I know our culture and our courts recognize it, but I can't, because God doesn't. How do I know that? Because when Jesus is asked about divorce, he only legitimizes what the Book of Genesis legitimizes, and that is one man and one woman in marriage. I'm not picking on homosexuality. In fact, when we talk about polygamy among hetero-sexuals in today's culture, that's not really *multiple marriages*; that's one marriage and a lot of adultery. Do you see what I'm saying?

The reason I see it that way is not because I want to be antagonis-tic; it's because of what Scripture clearly defines. I don't care who tries to say otherwise. King Jesus says marriage is for a man and a woman. You don't have to believe that. But if you believe in Jesus, why wouldn't you believe what Jesus believed?

Let me offer a word of caution here. One reason I feel compelled to remind us often about our belief in the Bible is because even among so-called (there's that phrase again) Bible-believing people, *waffling* is the word of the day. Let me be clear: I'm not concerned about minor issues of interpretation. We know these are present. Some people see the world coming to its appropriate end one way; others see it happening another way. The key is that we believe God is in charge of it, regardless.

So, we know there are varying interpretations of some things. These are not my concern. My concern is that some people calling themselves "Christians" have abandoned the very basics the Lord of the church (Jesus) has made clear as bedrock, foundational issues for our faith.

For example, whereas Christians used to stand strong on moral issues, these days far too many do not. Because they're concerned about acceptance, or they want to avoid conflict, they no longer stand on Scripture. Rather, they seek to explain it away so as to be acceptable in the culture's eyes. That's the contemporary version of selling one's birthright!

There are so-called (there's that phrase again) churches that say "Jesus is our way to get to God, but God may have a different path in mind for others." No. No, he doesn't! That's what I'm talking about. You can't say you belong to Jesus and not adhere to the Word of Jesus, which is the Word of God, which is the Bible.

I was in my early twenties when someone fully explained the process of how the Bible came into existence. And I determined right then and there I would make sure other people knew how it happened, too. That's so they wouldn't become victims of a culture that sometimes knows more about the basics of the Christian faith than Christians do, although their main agenda is to discredit the Christian faith.

I believe what I believe because of what Jesus believed. Jesus believed the Old Testament to be the Word of God. I do, too. So, whether we're talking about creation or so-called gay marriage, or drunkenness, I'm going to stay on the side where Jesus is standing.

The words Jesus utters don't contradict what has already been written in Scripture. Remember when he was at the Temple at the tender age of twelve, and how he showed astonishing knowledge of the content of Scripture? That knowledge only grew during his earthly life. And I promise, Jesus didn't waffle at any point because he was concerned about acceptance.

But Jesus didn't just believe the Old Testament. I believe he also set his seal of authority on the New Testament, as well. How could this be, since it wasn't yet written?

As W. A. Criswell masterfully notes in his book, *Why I Preach that the Bible is Literally True*, "The answer lies in the fact that Jesus placed His stamp of authority upon the writings of the apostles by anticipation."[2]

Look at John 14:26:

> *But the Helper, the Holy Spirit, whom the Father will send in my name, he will teach you all things and bring to your remembrance all that I have said to you.*

Here's the key: According to Jesus, the apostolic records don't merely feature what the apostles recall Jesus saying. No! We have the Holy Spirit's recollection of what Jesus said. And Jesus said the Spirit — who is God, the third person of the Trinity — is the one who ensures the faithful memory of the apostles.

I TRUST THE BIBLE BECAUSE IT TELLS THE TRUTH

Sanctify them in the truth; your word is truth (John 17:17).

You may ask, "Do you believe Jesus because the Bible speaks of him, or do you believe the Bible because Jesus says it's true?" My answer is, "Yes!"

I trust the Bible because the Bible tells the truth. We have witnessed its inherent power in what it does to clarify the need for God in our hearts. We don't just read the Bible; the Bible, in fact, reads us!

The prophecies contained in Scripture validate the Bible in their fulfillment. We see the power of God's Word to convert people, to guide people, to give peace to people, to sometimes give necessary unrest to people (you know the idea about "comfort the afflicted and afflict the comfortable"). The Bible's influence upon the human race is so massive, it cannot be fully measured.

These points alone may not seem sufficient for a person to say, "I trust the Bible." But when you see how God's Spirit has pointed a person to Jesus through the reading of Scripture, you begin to understand.

I believe that when we hear the Word, it can change us. Look at these verses:

For God so loved the world, that he gave his only Son, that whoever believes in him should not perish but have eternal life (John 3:16).

And they said, "Believe in the Lord Jesus, and you will be saved ..." (Acts 16:31).

Even though I walk through the valley of the shadow of death, I will fear no evil, for you are with me ... (Ps. 23:4).

In the beginning, God ... (Gen. 1:1).

Let not your hearts be troubled ... (John 14:1).

You have heard that it was said, "You shall love your neighbor and hate your enemy." But I say to you, Love your enemies and pray for those who persecute you ... (Matt. 5:43-44).

And behold, I am with you always, to the end of the age (Matt. 28:20).

Trust in the LORD with all your heart, and do not lean on your own understanding. In all your ways acknowledge him, and he will make straight your paths (Prov. 3:5-6).

He will wipe away every tear from their eyes, and death shall be no more, neither shall there be mourning, nor crying, nor pain anymore, for the former things have passed away (Rev. 21:4).

You see, there is great power in the Bible. The writer of Hebrews tells us:

For the word of God is living and active, sharper than any two-edged sword, piercing to the division of soul and of spirit, of joints and of marrow, and discerning the thoughts and intentions of the heart (Heb. 4:12).

A doctor was won to Christ under the preaching of Dwight L. Moody. Someone asked the doctor how it happened. He said:

I went to hear Mr. Moody preach with no other idea than to have something to laugh at. I knew he was no scholar and I felt sure I could find many flaws in his argument. But I found I could not get at the man. He stood there hiding behind the Bible and just fired one Bible Scripture after the other at me until they went home to my heart straight as a bullet from a rifle, and I was converted.[3]

The doctor said Moody was *hiding* behind the Bible. Would to God the same could be said of all Christians.

Well, let's continue our conversation about why we can trust the Bible. You know as well as I do there's a lot of misinformation about the Bible.

Perhaps you've heard the story of the person interviewed as a candidate for church membership. It's unclear where the story originated, and I think in a minute, you'll see why. The candidate was asked, "What part of the Bible do you like best?"

He said, "I like the New Testament best."

Then he was asked, "What book in the New Testament is your favorite?"

He answered, "The Book of the Parables, Sir."

They then asked him to relate one of the parables to the membership committee. And with a bit of uncertainty, he began ...

"Once upon a time a man went down from Jerusalem to Jericho, and fell among thieves; and the thorns grew up and choked the man. And he went on and met the Queen of Sheba, and she gave that man a thousand talents of silver, and a hundred changes of raiment. And he got in his chariot and drove furiously, and as he was driving along under a big tree, his hair got caught in a limb and it left him hanging there! And he hung there many days and many nights. The ravens brought him food to eat and water to drink. And one night while he was hanging there asleep, his wife Delilah came along and cut off his hair, and he fell on stony ground. And it began to rain, and it rained forty days and forty nights. And he hid himself in a cave.

"Later, he went on and met a man who said, 'Come in and take supper with me.' But he said, 'I can't come in, for I have married a wife.' And the man went out into the highways and hedges and compelled him to come in! He then came to Jerusalem, and saw Queen Jezebel sitting high and lifted up in a window of the wall. When she saw him she laughed, and he said, 'Throw her down out of there,' and they threw her down. And he said, 'Throw her down again,' and they threw her down seventy-times-seven. And the fragments which they picked up filled twelve baskets full! Now, whose wife will she be in the day of the judgment?"

The membership committee agreed that this was indeed a knowledgeable candidate!

There's a lot of misinformation about the Bible, so why trust it? Maybe what we've said so far isn't convincing. Let's look at this from a little different angle.

THE BIBLE IS "BREATHED OUT" BY GOD, AND IT'S A PROCESS

> But as for you, continue in what you have learned and have firmly
> believed, knowing from whom you learned it and how from childhood you
> have been acquainted with the sacred writings, which are able to make
> you wise for salvation through faith in Christ Jesus. All Scripture is
> breathed out by God and profitable for teaching, for reproof, for correction,
> and for training in righteousness, that the man of God may be complete,
> equipped for every good work (2 Tim. 3:14-17).

Paul is telling Timothy to continue in his learning of Scripture —
these "sacred writings" — because they make one wise for salvation
through Jesus. Even beyond that, the Bible makes one wise for living
day-to-day in a really messed-up world.

Paul's phrases, *sacred writings* and *All Scripture,* are synonymous.
What I'm going to share at this point certainly isn't exhaustive, but for
some, it may be *exhausting.* Even so, this at least offers a good basis for
our common understanding. It's important to know how we ended
up with the Bible in its current form.

The list that begins on page 14 is compiled from books on biblical
interpretation, most notably *Grasping God's Word* by J. Scott Duvall
and J. Daniel Hays; *A History of the Christian Church* by Williston
Walker, Richard A. Noris, David W. Lotz, and Robert T. Handy; *Introduction to Biblical Interpretation* by William W. Klein, Craig L.
Blomberg, and others. It also comes from websites, charts and graphs
by various publishers, and snippets from various study Bibles. I will
do what I can to simplify the explanation, so here goes.

The twenty-seven books of the New Testament were formally
confirmed as canonical (accepted as being accurate/Scripture) by the
Synod of Carthage in AD 397. By AD 400, the standard of twenty-
seven New Testament books was accepted by the East and the West
as confirmed by Athanasius, Jerome, Augustine, and three church
councils.

It is neither a secret, nor even a great mystery, how this came about. People were "moved by God" to write. The Holy Spirit "superintended" the writing of Scripture so that it is completely "truth without any mixture of error." That is what my denomination, the Southern Baptist Convention, believes. This is just a portion of our (Southern Baptist) doctrinal statement, *The Baptist Faith & Message* 2000:

I. The Scriptures

The Holy Bible was written by men divinely inspired and is God's revelation of Himself to man. It is a perfect treasure of divine instruction. It has God for its author, salvation for its end, and truth, without any mixture of error, for its matter. Therefore, all Scripture is totally true and trustworthy. It reveals the principles by which God judges us, and therefore is, and will remain to the end of the world, the true center of Christian union, and the supreme standard by which all human conduct, creeds, and religious opinions should be tried. All Scripture is a testimony to Christ, who is Himself the focus of divine revelation.

Exodus 24:4; Deuteronomy 4:1-2; 17:19; Joshua 8:34; Psalms 19:7-10; 119:11, 89, 105, 140; Isaiah 34:16; 40:8; Jeremiah 15:16; 36:1-32; Matthew 5:17-18; 22:29; Luke 21:33; 24:44-46; John 5:39; 16:13-15; 17:17; Acts 2:16ff.; 17:11; Romans 15:4; 16:25-26; 2 Timothy 3:15-17; Hebrews 1:1-2; 4:12; 1 Peter 1:25; 2 Peter 1:19-21.

These sacred writings came to us through a "divine process."

Under the inspiration of the Holy Spirit, the Bible was written by some forty authors in Hebrew, Aramaic, and Greek in about thirteen different countries on three different continents over a period of sixteen hundred years. Yet, remarkably, its story line is unified.

This is one reason the "King James only" argument is flawed. I still cherish the King James Bible my parents gave me more than forty years ago, but Jesus didn't speak English, and neither did Moses,

Daniel, Peter, Paul, or any other human author of Scripture. The King James Version is an English *translation* from manuscripts based on the original languages, just as other translations are.

I've often wondered why we don't have the originals, known as *autographs*. Who would have kept them? How many nations would have fought for them? How many groups would have killed to possess them? How many so-called holy wars would have been fought to own them? How many people would have chosen to worship the written words? We don't worship the Bible of our God, but we worship the God of our Bible. It is his revelation of himself to mankind.

While we do not have the autographs, God has ensured the fundamental doctrinal integrity of tens of thousands of manuscripts throughout centuries of copying and translating his Word.

For example, a comparison of the Isaiah scroll discovered in the Qumran library agrees almost verbatim with the Masoretic text from which we have our Hebrew Bible, and which comes to us after a full thousand years of copying.[4]

Indulge me, and let's trace the history of Scripture, quickly, up to our modern era. Just pretend you're in a classroom. And I promise, I'm taking the fastest route to the finish with this:

1500 BC – God tells Moses to write down the Law for the people. The first five books of the Old Testament are called the "Law of Moses" (the Pentateuch).

1500-400 BC – Samuel, David, Solomon, Daniel, Ezekiel, Jeremiah, Amos, and others write the books of history, prophecy, and poetry. Scribes copy books as the originals wear out.

450 BC – Ezra collects and arranges the books, according to Jewish traditions. These books make up the Hebrew Scriptures (called the *Old Testament*).

250-100 BC – Jewish scholars translate the Hebrew Scriptures into

Greek. This Greek translation is called the *Septuagint* (meaning *seventy*) for the tradition that 70 (or perhaps 72) men translated it.

100 BC-AD 100 – Dead Sea Scrolls: copies of portions of Old Testament books and other writings are sealed in clay jars and hidden in caves.

AD 45-100 – Jesus' followers (Matthew, Mark, Luke, John, Peter, Paul, Jude, James) write letters and historical accounts to churches and friends throughout the Roman Empire. They quote from *all but eight* of the Old Testament books.

AD 100-500 – The writings of Jesus' followers are copied and translated from Greek into other languages and spread across the world as far as India and China.

AD 200-300 – Christianity reaches Britain.

AD 250-350 – Church fathers accept the writings of the Gospels and Paul's letters as "canonical" (from a Greek word referring to the rule of faith and truth). The Council of Carthage lists 27 New Testament books as authentic. These are the 27 in our New Testament today.

AD 313 – Christianity is legalized in the Roman Empire.

AD 325 – Codex Vaticanus: an early handmade copy of nearly all the Bible. It resides in the Vatican Library from 1481 and is released to scholars in the late 1800s.

AD 350 – Codex Sinaiticus: an early handmade copy of all the New Testament and part of the Old Testament. It is discovered in 1844 in St. Catherine's Monastery at Mt. Sinai.

AD 410 – Pope Damascus commissions Jerome to translate the Bible into Latin. This is called the *Latin Vulgate* and takes 22 years to complete. It is the Bible used for the next 1,000 years.

AD 450-600 – The Roman Empire falls.

AD 500-900 – Jewish scribes (Masoretes) develop a meticulous system of counting words to ensure the accuracy of each copy of the Hebrew Scriptures.

AD 1382 – First whole Bible in English is translated from Latin and named the Wycliffe Bible after John Wycliffe, Oxford scholar and priest.

AD 1455 – First printed book: Gutenberg prints the Latin Bible.

AD 1516 – Erasmus, a priest and Greek scholar, publishes a new Greek edition of the New Testament.

AD 1525 – William Tyndale, an Oxford scholar, translates the New Testament from Greek.

AD 1535 – The Coverdale Bible is the first printing of the complete English Bible.

AD 1555 – England's Queen Mary Tudor outlaws English Bible versions by Protestants and persecutes Protestant leaders.

AD 1560 – Geneva Bible appears. Hundreds of people flee to Switzerland to avoid persecution. A new English translation is printed in Geneva and contains theological notes by Protestant scholars.

AD 1611 – King James I of England commissions fifty-four scholars to translate a Bible without theological notes. They utilized the Bishops Bible and some available Greek and Hebrew texts. Revised in 1769.

AD 1881 – Revised Version printed.

AD 1901 – American Standard Version printed.

AD 1952 – Revised Standard Version printed.

AD 1971 – New American Standard Bible printed (revised in 1995).

AD 1978 – New International Version printed (revised in 2011).

AD 1982 – New King James Version printed.

AD 1989 – New Revised Standard Version printed.

AD 1996 – New Living Translation printed (revised in 2004, 2007, 2014, and 2015).

AD 2001 – English Standard Version printed (revised in 2011 and 2016).

AD 2004 – Holman Christian Standard Bible printed.

AD 2005 – NET Bible released (originally online, later printed).

AD 2017 – Christian Standard Bible, a revision of the Holman Christian Standard Bible, released.[5]

So, why the need for all these? Because the work of translation is never done! Remember when you were a kid and you said, "Oh man, I'm down with that!" It meant you had the flu. Now it means "I'm okay with that," or "I'm in." The process of translation is "more than just finding matching words and adding them up."[6] The usage of words changes, and words have shades of meaning, so we need to keep updating to make sure the truth of the Word is communicated to a current generation.

Can we trust the Bible? How reliable is it? Of the thousands of copies made by hand before AD 1500, more than 5,300 Greek manuscripts from the New Testament alone still exist today. The text of the Bible is better preserved than the writings of Caesar, Plato, or Aristotle. Even if no New Testament manuscript copies existed, we could reconstruct nearly all of the twenty-seven books because the early church fathers quoted the NT more than 36,000 times.[7]

TRUST THE BIBLE OVER TRADITION

I'm not down on traditions generally, but when it comes to choosing between traditions and the Bible, I'll take the Bible every time. Let's look at Mark 7:1-13 to help us see the importance of maintaining faithfulness to the Bible over tradition:

Now when the Pharisees gathered to him, with some of the scribes who had come from Jerusalem, they saw that some of his disciples ate with hands that were defiled, that is, unwashed. (For the Pharisees and all the Jews do not eat unless they wash their hands properly, holding to the tradition of the elders, and when they come from the marketplace, they do not eat unless they wash. And there are many other traditions that they observe, such as the washing of cups and pots and copper vessels and dining couches.) And the Pharisees and the scribes asked him, "Why do your disciples not walk according to the tradition of the elders, but eat with defiled hands?" And he said to them, "Well did Isaiah prophesy of you hypocrites, as it is written,

> *'This people honors me with their lips,*
> *but their heart is far from me;*
> *in vain do they worship me,*
> *teaching as doctrines the commandments of men.'*

You leave the commandment of God and hold to the tradition of men."

And he said to them, "You have a fine way of rejecting the commandment of God in order to establish your tradition! For Moses said, 'Honor your father and your mother' and, 'Whoever reviles father or mother must surely die.' But you say, 'If a man tells his father or his mother, "Whatever you would have gained from me is Corban"' (that is, given to God) then you no longer permit him to do anything for his father or mother, thus making void the word of God by your tradition that you have handed down. And many such things you do."

The context here involves a situation with a son becoming angry with his parents. If the young man declares what he has to be "Corban," he can dedicate his money and property to God (which sounds really good at first). The problem is, in this situation, the son is making a vow to God (knowing that according to Num. 30:2, a vow to God can't be violated). Therefore, his possessions cannot be used except in service to God. That means (and here's the subversive part) he cannot use what he has in any way to offer financial assistance to his parents.

What Jesus is offering here is a word of condemnation for that kind of practice. He's reminding those listening that tradition doesn't trump the Word of God. Jesus is saying to the scribes and Pharisees that, in this scenario, they are guilty of ignoring God's Word. After all, doesn't the Word of God say something about honoring one's parents?

Jesus has nothing good to say of this sneaky son's subversive strategy.

So, all this talk of the Bible being sacred writing and Jesus being "the only way" may seem quite narrow — and, in fact, it is. But you know what? It's true!

I love the way W. A. Criswell expresses this:

All truth is narrow. Mathematical truth is narrow. Two plus two equals four, no more, no less. If a person does not believe that narrow truth, he will find himself in trouble with the bank ... Scientific truth is narrow. There is no exception. Historical truth is narrow. An event happens at a certain place at a certain time in a certain way. The whole purpose of a jury and the whole purpose of court testimony is to arrive at that narrow truth.

If a person were to say, "But I am liberal and broad-minded in my history. I believe that Julius Caesar or Alexander the Great or Napoleon Bonaparte could live at any time in any place; in fact, we can go visit George Washington now." The person who would say that would not be taken seriously. Historical truth is narrow. Geographical truth is narrow. What would you think of a person who would say, "I am no geographical bigot. I am broad-minded in my geography. I believe that the Gulf Stream is in the Pacific Ocean"? Such broad-mindedness is preposterous.

Ecclesiastical truth is no less narrow. In the days of Noah there was no salvation outside of the ark. In the days of Moses there was no deliverance from the judgment of God except for those who were under the blood. Likewise in our day the same truth still stands![8]

Consider:

He that believes on the Son has everlasting life; he that believes not the Son shall not see life; but the wrath of God abides on him (John 3:36).

There are too many Christians and too many churches that haven't settled this issue about what they believe about the Bible. Until that issue is settled, a person, a church, or a denomination is never as effective as possible. Trusting the Bible as the Word of God is foundational to life as a Christian.

A few years ago, on New Year's Eve, my wife, Lori, and I went to The Cheesecake Factory. She ordered her beverage of choice: Cherry Coke. Then it was my turn. I drink about two sodas a month, and I was thinking, "It's New Year's Eve. I should probably live a little." And I was going to get a Cherry Coke, but then I thought we might get dessert and I'd want coffee. And while I'm happy for everyone else to have a soda and then coffee, I can't bring myself to do it; I'm tighter than bark on a tree.

So, I ordered coffee. Decaf, no less. Two minutes. Five minutes. Ten minutes. Finally, the waitress returns. She has the Cherry Coke and the coffee. The coffee is as cold as that stare a preacher gets from a nursery worker after a fifty-five-minute sermon. It's not warm at all. And I said, very graciously, "Ma'am. This isn't very hot."

Our waitress looked stunned. She was speechless. And then do you know what she said? "Would you like me to add some warm water to that?"

And I thought, "No ma'am. I don't want a watered-down version of something that's lukewarm already."

And then it struck me: *a watered-down version of something that's lukewarm already.* Sadly, that describes too many believers and too many churches in our world. I hope that never is said of you or me.

QUESTIONS FOR PERSONAL OR GROUP STUDY

1. What do you believe about the trustworthiness of the Bible, and why?
2. How does what you believe about the Bible impact how you respond to its teaching?
3. Why is Jesus' opinion about the Bible so important?
4. How would you respond to someone who says, "The Bible isn't from God; it was written by people"?
5. How can Christians say the Bible is without error when sinful men are attributed with writing it?

CREATION VS. EVOLUTION

IF GOD DIDN'T MAKE EVERYTHING, THEN WE ALL DESERVE
PARTICIPATION TROPHIES.

Three monkeys sat in a coconut tree
Discussing the things that are said to be —
Said one to another: "Now listen you two
There's a certain rumor, but it can't be true
That man descended from our noble race —
Why, the very idea; it's a disgrace.
No monkey ever deserted his wife,
Starved her babies and ruined her life.
Nor did ever a mother-monkey
Leave her babies with others to bunk,
Or pass them on from one to another
'Till they scarcely knew who was their mother.
And another thing you'll never see
A monkey building a nest around a coconut
    tree,
And let the coconuts go to waste,
Forbidding all other monkeys to have a taste.
Why, if I build a fence around a coconut tree,

Starvation would cause me to distribute to you.
Here's another thing that a monkey won't do:
Go out at night and get on a stew;
Or use a gun, a club, or a knife
To take another monkey's life.
Yes, Man descended, the ornery cuss!
But Brother, he didn't descend from us."[1]

That's a funny little poem, but this statement is anything but humorous. As John MacArthur notes, "By embracing evolution, modern society aims to do away with morality, responsibility, and guilt."[2]

My goal in this chapter is not to convince unbelievers that God did the creating, or that God did the creating in a compact period of time. Neither is my goal to convince unbelievers of God's existence. Rather, my goal is to remind believers, and in some cases perhaps *convince* believers, that God did do the creating and that he did it in the way depicted in Scripture.

What we believe about how the universe was created is vitally important. We'll unpack this as we go along. Let me further state something quite obvious: I write as a pastor, not a scientist. Saying that and owning that in no way disqualifies me from what I share on these pages. I'm not an ethicist by discipline, but when I talk or write about what the Scripture says related to ethics, I'm on solid ground. Agree? I'm not a prophet in the sense of predicting that which is to come, but when I talk about what Scripture says related to future events, I'm on solid ground. Agree? I'm not a historian by discipline, but when I talk about what Scripture says about history, I'm on solid ground. Agree?

As long as I'm teaching, explaining, and applying Scripture, utilizing sound rules of hermeneutics (the discipline of interpretation), I'm on solid ground. So even though I'm not a scientist, I am, in fact, equipped to teach about creation because my teaching about creation is based on what Scripture says about creation. Do you follow? So that's what we're going to do.

EMBRACING EVOLUTION ULTIMATELY DENIGRATES MORALITY

In the beginning, God created the heavens and the earth (Gen. 1:1).

Please don't miss the reality of what Scripture plainly states: God created. If we deny the creation of God, we're well on the way down a slippery slope. Look again at what MacArthur says: "By embracing evolution, modern society aims to do away with morality, responsibility, and guilt."

There may have been a time that statement would not have seemed to ring *so true*, but we simply cannot escape the reality that the statement is indeed true today. We have seen it in our own nation. In less than a decade, what used to be considered abhorrent behavior is now considered mainstream.

Our children are being taught not just to be kind to the LGBTQ community (I'm in complete agreement that we should be kind to all people), but the wider culture is teaching them they ought to be open to exploring these various lifestyle choices, regardless of what their faith has taught them or their family has instilled in them. So, I think it's fair to say MacArthur is right. In fact, we see what he said being validated every day: modern society aims to do away with morality.

Let me remind us of Paul's words from Romans 1:26-28:

> *For this reason God gave them up to dishonorable passions. For their women exchanged natural relations for those that are contrary to nature; and the men likewise gave up natural relations with women and were consumed with passion for one another, men committing shameless acts with men and receiving in themselves the due penalty for their error. And since they did not see fit to acknowledge God, God gave them up to a debased mind to do what ought not to be done.*

The culture may say it's an alternative lifestyle, or an orientation from birth, yet God says it's a dishonorable passion. We are living as recipients of this kind of sinful behavior. And one reason this kind of behavior is culturally acceptable is because people no longer believe there is a God who created; therefore, there is not a God to whom they must answer. But we know better, don't we? And I know a lot of unbelievers say, "See, God hasn't brought judgment." And with great sadness for them I would say, "It's not over yet."

Some people may think it's petty, but the whole restroom debacle in our culture (people choosing which restroom to use based on how they "feel" as opposed to the actual physical gender they are) clearly illustrates how far off the rails we've gone. Let me clarify: I don't think someone who identifies as a transgendered person is necessarily out to harm children in a restroom. In fact, statistically speaking, let's be fair: most don't. I'm just saying the ridiculous thinking process that has gotten us to this point *is harmful* to children as well as adults. I'm not a physician, but I know the difference between male and female. The whole purpose in this broader agenda is to further drive people away from basic tenets of morality. MacArthur is right.

While I'm on a roll here, let me say I think it is child abuse for parents to allow their children to consider changing gender. Gender is a gift from God. You were created just as God saw fit. We don't let children under sixteen drive. Why in the world would we think they should be allowed to make such life-altering decisions at even younger ages?

I saw a college entrance form not long ago with listings for gender. There were at least six. Again, it's not rocket science. The reality is, contrary to what the talking heads at Harvard or Berkeley tell you, you're either male or you're female. (Granted, there are rare anatomical exceptions.) It's not that complex!

We even see MacArthur's statement proven true in politics with respect to the debate about gun violence. I'm all for common-sense gun laws, and I'm also good with the Second Amendment. As much as it's tempting to say, "Let's have stricter gun laws," or even, "Let's limit the number of rounds a gun you purchase may fire," it comes down to people — to individuals. The mass shootings to which we've grown accustomed in America are so tragic. I'm not opposed to strong gun laws and stringent background checks. I'm really narrow about gun laws — probably more so than you. In fact, I don't think anybody that doesn't like me should be able to own a gun ...

But can we talk? What's changed? Why are things so different today concerning gun violence in our nation? Here's what's changed: For decades now, we have been devaluing life. We have allowed our kids to be influenced by ideologies that don't even recognize there is a God. We've stopped teaching moral absolutes. We've been killing babies legally — more than sixty million, in fact — since 1973. We've allowed the loudest voices to drown out common sense.

I really think MacArthur is right: "By embracing evolution, modern society aims to do away with morality, responsibility, and guilt."

These days everybody has to get a participation trophy. A "speedy trial" nowadays may take years, so there's little connection between crime and punishment. One can be given the death penalty and die of old age getting better health care than someone who has worked for fifty years.

We don't make people take responsibility for their actions. "It was my dad's fault." "It was her fault." "It was the gun's fault." We got that, by the way, from our original father. Didn't Adam say, *"The woman whom you gave to be with me, she gave me fruit of the tree, and I ate"*? We've been playing the blame game since the beginning. That really needs to stop.

Whoever paints graffiti on the wall is guilty, not the spray paint company. Whoever breaks into the store is guilty, not the crowbar company. Whoever cheats on his taxes is guilty, not the pencil company. Whoever pulls the trigger is guilty, not the gun company, not the people who didn't like the shooter in grade school, and listen ... not even the NRA.

Lots of things and lots of people can influence a person. Just a guess here, but maybe half the people who read these pages were bullied as kids. But they're not toting weapons, bent on settling the score at school or work today. At least I hope not. And you ... maybe you didn't get everything you needed from your parents. Maybe you didn't make the basketball team. Maybe you didn't get the college scholarship you think you deserved. But you're not posting terrorist manifestos on the Internet, are you?

I really think there is a connection between not believing in God (evolution) and the mess that our culture is in on so many fronts. I'm not sure we've been able to see that connection so clearly until the last few years, at least not in American culture. You see, if we believe no one did the creating, we think we have no one to whom we must answer. We need a simple reminder: *"In the beginning, God created the heavens and the earth."*

CREATION WAS IMMEDIATE

Genesis 1:3 records, *"And God said, 'Let there be light,' and there was light."* When you have some time, read the rest of Genesis 1. We get to the end of the first chapter and the Bible records, *"And God saw everything that he had made, and behold it was very good. And there was evening and there was morning, the sixth day"* (v. 31). Creation was immediate. I just chose these two verses to remind us of what all the others say. God speaks and something is created. That's the pattern. He says it and it is. It is *instantaneous*.

One of the first rules of biblical interpretation is to take something at face value unless there's a compelling reason to do otherwise.[3] So when we read, *"For God so loved the world,"* most everybody says, "Okay. I get it. God loved the world." Right? No reason to complicate it. Would anybody say, "I know the Bible says God so loved the world, but really I don't think that's what that means"? Of course not.

In the case of creation, I suppose I understand why some want to see this as a depiction of God's handiwork over a long period of time. But why? You see, the main compelling reason to think it has to be a long period of time — or epochs — is because some people who want to elevate science over God have told us to believe that. Scripture hasn't said that, but science has, to some degree. And for the record, I'm in favor of good science. But some scientists serve as priests in the church of evolution. I'm grateful for good science. In fact, I appreciate clean water to drink and anesthesia to put me out when I undergo surgery. Nobody appreciates ibuprofen more than I do. I love science. I just don't worship it. No surprise, I don't believe in evolution; not even *theistic evolution*.

MacArthur notes:

> The notion that natural evolutionary processes can account for the origin of all living species has never been and never will be established as fact. Nor is it "scientific" in any true sense of the word. Science deals with what can be observed and reproduced by experimentation. The origin of life can be neither observed nor reproduced in any laboratory. By definition, then, true science can give us no knowledge whatsoever about where we came from or how we got here. Belief in evolutionary theory is a matter of sheer faith. And dogmatic belief in any naturalistic theory is no more "scientific" than any other kind of religious faith.[4]

Again, I'm not trying to convince unbelievers that God created the heavens and the earth; I'm trying to assure believers that God actually did *exactly* what the word of God states that he did. Somebody said to me not long ago, thinking they were getting in a dig, "You believe in a literal creation by God. You think all this happened the way the Bible says it did." Listen, that's not a dig to me. That's a compliment; that's exactly what I believe!

So, what does Scripture say? It gives an account of a six-day creation. Now, I know this is troubling for some people because they want to believe the world is 4.54 billion years old, give or take some 50 million years.[5] The point is, the Bible says God created it all in six days. It says that throughout Genesis chapter one, and then chapter two offers a summary of sorts:

> *Thus the heavens and the earth were finished and all the host of them. And on the seventh day God finished his work that he had done, and he rested on the seventh day from all his work that he had done* (Gen. 2:1-2).

So, here's my question: If God wanted us to believe that creation took place in six days, could he have said it with any greater clarity? The days are marked by the passage of morning and evening. Human labor and rest are patterned after the week of creation. There's a beautiful order and symmetry offered with this six-day creation.

Some people hold to a concept known as the *Framework Hypothesis*.[6] This is a belief that the days of creation aren't necessarily distinct periods of time. Instead, they're stages that overlap throughout a long evolutionary process. For a lot of people, this sounds plausible. But there's a problem. The Framework Hypothesis essentially dismisses the creation account as it's given in Genesis 1.

If the language, as they say, is simply a literary device, designed to give us a symbolic picture of what God was up to, then how far do we go with thinking Scripture only offers symbols? When do symbols end, and where does true history begin? Does it happen at the time of the flood, or is the flood symbolic? What about Jonah and the great fish? Maybe Abraham didn't really intend to sacrifice Isaac, and the story was made up to make him look good. And the resurrection of Jesus? Merely symbolic? Maybe it's just a story that depicts God's love for humankind, and the grave symbolizes love being brought out of darkness. I don't think so!

If Genesis doesn't offer us a true chronological view of creation, then what in the world is the purpose of mentioning six days? Nothing in the Genesis account suggests it is meant as symbolic, poetic, or allegorical. Take a second or two and read that last sentence again. People say, "Well that can't be! The plants were created on the third day but the sun wasn't created until the fourth. And we all know plants can't survive without sunlight." Does that really bother you, Christian? We believe a dead carpenter walked out of the tomb. If God can do that, don't you think he can keep some plants alive for a day before he created the sun?

Do you ever wonder why the faith of so many Christians is weak? I think in some cases it's because we want to be *in* but not *all in*. You see, it's socially acceptable to say you believe in God — and even in creation perhaps. But attend a dinner party and tell people you think

God actually spoke all this into existence in six days. Suddenly, you're *that guy*. I'm afraid a lot of Christians have a fear of being *that guy*. You know, the one who believes the stuff that really takes faith.

I believe that in six days God created everything in the heavens and the earth, and then he rested. Do you know why I believe that? Because that's what God said happened. If I believe God could do it, is it a stretch to believe he did it in the time frame laid out in Genesis? Six days, and that's the truth.

Augustine said, "When regard for truth has been broken down or even slightly weakened, all things will remain doubtful."[7] Didn't James say something about being a "double-minded man" (Jas. 1:8)? I realize this is an issue of faith. Let's face it, apart from faith the whole thing is nuts. But I believe. Augustine also wrote, "God does not expect us to submit our faith to him without reason, but the very limits of our reason make faith a necessity."

SOME THINGS GO TOGETHER; SOME THINGS DON'T

Some things in life go together. Some things don't, and for good reason. Sometimes I eat Chinese food. My favorite Chinese place is a little restaurant in Kansas City called China Wok (I know, that's original, right?). I'm always amused and maybe feel a little guilty every time I go there. The reason is simple: Every time I come out of China Wok, I see somebody running on the sidewalk, testing a pair of running shoes. Just a couple doors down from the restaurant is a place called The Running Well Store. How ironic — a Chinese restaurant and a running-shoe store in such close proximity. Near my home there's a somewhat famous shop called LaMar's Donuts & Coffee. The founder was once on The Tonight Show with Johnny Carson. Anyway, right next door to LaMar's is a Nutrition Store. Can you say, "Ironic"?

Some things in life go together. Some things don't. And then, there are some things that people *want* to go together, but they really don't work well together. I know there are some Christians who have been influenced so strongly by the secularization of our culture that they believe more from Darwin than from deity. I'm not here to offer a treatise on all things "evolution," but let me clarify that I'm not knocking the notion of adaptation; this is clearly something we have observed throughout history.

We still see it taking place. I'm not arguing against that. People living closer to the equator look different than lifelong Missourians. People today look somewhat different than our ancestors. Height, weight, skin tone, and so forth are different from one period of time in human history to another as we have adapted to climate changes, food supplies, medical advances, and so on. And, of course, we've all seen the examples of finches' beaks of different lengths and moths' wings of different colors in our kids' science books. These are examples of adaptation. Some might refer to what I'm describing as "evolution," but that's not what I mean. Let me explain what I mean when I use the term "evolution."

Living things change. Changes occur in organisms over time. And if that's what comes to mind when you hear the word "evolution," I'm not debating that. What I am saying is that human beings, whatever they look like — however tall, short, dark, light, heavy or thin — they have always been created in the image of God. Since the days of Adam and Eve, the first parents, we were created with the ability to know God and be recognized as image-bearers of God.

If you want to name a specimen — a "missing link" or "transitional fossil" — that scientists say they've discovered in the last few hundred years, I will say either that discovery is a human being, created in the image of God, or it isn't. Lucy, the alleged human ancestor on which science so often hangs its hat, was either a human being or she wasn't. There's no in-between. The Bible gives no wiggle room for such. I don't believe that other creatures over time *became* human beings; human beings, according to Scripture, are the distinct and crowning achievement of God.[8]

So, when I talk about evolution, I'm talking about a theory of origins — the idea that human beings came into existence over a period of thousands, if not millions of years. Not that humans merely adapted to changes in the environment, but that humans actually evolved from lower life forms over eons of time. I don't believe that. I believe from the beginning that God created man *in his own image.* And I believe that because that's what the Bible says.

In case you don't realize this, most of Darwin's theories about the mechanisms of evolution were long ago discarded.[9] Even some of the most strident opponents to faith readily admit Darwin's views cannot be maintained. Richard Dawkins writes, "We must acknowledge the possibility that new facts may come to light which will force our successors of the twenty-first century to abandon Darwinism or modify it beyond recognition."[10]

The challenge is that the doctrine of evolution has itself become entrenched in American culture. Like Chinese food and running shoes, or a donut shop and a nutrition store, there's incongruity when we look at these things together, because in many ways they're on opposite ends of a spectrum. But like a lot of other things in Scripture, if we claim to be followers of Jesus, we don't have the luxury of picking and choosing what we want to believe.

IS SCRIPTURE SUFFICIENT?

Do you believe Scripture really is the inspired word of God? Okay. So, do you believe the New Testament is the Word of God? The Gospels? What about the Old Testament? Do you believe Psalms or Proverbs or Exodus? Are they part of the Word of God? How about Genesis?

Think about this: You wouldn't read the Gospel of John and say, "I just don't think what John says squares with modern culture; therefore, I can't commit to believing what John wrote. The miraculous feeding of five thousand, or Jesus supposedly walking on water — there just has to be a more sophisticated explanation." I doubt any professing Christian would say that.

But is John's Gospel any more inspired than Genesis? Is the Book of Genesis any less the Word of God? So, why would anyone say of the Genesis account, "There has to be a more sophisticated explanation"? Is the Word of God sufficient or not? As a Christian, do you feel compelled to believe only the things that line up with modern philosophy, contemporary culture, or current scientific views? Is the Word of God primary, or is some other discipline primary?

Let me be blunt and offer a warning: If you don't accept the Genesis account of creation, I don't think you can be on solid ground in your belief related to the other truths of the Bible. I'm not talking about those of you who might say, "I don't fully understand all this, but I'm learning." I'm talking about someone who would say, "Of course I believe Jesus is the Son of God; I just can't buy that God created the heavens and the earth the way the Bible records." If you say that, you're on a slippery slope.

CREATION — REPRISE

Scripture indicates that the future new creation is an immediate work of God: *"For behold, I create new heavens and a new earth, and the former things shall not be remembered or come into mind"* (Isa. 65:17).

Remember what we noted earlier: God spoke, and things came into existence. God's powerful word brought the universe — the planets, the sun, the stars, the earth, living things, humankind — he brought it all into existence with his word.

Let me take you to some more verses to illustrate what I'm saying. Remember we noted that Genesis offers a picture of an immediate creation, not creation over billions of years. Genesis provides an account of a relatively brief period of time: six days, in which God did the creating.

In fact, we ought to take note that the original creation is the model for the new creation. Look at what Scripture says:

> For I consider that the sufferings of this present time are not worth comparing with the glory that is to be revealed to us. For the creation waits with eager longing for the revealing of the sons of God. For the creation was subjected to futility, not willingly, but because of him who subjected it, in hope that the creation itself will be set free from its bondage to corruption and obtain the freedom of the glory of the children of God (Rom. 8:18-21).

The "creation and creation reprise" concept suggests that the original creation is waiting for the world to be "made right." The picture is that of the original creation being destroyed ("set free from its bondage") and ultimately recreated ("obtain the freedom of the glory of the children of God"). Drum roll please ... there's no mention of anyone waiting around billions of years for this to occur.

Look at some other biblical texts:

Then I saw a new heaven and a new earth, for the first heaven and the first earth had passed away, and the sea was no more (Rev. 21:1).

And he who was seated on the throne said, "Behold, I am making all things new" (Rev. 21:5).

Again, the picture here in Revelation is that of a new heaven and new earth that is viewable to people in short order, not in a time frame of millions of years to create.

Both of these texts in Revelation fit the idea of an immediate new creation. For example, if the new creation takes a long period of time to accomplish, based on a belief that the original creation took a long period of time, then Revelation 21:5 would not seem to offer a whole lot of promise. Or, at the very least, it would read differently to indicate that everybody ought to sit tight; this is going to take *forever!*

EVOLUTION BEGETS UGLY OFFSPRING

Evolutionary ideas can be seen as the parents of all kinds of ugly offspring: naturalism, Marxism, and the Nazi movement, just to name a few. The idea of not believing God as creator is known as *naturalism*. *Naturalism* is the belief that everything operating in the universe is natural rather than moral, spiritual, or supernatural.[11] Naturalism has, in fact, become a key religion in our day, although naturalists typically wouldn't identify it as such.

You may be familiar with the name Carl Sagan. Sagan — an astronomer, planetary scientist, cosmologist, astrophysicist, astrobiologist, and best-selling author — was antagonistic to biblical theism. He was a naturalist in his orientation; that is, he didn't believe in the supernatural at all. Toward the end of his life, Sagan wrote, "Our planet is a lonely speck in the great enveloping cosmic dark. In our obscurity, in all this vastness, there is no hint that help will come from elsewhere to save us from ourselves."[12]

That's a picture of the naturalist. And the naturalist's views are rooted in the doctrines of Darwinism. I trust you're familiar with the name Karl Marx, the German philosopher and revolutionary. Much of his economic and social theories were rooted in the doctrines of Darwinism. Marx once said that Charles Darwin's *Origin of Species* was "the book which contains the basis in natural history for our view."[13]

Evolution is ultimately degrading to humanity. It not only casts doubt on God; it casts doubt on God's care for his creation. Even if you believe in God, if you don't think he cares for his creation (and I mean both the material world and the inhabitants of it), that's ultimately going to degrade humanity. In other words, if you don't think you're a special cog in the wheel of all that God has made, then really, what's the point?

Let me simply remind us again of this connection. It is a firmly grounded belief in evolution that devalues our humanity. You can connect the dots between evolutionary thought and abortion and euthanasia, and even some forms of genetic manipulation seeking to form a master race, where the weak among us or the less intelligent among us are disregarded or eliminated altogether. A cursory reading of world history sheds much light on this concept.

You know I am an animal lover. But listen, there's a big difference between us and our beloved pets. But many evolutionists don't think so. In fact, to cite just one example let me offer you a quote from Ingrid Newkirk. She was the controversial founder of PETA, People For the Ethical Treatment of Animals. She wrote, "There is no rational basis for saying that a human being has special rights ... A rat is a pig is a dog is a boy." She told a *Washington Post* reporter that the atrocities of Nazi Germany pale by comparison to the killing of animals for food. She said, "Six *million* Jews died in concentration camps, but six *billion* broiler chickens will die this year in slaughterhouses."[14]

I have seen some beautiful things in this world, yet I haven't seen a tenth of the glory of God's creation. I've never been to the Grand Canyon or Niagara Falls. But the mountains and the rivers and the oceans I've seen, not to mention the golf courses ... God is a master creator. But the crowning achievement of God's creative week is found in verse 27 of Genesis 1: *"So God created man in his own image, in the image of God he created him; male and female he created them."*

So how did God do that? With great care! Pay attention because this is beautiful. In Genesis 1:2, the Bible says, *"And the Spirit of God was hovering over the face of the waters."* I believe the earth was created, as verse 1 reminds us, but it is undeveloped, unformed, and a lifeless mass of matter hung in space. It would stand to reason based on the whole of Genesis 1 that the earth was covered by water and engulfed in darkness.

Remember, light hasn't yet been created, and not until verse 9 do we see God command that *"the dry land appear."* So, in verse 2, we read the Spirit of God was hovering over the surface of the earth. The Spirit surrounded it, engulfed it, and guarded it. The Spirit of God would oversee formation out of the formlessness.

This is what is *so* beautiful. As MacArthur notes, "The Hebrew word for *hovering* evokes an image of a hen brooding over her chicks. It indicates superintending, divine care, and supervision."[15] God is present in the moment, overseeing this whole project. He didn't speak and walk away. When someone says they believe in "Open Theism," run! That's not a biblical picture of God's involvement in creation, much less the rest of the ages since.[16] Either God really is sovereign or we really are in trouble.

Let me use a food analogy. The difference between evolution and creation would be the difference between you pulling out a bunch of stuff from your refrigerator, throwing it all in a pan and serving it, versus going to a five-star restaurant where there are various courses, designed to make sense to the palate, and all served beautifully with great creativity, order, and distinction, yet all working together to ultimately comprise a wonderful meal.

EVOLUTION DISREGARDS REASON

Some of what must be said about evolution is harsh. And the truth is, I don't wish to be unkind. However, I do feel a certain edge and a certain unction related to addressing this because of how detrimental evolutionary teaching and philosophy are to human kind.

If we were to take a poll of professing Christians, a good percentage of them, sadly, would likely indicate they believe in some form of evolution (again, remember what I offered as the definition: not just changes over time, but human beings descending from something other than that which is human).

For some, the Genesis account is too fanciful, or they're afraid of being seen as anti-intellectual. Let me reiterate something I've often said: I'm a product of public education. My parents worked for the public-school system. My in-laws worked for the public-school system. My wife has spent her career working for the public-school system. I don't expect public schools to spiritually educate our children. That's not their job. But the problem is that for decades now, in many cases, we've been teaching children in public schools that they are not special creations of God, or even the highest form occupying the food chain.

I'm not blaming teachers who have to teach evolution. In fact, teaching it as a theory of origins doesn't blow me away. But it *is* a theory — and one that a lot of people believe. Believing we came from something other than that which is human is not compatible with the Judeo/Christian ethic, much less the Christian faith.

Is it any wonder our children are raised with no concept of the value of human life? Is it any wonder a human being kills another for just a few bucks, or to settle a petty dispute? Is it any wonder we legally allow a doctor to take forceps and invade a baby's sacred space, while the child recoils in pain and fear awaiting impending demise?

It's no wonder because, for decades, our public schools, and in some cases even private parochial institutions, have been teaching children that they are not created image-bearers of God, but rather, they are a compilation of matter subject to the whims of time and chance.

What the evolutionists believe is pretty ridiculous, actually. I don't ever want to be crude, but here's about the best way I can think of to say this: We've been teaching our kids for decades that they are the product of some kind of *cosmic belch* that scientists call the "Big Bang." Should we be surprised that they act the way they do, believing that's how it all began?

We've been teaching that there was nothing. And then, suddenly, there was something out of nothing, but God had nothing to do with it. Shame on our culture. Shame on us. Shame on schools that teach this nonsense, communities that put up with it, and churches and pastors that remain silent about it. We are reaping as a people what we've sown as a collective culture.

Evolution, theistic evolution, billion-year-old-earth theories, and so-called "progressive creationism" are all refuted if we simply take the statements of Genesis at face value.

EVOLUTION OPPOSES GOD

If you don't believe *"In the beginning,"* you can't believe "in the end." And if you don't believe in the end, as God has decreed it, you're in trouble. We see throughout the evolutionist's argument that believing in evolution in terms of where we human beings came from is tantamount to *not* believing in God. How can you believe in a God whose word is uncertain? If God is not completely truthful, why believe in him?

Think about this logically. I know a lot of believers who stick their heads in the sand and say, "I believe in Jesus. I trust the Bible. I just don't know that God really did the creating in six days." What did Jesus have to say? And bear in mind, as a man, Jesus knew the contents of the Book of Genesis. Remember Jesus, speaking to the

Father, said, *"Your word is truth"* (John 17:17). And in Matthew 19:4, Jesus said, *"Have you not read that he who created them from the beginning made them male and female ..."*

How firm are you in your beliefs about God, Jesus as Savior, eternal life, creation, and Scripture? If you're contemplating whether to believe the Genesis account of how the universe came to be, I want to remind you of a quote I shared earlier from Augustine: "When regard for truth has been broken down or even slightly weakened, all things will remain doubtful."

QUESTIONS FOR PERSONAL OR GROUP STUDY

1. Why is evolution contrary to the teaching of Scripture?
2. Do you think belief in a literal six-day creation is important? Why or why not?
3. What are the challenges to believing in a six-day creation?
4. How might decades of teaching that human beings are the product of chance lead to a devaluing of human life?
5. What are the most important reasons Christians should believe in the creation account as given in Genesis 1-2?

SOCIAL MEDIA AND HOW WE SPEAK

OUR WORDS CAN BE DEADLY — OR SOOTHING SALVE.

I t could be argued that it's not really fair for me to talk about what I'm going to talk about in this chapter. I watch what I say. In fact, I always have to watch what I say. I make my living with words. I'm a pastor.

I'm sure I don't do this perfectly, but I try not to say or write anything that would prove embarrassing if it appeared on the screens at the church where I serve. So, it's true that I watch what I say because I'm a pastor. But let me be clear: I watch what I say because I'm a Christian.

I make my living with words, so you may feel the playing field is tilted in my favor when I talk about *how* we use our words. That may be true. Even so, we all know what constitutes positive speech — speech that honors Jesus. And I think we all know about speech that does and doesn't honor Jesus. We know that words have various meanings and usages, and they even change over time, which causes us to be even more cautious — or at least, it should.

"I'm down with that" used to mean you had the flu or some other illness. When I was a kid, had I used the word *queer* of someone in a pejorative sense, my dad would have whipped me worse than the St.

Louis Cardinals usually beat the Chicago Cubs (okay, now I've made some of you angry). But you know the word *queer* is now a label commonly used to identify certain people. Those who identify as queer don't see it as a negative label anymore. At any rate, some words are used in helpful ways and some in hurtful ways. I'm saying, when you tell someone, "I think you're ugly and your mother dresses you funny," you know that's not nice, right?

As we see from the Bible, our words have power. We may bless God or curse people, and if we belong to Jesus, we know which of these is proper. Some of us are blessed by the words of others. When someone says, "Good job," "I appreciate you," "You're so kind," or "I love you," we're blessed. But if you've been called *fat* or *stupid* or *lazy* or *arrogant* or *racist* or *misogynistic*, you know these words aren't complimentary.

My point is to deal with *how* we speak, generally speaking that is, as well as how we *speak* via social media. I'm not going to name each platform, but whether we're talking about Facebook, Twitter, Snapchat, Instagram, and so forth, the rules of engagement need to be the same as when we speak to people on the phone or face-to-face. All of this applies to how we communicate.

I'm sure we've all had the wonderful experience of having someone blast us, drag our name, our views, or our faith through the mud — all from behind the safety, security, and sometimes anonymity of a personal-computer keyboard. In fact, you know as well as I do, some people say things from that vantage point they would never say to someone's face.

You might wonder why I'm including the topic of how we speak in this book. Well, I'm glad you asked. First, it's important because we're raising a generation that doesn't know how to simply talk with one another. They'll text, tweet, Snapchat, Messenger, and use Instagram. They use apps such as Tik Tok, Tumblr, WhatsApp, Discord, House Party, Live Me, Whisper, Monkey, MeetMe, Omegle, and one called Yubo, formerly Yellow, which is often called the Tinder for teens. You just need to know that's not healthy. And it's likely that by the time you read this, some of these platforms will have gone away and others will have taken their place.

There are other reasons to talk about how we use social media. Sometimes Christians don't understand (or don't want to admit) that people connect what we *say* to what we *believe*. If a non-Christian blasts a politician on social media, everybody thinks it's business as usual. But if a Christian says something derogatory about someone on social media, it's a reflection of his or her faith, family, local church, denomination, and most importantly Jesus himself. Let that sink in!

Please don't hear me call for Christians to be mute. We have opinions. In fact, they should be *sanctified* opinions. They ought to be *informed* opinions. So, we can and should speak. I just think we have to be very careful in *how* we speak, and we need to realize every opinion we have doesn't necessarily need to be shared.

It should not go unnoticed that God "spoke" and the world "became." Remember? *"And God said, 'Let there be light,' and there was light"* (Gen. 1:3). With just a word, God brings the universe to life. Our words have life-giving power of a different sort.

Remember what Jesus said about words: *"For out of the abundance of the heart the mouth speaks"* (Matt. 12:34).

So, let's talk about our words and what they say about us. And in the process, let's talk about social media and how we speak through these various platforms. And I can't help but talk about politics, as well, because so much about social media is politically driven, and social media has done a lot to influence America's political landscape.

I debated how to title this chapter. I wanted to call it *Be Careful Little Mouth What You Say & Be Careful Little Hands What You Type*, along with about twenty other titles. But I went with the current title. So, let's discuss what our words say about us.

OUR WORDS SPEAK VOLUMES ABOUT OUR PROCLIVITY TO STUMBLE

Not many of you should become teachers, my brothers, for you know that we who teach will be judged with greater strictness. For we all stumble in many ways. And if anyone does not stumble in what he says, he is a perfect man, able also to bridle his whole body (Jas. 3:1-2).

People stumble; nobody's perfect. Do you ever put your foot in your mouth? There's a reason that phrase is so popular: that practice is so common! One of the greatest traits we can teach and model is the importance of carefully choosing words. The point is, throughout life we learn that words are a big deal. And one truth we need to underscore is that our words far too often remind us about our proclivity to stumble.

When someone drops the "F-bomb" in a television interview, do you know why that happens? Because that person is comfortable dropping it elsewhere. Jesus said, *"For out of the abundance of the heart the mouth speaks,"* right? So, listen: This is convicting, not just about this word, but about a lot of words, phrases, paragraphs, and even thoughts we never utter. The reason someone drops the "F-bomb" is because that person's heart has made room for "F-bombs."

That's also true for sexually charged innuendo, racial slurs, or phrases meant to denigrate someone else in some way. Frankly, it's convicting as I search my own heart and consider things I've said and things I've thought.

The context, of course, for James' remarks has to do with the responsibility of those who teach spiritual truths. They need to be sure they don't teach things that are false. And those who teach spiritual truths face a stricter judgment. The stumbling to which James alludes is related to the teacher of spiritual things who teaches something that's not right, or not *exactly* right, or perhaps completely wrong, and how that causes disciples of Jesus to stumble.

Teachers of spiritual truth should exercise caution with words and actions because of influence and accountability. There were some in the early church who sought to be teachers because of the status; teachers were held in high esteem. Teaching spiritual truth is a great privilege — and an awesome responsibility. The older I get, the more I realize how much there is to learn. Each preaching and teaching engagement demands my best. Every writing project must be undertaken with great care. In fact, even simple things, like notes I send to others or words I post on my personal Facebook account, matter. I have to give all of these my best — my best self, my best preparation, my best delivery, my best heart, my best commitment.

Teachers of spiritual truth are held to a higher standard of accountability. There are many things I just don't do, and wouldn't even consider doing, or wouldn't say or wouldn't write or wouldn't post, simply because I'm a Bible teacher.

I willingly accept this responsibility. We ask all those in teaching positions in our church to sign a teacher's covenant, not because we're legalistic, but because we're seeking to protect them! We want them to realize what a huge spiritual obligation this is, based on James 3.

I don't think it's a stretch to recognize that, as followers of Jesus, the world is judging us strictly, too. And sometimes, we cause them to stumble because our words don't match what we purport to believe. The fact that James says, in essence, "Be careful," should be a warning to us. James said it (under the inspiration of the Holy Spirit) because he knew (and the Holy Spirit knows) our tendency toward stumbling and causing others to stumble because of our words.

OUR WORDS SPEAK VOLUMES ABOUT OUR PROCLIVITY TOWARD PRIDE

If we put bits into the mouths of horses so that they obey us, we guide their whole bodies as well. Look at the ships also: though they are so large and are driven by strong winds, they are guided by a very small rudder wherever the will of the pilot directs. So also the tongue is a small member, yet it boasts of great things (Jas. 3:3-5).

We know that small things exert large influence. A bit in a horse's mouth gives direction to the horse. A rudder of a ship is small but steers a large ship. A small fire can ignite a huge forest. An atom is small, but think of the inherent power it possesses.

Currency in America is not very big, but think of the power money holds to do good or evil. A hundred-dollar bill is only about six inches in length and two and a half inches in width, yet think of what people do to gain it.

What we say speaks volumes about who or what controls us. The tongue is evil — not merely passive, but active and on the attack. It is deadly poison that can be used for evil, or it can be a salve to soothe the hurting.

There's a reason for the limits of "free-speech." I know many people today don't see it this way, but the Constitution, as I understand it, really doesn't give you the freedom to say anything that you want, anytime you want, anywhere you want.

I have three grandchildren: Ryann, Hudson, and Jack. And when they get older, if I were to pick them up at the airport and they came running, I can say, "Hi, Ryann!" and "Hi, Hudson," but I had better not yell, "Hi, Jack!" at the airport. Understand? Even if I'm simply addressing my grandson, Jack. You just can't yell, "Hi, Jack!" at an airport.

The tongue quickly reveals our level of pride. Don't you have to fight to hold your tongue sometimes? Oftentimes my wife, Lori, has said, "I wish I had your wit." I say, "No you don't." And I'm serious when I say it. It's a battle not to cut with the tongue when someone cuts me first. It's an internal struggle not to lash out when someone has lashed out at me.

Let me illustrate what I mean. Knowing I'm about to be rebuked as someone says, "I just have a little thought I want to share with you," my first internal response is, "Good thing you said little ... at least you recognize your limitations."

Someone says, "I want to get something off my chest." My first thought is, "Why not, you've already removed your heart."

Someone says, "I have half a mind to really tell you off." I think, "Be careful, remember, you only have half to start with."

Pride. That's all that is. So before you select "Post" or hit "Send," give ample consideration to what your words are about to do. Is what you're saying true? Is it accurate? Is it necessary? Is it helpful?

OUR WORDS SPEAK VOLUMES ABOUT OUR PROCLIVITY TOWARD ALL KINDS OF SIN

And the tongue is a fire, a world of unrighteousness. The tongue is set among our members, staining the whole body, setting on fire the entire course of life, and set on fire by hell. For every kind of beast and bird, of reptile and sea creature, can be tamed and has been tamed by mankind, but no human being can tame the tongue. It is a restless evil, full of deadly poison. With it we bless our Lord and Father, and with it we curse people who are made in the likeness of God. From the same mouth come blessing and cursing. My brothers, these things ought not to be so (Jas. 3:6-10).

The tongue expresses the sinfulness of the world. Verse 8 reminds us the tongue is a restless evil. How often we hear words from people's lips that express the sinfulness of the world. And lest I come across as more self-righteous than I am, I need a constant reminder of this truth — not for the outside world, but for me.

My best friend is Larry Brant. He was my best friend growing up. He's now Lieutenant Commander Larry Brant, Chaplain Corps, United States Navy. I'm so proud of him, and if I had a brother, I couldn't love him more than I love Larry. But when we were kids, I did what most kids do. When I wanted to do something my parents forbade, I'd say, "But Larry got to!" And my parents swiftly reminded me, in ways that were quite memorable, that I wasn't Larry. And then if I did the thing I wasn't supposed to, they'd say, "You know better." And they were right.

Listen, if you're not a Christian, I think you would do well to clean up your speech, but you're not my responsibility. But the people of the church I serve, at least to some extent, are. And I feel a certain responsibility for the wider Christian community, too.

Sometimes I scroll through Facebook. I don't deal with much else social media-wise, because it's only my body that goes "snap," and my mouth that will "chat," and my memory loss is "Insta," and a "gram" is a cracker. And at my age when someone says they're "tweeting," I'm concerned it's a medical malady.

So, when I'm on Facebook (and that's enough for me) and I read some Christian criticizing someone else, or I read words that someone has typed that I know they wouldn't have said in a group of people, or I see someone lash out with all kinds of ugly against an unbeliever (who, by the way, is only acting as his nature allows), I want to say what my mother used to say, "You know better."

You see, there are more important things in life, especially for Christians, than just trying to convince somebody that our sports team is better than theirs or that our political persuasions are superior to theirs. Why in the world would we risk the ability to influence others for the gospel and settle instead for speaking our mind about _____ (fill in the blank here)?

I'm not saying you shouldn't share what you think, feel, or believe. However, a lot of social media posts and tweets would be better shared in face-to-face dialogue. Be careful! If you're going to engage with people on social media, you need to imagine that just under your post you have signed your name, told where you go to church, given your personal address, your mother's phone number, and your kids' social security numbers. And then imagine everything you post being put up on the screen at church on a Sunday morning.

Sometimes, I type one of those computerized "sticky notes" and post it in the corner of my screen. I have one there now. Do you know what it says? "Don't post on social media today. You don't have the time or the energy necessary to defend all the things you're prone to say today. And besides that, people are crazy!"

Listen, I know they're doing it. People are posting all kinds of ugly things. But *you* are not *them*. If you belong to Jesus, you're different than the rest. Like my parents would tell me when I did something just because Larry did, "But you know better." For the record, Larry was and is a good guy!

I think you should still engage people, but be winsome about it. One of my atheist friends posts frequently on Facebook, and he's always negative about Christians. In fact, he's been fuming since the presidential campaign of 2016 because he says evangelical Christians sold their souls in that election. Now, bear in mind, he hasn't cared about anything else we've done or haven't done, but he's vocal about his political views, and he's negative about most everyone else's. For the record, I don't engage him about politics. I'm practicing what I preach! Anyway, he shared a picture of a great fish and a character meant to be Jonah. The caption read:

Science from the Bible: Jonah lived in the stomach of a large fish for three days and nights and survived! Jonah 1:17

Fact: No human being could survive in the stomach of a large fish as there would be methane gas and a total lack of oxygen within the stomach!

Now, I could let that make me mad. But my friend, who is an unbeliever, is just acting naturally. If you don't believe in God, you'll live opposed to God. So, he's just doing what comes naturally. And he yanks my chain all the time about being a Christian.

I know some people might respond, "Go to Gehenna." I do believe those without Christ go to hell, but that's not a good response at that point. My friend and I have talked about this before, but calmly and without angst. So, what do you suppose I said in response to his post? I said, "Man, I'm glad nobody told God this." Do you see the difference? I was pushing back, but I wasn't being ugly about it. I love my atheist friend, and as much as it might pain him to admit it, I think he loves me, too.

I also love my gay friends. While I try to be kind to everybody, I do post statements with which not everyone agrees. Our church puts all of my sermons on the web, and some of my gay friends commented on a recent sermon I preached about homosexuality. But I'm not out to bash atheists or gay people. I don't want to say anything that in any way tramples the message of Jesus. In fact, not too long ago, one of my gay friends posted, "Ken, I'd like to visit your church. I don't believe everything you believe, but I'd like to hear you preach in person because I'm convinced you're charitable and you believe everything you say." At the risk of feeding my already-prone-to-prideful ego, that, my friends, is a beautiful endorsement.

The negativity seems to show up mostly on political posts. I don't want to waste whatever influence I have trying to convince somebody else of my political persuasion, especially not on Facebook — and especially if there's not some kind of "gospel issue" (like abortion) tied to my views. And guess what? I have yet to observe anyone changing his or her mind about anything based on any post on social media.

I've prayed for every U.S. president elected during my adult life. Some I've liked and some I haven't. I usually post every four years about my belief that it is God who ultimately puts people in positions of authority (see Dan. 2:21). And with all due respect, in case you haven't figured it out, President Obama couldn't bring hope and change, and President Trump couldn't make America great again. In the ultimate sense, only God can do that.

OUR WORDS SPEAK VOLUMES ABOUT OUR PROCLIVITY TOWARD INCONSISTENCY

Does a spring pour forth from the same opening both fresh and salt water? Can a fig tree, my brothers, bear olives, or a grapevine produce figs? Neither can a salt pond yield fresh water (Jas. 3:11-12).

James is talking about consistency. He's saying, "It's not consistent to say we love Jesus and then spew hateful words on one of his creatures." It doesn't matter if the words are spoken in person or written online. You can't tell your kids a beautiful Bible story, tuck them in with a prayer, and then wake up the next day screaming at them. They don't know which message to believe. But I guarantee they remember the screaming.

You can't post John 3:16 all over your Facebook page, then chime in with ugly words about other human beings. The people forget John 3:16; they remember your ugly words (or maybe they remember your ugly words in light of the fact that you posted John 3:16, which is even worse). It's important not to shake your fist as you drive by someone if your car boasts an "I LOVE JESUS" bumper sticker. Get it?

Consistency. We have a predisposition to the opposite, don't we? Think how silly we are. We come to church and talk about how much we love Jesus and the people made in his image. Then, on the way to lunch, someone turns into our lane, and we want to give God competition in occupying the Great White Throne in judgment! And just as we pass them with a scowl on our face, they look up and see that Jesus fish on our bumper.

We're prone toward being inconsistent, aren't we?

Many of you know the words to this great old hymn:

> *Come, Thou Fount of every blessing,*
> *Tune my heart to sing Thy grace;*
> *Streams of mercy, never ceasing,*
> *Call for songs of loudest praise.*
> *Teach me some melodious sonnet,*
> *Sung by flaming tongues above;*
> *Praise the mount—I'm fixed upon it—*
> *Mount of Thy redeeming love ...*

And then there's this stanza:

> *O to grace how great a debtor*
> *Daily I'm constrained to be!*
> *Let Thy grace, Lord, like a fetter,*

> *Bind my wand'ring heart to Thee.*
> *Prone to wander, Lord, I feel it,*
> *Prone to leave the God I love;*
> *Here's my heart, O take and seal it;*
> *Seal it for Thy courts above.*[1]

Robert Robinson wrote that hymn in 1758, and there's a widely told (but unverified) story about him and the hymn. Supposedly, it wasn't long after he wrote this great hymn that Robinson struggled with issues related to the faith about which he'd written. It wasn't that he no longer believed. As I understand it, he believed in the doctrine, but his own failure and sin caused him to doubt his belief that God could love him.

Years later, he was riding in a carriage with a lady friend. As the story goes, the lady was humming the tune of "Come, Thou Fount of Every Blessing." She asked Robinson what he thought of the hymn she was humming. He said, "Madam, I am the poor unhappy man who wrote that hymn many years ago, and I would give a thousand worlds, if I had them, to enjoy the feelings I had then."[2]

I can't help but wonder sometimes how many people feel like Robert Robinson — longing for a peace they used to have; dwelling on their sin and shortcomings; wondering if God could really love them. We are prone to wander, after all. Robert Robinson could have written the last point. He understood. The truth is, so do you. So do I. The question is: What are we going to do about it?

QUESTIONS FOR PERSONAL OR GROUP STUDY

1. What questions should you ask yourself before posting on social media?
2. What practices could you utilize that would enable you to post when you're clear-headed and not reactionary?
3. If you were to draft a "Social Media Covenant" to ensure that your posting always honors the Lord, your family,

your church, and your own personal faith, what elements would you include?

4. How much time should you actually spend interacting with others via social media?

5. Suppose the leader of your Bible study group declares that social media platforms like Facebook are inherently evil and thus should be avoided altogether. How would you respond?

SAME-SEX ATTRACTION

IT'S NOT THE UNPARDONABLE SIN, BUT IT GRIEVES THE
HEART OF GOD.

C hange often is hard for us. When a new store replaces an old one, people have a hard time with it. When a popular street is renamed, it's hard for people to adjust. It's difficult sometimes to wrap our minds around change. I realize how hard it is to cope with change when I meet someone who, in the past, attended the church I now serve. They say, "Oh, so you must be the new pastor at First Baptist Church." I'm starting my sixteenth year as pastor there!

Changes in stores, streets, and offices are one thing — and that's hard enough for some people. But what about change related to our understanding of long-held and long-cherished beliefs? I tell students at Midwestern Seminary that as they contemplate change in their churches, they should make sure there's a good reason for it. Don't discount the wisdom of what people did a generation ago; they likely had good reasons for doing what they did. In fact, it might surprise all of us to know that there was actually much wisdom on the planet before we got here!

Some things need to change, however. Change can be a good thing. I'm glad, for example, that we have running water in houses now. I like the fact that my dentist can numb my mouth before she drills. I'm totally cool with filling up the gas tank in my Jeep and not having to feed horses in preparation for a trip. But some things really shouldn't change. Nowhere is this concept clearer than in our understanding of human sexuality today.

I'm fairly well-connected to culture. I like to keep up with what's happening in our world. But there are trends, and even terms, I have to look up every few weeks because everything is changing so quickly. When I was in school, children were labeled either male or female. Today, according to the culture, gender consists of more than sixty classifications.[1] For the record, I think there are, in fact, two genders: male and female. Further, I think God created gender as a gift to his creation.[2] But I'm getting ahead of myself.

Let me be clear: I'm not opposed to change when it makes sense, doesn't violate my conscience, or contend with my biblical convictions. So, what does the Bible actually say about same-sex attraction and behavior, and what does that mean for us today? Let's look at the Scripture together.

For the wrath of God is revealed from heaven against all ungodliness and unrighteousness of men, who by their unrighteousness suppress the truth. For what can be known about God is plain to them, because God has shown it to them. For his invisible attributes, namely, his eternal power and divine nature, have been clearly perceived, ever since the creation of the world, in the things that have been made. So they are without excuse. For although they knew God, they did not honor him as God or give thanks to him, but they became futile in their thinking, and their foolish hearts were darkened. Claiming to be wise, they became fools, and exchanged the glory of the immortal God for images resembling mortal man and birds and animals and creeping things.

Therefore God gave them up in the lusts of their hearts to impurity, to the dishonoring of their bodies among themselves, because they exchanged the truth about God for a lie and worshiped and served the creature rather than the Creator, who is blessed forever! Amen.

For this reason God gave them up to dishonorable passions. For their women exchanged natural relations for those that are contrary to nature; and the men likewise gave up natural relations with women and were consumed with passion for one another, men committing shameless acts with men and receiving in themselves the due penalty for their error.

And since they did not see fit to acknowledge God, God gave them up to a debased mind to do what ought not to be done. They were filled with all manner of unrighteousness, evil, covetousness, malice. They are full of envy, murder, strife, deceit, maliciousness. They are gossips, slanderers, haters of God, insolent, haughty, boastful, inventors of evil, disobedient to parents, foolish, faithless, heartless, ruthless. Though they know God's righteous decree that those who practice such things deserve to die, they not only do them but give approval to those who practice them (Rom. 1:18-32).

As we begin this chapter, I need to give you some foundational ideas. Then, we'll get to an explanation of the biblical text. As we deal with the issue of homosexuality (I am using this term as a synonym for same-sex attraction and behavior), I want us to address four realities: 1) What the world says; 2) what the Word of God says; 3) what the church does; and 4) what Jesus would do. But let's look at some foundational thoughts first.

THERE IS A LOT TO CONSIDER IN THE ISSUE OF SAME-SEX ATTRACTION

Hermeneutics, the discipline of interpreting Scripture, is vitally important to this discussion. That's because the Bible speaks about homosexuality. But when you say that, the so-called progressives in the culture remind you that the Bible also talks about not eating shellfish or mixing fabric. Sadly, they think, "Gotcha!" when they mention this, as if you haven't noticed a change of tone between the Old and New Testaments. I talk about this reality often, but suffice it to say, you have to work hard at understanding how to interpret the Scripture. You have to distinguish between a once-for-all command

and a law God laid down in antiquity as he was in the process of establishing a people for himself.

So, when someone says, "The Bible talks about stoning immoral people," just say, "You're obviously stoned yourself, or you don't understand hermeneutics, if you're trying to offer that weak argument just because I hold to a Judeo-Christian sexual ethic." No, *please* don't say that, even if you're tempted to do so. Did they stone people for adultery in so-called biblical days? Yes. Should we stone people for adultery today? No. And the reason we can say that is because of hermeneutics.

One of the hardest things about discussing a sensitive subject, even one about which Scripture is crystal clear, is that people have a hard time separating principles from persons. If homosexuality is wrong, then it's *always* wrong, even if it's your brother or sister, son or daughter, niece or nephew, grandson or granddaughter who engages in same-sex behavior. The relationship we have with people doesn't change the principles of Scripture.

I've had countless conversations with individuals about homosexuality, and after they've heard me talk about what the Bible says, someone will then say, "Ken, you know my brother is gay," as if that's going to be a game changer. It's not! It certainly should be a reminder to all of us that when we talk about anything, especially a situation real people are dealing with (not just abstract ideas), we ought to convey our views with compassion and sensitivity. Far too often we might be correct, but the way we communicate causes people to ignore what we're saying.

Steve Brown recently wrote a book about this very phenomenon among Christians. It's called *Talk the Walk: How to Be Right without Being Insufferable*. Stick to the truth; just don't be ugly about it in the process! You can be right, but please be right without being insufferable!

Principles don't change just because people we know don't like the principles or don't measure up to them. Just because some Christians say something is okay, or even if a national or world leader says something is okay, that doesn't make it so. Anyone's opinion always needs to be subservient to the Word of God. I know that I'm preaching to the choir, so to speak. In other words, I'm not trying to convince pagans about all this. If that were the case, I'd write differently. I am trying to convince you, as a follower of Jesus, of the biblical truth about homosexuality.

There are some other foundational statements we need to make with respect to same-sex attraction. For starters, gay people are more than their "gay-ness." That's a part of who they are, but that's not all. Just like heterosexuals, gay people are doctors, lawyers, teachers, factory workers, and so forth. There's more to their lives than their sexuality (and that's true for all of us, regardless of what sexual label we embrace for ourselves). So, we can still converse with, relate to, show appreciation for, and genuinely care about *all* people — and recognize they are more than the sum of their sexuality.

Gender is another foundational issue. As we've noted already, contrary to what you've been told, there really are only two genders. We believe, in fact, that gender (as my denominational confessional statement reminds us) is actually a gift from God. I understand that there are some children (statistics vary about the incidence of this) that are hermaphrodites (also known as "intersex"), essentially human beings whose physical characteristics don't neatly fit male or female classifications. While the medical and psychological community may add variations to the description, if we're talking about babies with "ambiguous genitalia," the estimated birth rate worldwide is 1 in 4,500.[3]

In these cases, parents are left to make the difficult decision as to which gender to actually raise their child. The term *intersex* is often used for hermaphrodites, but that term actually carries even more concepts with it. Hermaphroditism is certainly a challenging scenario, and in no way do I wish to downplay the difficult decisions and challenging circumstances this situation brings to individuals and their families. We do need to be aware that this condition is a reality. Without a doubt, this condition complicates the understanding of one's sexuality and choices about sex into adulthood.

What other foundational issues need to be noted? Christians, and other people that hold to a traditional view of morality, have often been blamed for suicides among gay people. Some people say, "If you were more accepting of gays, they wouldn't kill themselves." The truth is, sadly, a lot of gay people kill themselves without ever having much, if any, interaction with Christians. Their depression and subsequent suicide often come as a result of their own feelings of not fitting in, of not "being right," so to speak, but not because Christians disagree with their same-sex behavior.

Among circumstances that raise the risk for suicide in the general population are: childhood sexual abuse, which is more common among females; conflict with an intimate partner; intimate partner violence, which is more commonly perpetrated on females; social isolation (being single, divorced, widowed, or having lost a parent in childhood); firearm ownership, which tends to be higher in rural areas and among men; low socioeconomic status; chronic pain; homelessness; being a veteran; immigration; and sexual orientation.[4]

But recognizing that sexual orientation issues raise the risk for suicide isn't an indictment on Christians, or on those apart from faith who hold to a more traditional view of morality. In fact, among adults, one of the factors that often deter an individual from carrying out suicide is church attendance.[5]

Next, in terms of foundational concepts, it's important to remember that the urges we have, or our proclivities toward certain behaviors, don't necessarily rise to the level of sin. What separates temptation from sin is what we do with it, how we dwell on it, and how we act on it. I have tremendous respect for those who struggle with same-sex attraction and yet do not give in because they recognize it is fundamentally wrong to do so.

In fact, I've said for years we have to be very careful about being judgmental. In my own life, I find I'm most judgmental about sins I'm not tempted to commit. That's probably the same for you, too. But just because something isn't my temptation, doesn't mean someone else won't have a strong temptation toward that sin. But we do have choices to make about our behavior.

Our culture needs constant reminders that we don't have to give in to our urges. If we continue to follow the do-whatever-you-want mindset, then survival of the fittest is the end result. If I decide I want your car, and I'm bigger than you or have a bigger weapon than you, your car becomes mine. The same is true for your home, your spouse, or your money. And that's just wrong.

There's much to discuss about nature and nurture when it comes to same-sex attraction and behavior, but at the risk of sounding flippant, it really doesn't matter. What matters is *what we do* with our urges, regardless of their origin. All of us are born with certain proclivities, and nature affects them all. Our nurturing affects these proclivities as well. So, the crux of the matter is not nature or nurture, but rather what we do in terms of thoughts and actions with the feelings we have.

We don't have to give in to sin. You name the sin and I'll say the same thing: We don't have to give in to it. I recognize it takes the Holy Spirit and a strong resolve to heed the Spirit in order to forsake sin. But we can be strong! As Owen Strachan notes, "A man is never less strong than when he rejects God's moral will and succumbs to sin."[6]

And finally, beware of the slippery slope. The culture says it's okay to act on whatever urges you experience. Therefore, homosexuality and gay marriage are now legal and culturally acceptable. If you read much, you know there are pockets within the culture saying that sexual relations between blood relatives, between adults and children, and between human beings and animals should be viewed as acceptable, as well. Let me be clear: I'm not saying that's the agenda of your gay neighbors at all. I am saying there's a mob mentality in our world, ready to further most any sinful agenda. And it only takes one misstep in the snow to start an avalanche.

WHAT THE WORLD SAYS

Homosexuality has been around for much of humankind's existence. We understand that biblical literature points to the issue early, and it clearly condemns the practice of homosexuality (cf. Gen. 19). Further, much literature reveals the role homosexuality played in the Greco-Roman world. Perhaps the most common form of homosexuality was the first-century practice of *pederasty*, which means "the love of boys." Recognizing the Greco-Roman world was a male-dominated society, this practice involved an adult man courting a young boy to become his protégé in various pursuits, and quite often taking advantage of the young boy sexually.[7]

The world at that time, much like today, was enthralled with the physical. Young men would go to the gymnasiums of the day, where they were taught math, science, and music. An older man would become the younger man's mentor and work with him in all these facets of life. And, often, he would use the younger man to gratify himself sexually. Obviously, this is repugnant, but it serves our purpose to see that homosexual behavior has been around a long time, and some cultures have, to varying degrees, accepted it. It was not, however, accepted by all in ancient society.

Now, to a more contemporary look at the issue. Related to current views about homosexuality, no organization has done more to influence the American culture than the Institute for Sex Research at Indiana University (now known as The Kinsey Institute). Several years ago, the famous Kinsey report on sexuality supposedly revealed that approximately 10 percent of the United States' population was homosexual. For a detailed account of how Kinsey's research was flawed, I recommend Alan Branch's book, *Born This Way? Homosexuality, Science, and the Scriptures*.[8] To offer one example, Kinsey's identification of 10 percent of the population as being homosexual included a disproportionate sampling of prison inmates, many of whom were sex offenders.[9]

Much of what Kinsey called "data" was simply pornographic material. He even included graffiti from bathroom walls in his research.[10] Branch notes:

> The true number of people who are homosexual is much lower than
> Kinsey suggests. The pro-homosexual Williams Institute at UCLA's

School of Law reported in 2011 that about 3.5% of American adults self-identify as lesbian, gay, or bisexual and that a further .03% identify as transgender ... About 1.1% of women and 2.2% of men self-identify as exclusively homosexual.[11]

The truth is, the world may have some who are offended by homosexual behavior, but there are also those who see homosexuality as a simple expression of one's self. In other words, many simply voice their philosophy and say, "If it feels good, do it. It's not anyone else's business."

It's obvious that the world has gladly accepted skewed data in order to further the agenda of homosexuality as normative. The Board of Trustees of the American Psychiatric Association voted to remove homosexuality as a mental disorder from the DSM II (*Diagnostic and Statistical Manual of Mental Disorders of the American Psychiatric Association*) on December 15, 1973, and the push for more broad-based acceptance of homosexual activity has followed.[12]

While in office a few years ago, President Barack Obama said that his daughters had essentially helped him change his mind about homosexuality and gay marriage.[13] This signaled a significant shift in policy. Whereas, previously, members of both political parties had stood for the Defense of Marriage Act, President Obama's break from the ranks signaled a new era of pushing to change the definition of marriage in the United States. In changing centuries-long cherished views — and with the help of the U.S. Supreme Court — the president succeeded.

WHAT THE WORD OF GOD SAYS

Genesis 19 records God's harsh judgment on homosexual behavior. More liberal theologians have sought to describe the sin of Sodom as inhospitality. Suffice it to say, I have read their arguments and don't find them compelling in the least. It's difficult to imagine God raining down sulfur and fire for a breach of etiquette, don't you think?

Billy Graham often said, "If God does not bring judgment on

America, He will have to apologize to Sodom and Gomorrah." Obviously, Graham understood that the sin of those ancient cities — and of the U.S. — runs far deeper than violating accepted social customs. Leviticus 18:22 clearly prohibits homosexual behavior: *"You shall not lie with a male as with a woman; it is an abomination."* To "lie with," of course, implies sexual relations in this context.

Leviticus 20:13 says homosexuals must be put to death. Of course, contained in these laws are also the death penalty for adultery, and burning in fire a man who has relations with a woman and her mother. Also, men and women were to be cut off from their people if they had sexual relations during the woman's monthly period.

We may not endorse homosexual activity, but we don't think in terms of capital punishment for these other offenses, and the reason is hermeneutics. This is why I noted earlier that the discipline of hermeneutics — how to interpret the Bible — is vitally important. Without a proper understanding of biblical texts, we end up with all kinds of irrational notions.

I'm certainly opposed to violence against anyone, homosexuals included, but the Scriptures are clear on their depiction of homosexual behavior as an abomination in the sight of God.

Among the earliest-recorded written responses to homosexuality is 1 Corinthians 6:9-10. Paul writes:

Or do you not know that the unrighteous will not inherit the kingdom of God? Do not be deceived: neither the sexually immoral, nor idolaters, nor adulterers, nor men who practice homosexuality, nor thieves, nor the greedy, nor drunkards, nor revilers, nor swindlers, will inherit the kingdom of God.

Let me explain something important: Homosexuality doesn't send one to hell. Neither does adultery, lying, and so forth. Remember, it is a lack of repentance from these sins (and sinfulness in general) — in other words, self-righteousness (believing you don't need a Savior, therefore rejecting Jesus) — that sends one to hell.

Scripture is clear that unrepentant homosexuals will not inherit the kingdom of God. But don't be exclusive here. Neither will adulterers, liars, drunkards, etc., unless they repent. Scripture must be viewed in its entirety, and it is definitely anti-homosexual behavior, just as it is opposed to idolatry, adultery, thievery, greediness, drunkenness, reviling, and swindling.

Some people hold to the argument that they were "born this way." Lady Gaga made a fortune singing a song with that title. The truth is, we are all born with a bent toward sinning. I suspect every adult reading this book has entertained an impure sexual thought. The issue is not about *how* we're born; it is about *what we do* with our desires. We haven't all acted on those impure thoughts for a myriad of good reasons.

Homosexuality brings a penalty. Romans 1:26-27 records:

For this reason God gave them up to dishonorable passions. For their women exchanged natural relations for those that are contrary to nature; and the men likewise gave up natural relations with women and were consumed with passion for one another, men committing shameless acts with men and receiving in themselves the due penalty for their error.

I'm not being judgmental when I say this; it's the truth: There is a price to be paid for living as a homosexual without repentance. The penalty is received by the persons themselves. The Centers for Disease Control (CDC) reports that homosexuals are fifty to sixty times more likely to become infected with AIDS than other groups. Researchers note that "Life expectancy at age 20 years for gay and bisexual men is 8 to 20 years less than for all men."[14]

According to the CDC:

Sexually transmitted diseases have been rising among gay and bisexual men, with increases in syphilis being seen across the country. In 2014, gay, bisexual, and other men who have sex with men accounted for 83% of primary and secondary syphilis cases where sex of sex partner was known in the United States.... Gay, bisexual, and other men who have sex with men are 17 times more likely to get anal cancer than heterosexual men.[15]

While medical advances, especially related to HIV and AIDS, have been helpful in this regard, the statistical data indicates that gay people have a diminished life expectancy. According to a paper published in the *International Journal of Epidemiology* on the gay and bisexual life expectancy (in Vancouver), it was demonstrated that life expectancy at age 20 for gay and bisexual men is eight to twenty-one years less than for all men. The study notes, "If the same pattern of mortality continued, we estimated that nearly half of gay and bisexual men currently aged 20 years would not reach their 65th birthday."[16]

My point is not to berate the gay community, but rather to demonstrate that statistical data verifies what the Scripture clearly posits: There is a high price to be paid for living as a practicing homosexual.

Some have tried to argue for homosexuality and say that the Bible doesn't speak much about it; therefore, we should not say much about it. That's faulty reasoning. The virgin birth is only mentioned a couple times in Scripture, and the bodily resurrection of Christ isn't contained on every page, but orthodox Christians recognize its importance in the larger drama of doctrine.

Scripture clearly recognizes homosexuality as sin. It's not an alternate lifestyle; it is abhorrent behavior, but so is all sin. I think the church would do well to change how we communicate our views regarding sexuality. Rather than singling out homosexuality all the time, we need to put it under the umbrella of "sexual sin" along with all sex outside of marriage (with the understanding that marriage is a union between a man and a woman). That's not meant to water down the severity of the sin of homosexuality, but rather to help everyone understand the severity of all sexual sin.

WHAT THE CHURCH DOES

In his weblog from April 21, 2004, Southern Baptist Theological Seminary President Albert Mohler points out:

As Romans 1 makes absolutely clear, homosexuality is fundamentally an act of unbelief. As Paul writes, the wrath of God is revealed against all those *"who suppress the truth in unrighteousness."* God the Creator has implanted in all humanity a knowledge of Himself, and all are without excuse. This is the context of Paul's explicit statements on homosexuality.

Homosexual acts and homosexual desire, states Paul, are a rebellion against God's sovereign intention in creation and a gross perversion of God's good and perfect plan for His created order. Paul makes clear that homosexuality — among both males and females — is a dramatic sign of rebellion against God and His intention in creation. Those about whom Paul writes have worshipped the creature rather than the Creator. Thus, men and women have forfeited the natural complementarity of God's intention for heterosexual marriage and have turned to members of their own sex, burning with an illicit desire which is in itself both degrading and dishonorable.

This is a very strong and clear message. The logical progression in Romans 1 is undeniable. Paul shifts immediately from his description of rebellion against God as Creator to an identification of homosexuality — among both men and women — as the first and most evident sign of a society upon which God has turned His judgment. Essential to understanding this reality in theological perspective is a recognition of homosexuality as an assault upon the integrity of creation and God's intention in creating human beings in two distinct and complementary genders. This text may be dismissed and ignored by those who reject its message, but it cannot be neutralized.[17]

I think Mohler is right. Sadly, a lot of Christians are waffling. Even kids that have grown up in conservative churches under conservative preaching now say about homosexual behavior, "Well, I may not go along with it, but it's really none of my business. I just don't want to get into it." Frankly, I don't want to get into it, either, but if the Scripture isn't our proverbial "True North," then we've abdicated truth to being put on trial in the court of public opinion. And public opinion rarely vacillates to the side of biblical orthodoxy.

Churches may ignore the issue of homosexuality because they don't want to hurt anybody's feelings. Churches may stick their heads in the sand and act as if it will all go away. And a lot of churches may just give in and say it's not a sin anymore because, after all, "gay people are so nice." It is true; most of the gay people I know are very nice. But I also know a lot of nice problem gamblers. Alcoholics have been nice to me, too. People who have cheated on their spouses appear nice in many contexts. Niceness isn't the issue; holiness is. And holiness is connected to maintaining a biblical sexual ethic that includes sex only between a man and a woman in the bonds of monogamous heterosexual marriage.

Bible-believing Christians face an uphill battle on this. You've likely noted the self-righteous signs some denominations use: "All are welcome here!" Well, in a way, if you have to say it, they're probably not. But, of course, *all people* should be welcome at church. All people should be welcome to hear the gospel proclaimed. All people should be given a chance to meet people who care about others. In every church I've pastored, we've had gay people attending, just like we've also had people who are adulterers, liars, drunkards, and so forth. I'm always grateful anytime anyone (regardless of his or her sin) attends church. Everybody should be welcome to attend the church, but that doesn't mean we shy away from the truth.

So, practically speaking, what should you do? Be a person of conviction, but don't be a jerk about it. Love all gay people and demonstrate that love, just like we should love all heterosexual people and demonstrate it. Befriend them. Take them cookies when they move into your neighborhood. Be kind. I'm going to be as good a friend to all that I can, but I'm not officiating any gay weddings, and in fact I'm not attending any, either. But that doesn't mean I have to be unkind.

WHAT JESUS WOULD DO

I know a lot of people think the question — "What would Jesus do?" — is trite, and I get that. In fact, we ask that question about a lot of things that, frankly, we don't know what the answer would be. I think I know what the answer would *not* be. I don't know for sure what Jesus would do, but I think I know what he *wouldn't* do. Jesus wouldn't yell, scream, and point his finger. Jesus wouldn't instruct his followers to be unkind to people struggling with this sin. And I'm pretty sure Jesus *wouldn't* say, "All the grace and forgiveness I've been talking about is available to all sinners except you." I'm confident the blood Jesus shed to purchase the pardon for the drunkard, the liar, the thief, the adulterer, and the idolater is powerful enough to purchase the pardon for the homosexual, too.

To someone struggling with same-sex attraction, Jesus might say something like, *"Come to me, all who labor and are heavy laden, and I will give you rest"* (Matt. 11:28). Just like he said to his disciples. Just like he says to you. And just like he says to me.

QUESTIONS FOR PERSONAL OR GROUP STUDY

1. In what ways have you seen Christians respond well to those engaging in same-sex behavior?
2. What do you say to the person who says, "The Bible is archaic. If you follow the rules in the Old Testament, you can't even eat shellfish or mix fabric. Why should I care what you think about homosexuality if you don't follow the other Old Testament teachings?"
3. Why do you think Christians so often regard homosexuality as the worst of all possible sins? How does

the Bible place homosexuality in a proper context of sins that grieve the heart of God?

4. What can you do personally to be salt and light to people caught up in homosexuality (or any other sin, for that matter)?

5. How would you respond to a homosexual who asks, "Does Jesus love me?"

RACISM AND SEXISM

THEY DON'T EXIST IN HEAVEN, AND THEY HAVE
NO PLACE HERE.

When my sons were small and we lived in Fort Smith, Arkansas, one of them came home and told my wife, Lori, and me about his new friend. He went into great detail about his new buddy. He wore a certain kind of shirt (like Power Rangers or something), had a really neat cap, wore the coolest shoes, and could run really fast. I don't remember what set his new friend's shoes apart, but my son said something about how much he really liked Chris' shoes.

So, our son invited Chris to our house to play. We greatly appreciated that one of Chris' parents called us to talk before granting permission for him to come to the house. I appreciated their due diligence as parents. They wanted to know the family their son was going to visit. We had never met Chris. All we knew was he was a nice kid, a friend of our son, wore Power Ranger shirts, had some really cool shoes, and could run really fast. Chris shows up at our house, and he's black.

That was the coolest thing in the world. Neither of my two kids used skin color to describe Chris. They talked about his shirt and his cap and his shoes and his speed. Wouldn't the world be a much better place if grown-ups took their cue about other people from kids?

Listen carefully. Racism is *learned behavior*. I remember as a kid that two of my best friends in grade school, Lee and Vincent, were black.

It was never a big deal to us. We even talked as kids about how we were different. I remember in the spring of the year, when we were getting ready to go on a field trip, one of the kids in our class asked Vincent if he could get sunburned. He wasn't being insensitive; he really didn't know. In his childlike innocence, he was asking. And with a child-like innocence in return, Vincent answered him. And nobody thought anything about it. Little kids could talk about race, and nobody got angry.

Let's talk about race and racism. I know for some of you, your stomach started churning as soon as you read that. But, let's also talk about sexism in this chapter. Obviously, there are differences, but there are also many similarities in the sense that we need to understand how other people — that is, other races than our own and other sexes than our own — might feel in today's world.

Talking about such things is uncomfortable for many people. It's the equivalent of — maybe worse than — talking about politics. Let me say on the front end, one of the challenges we have in seeking to eradicate racism is that too many people don't feel comfortable talking about it. Or, at least it seems they can't talk about it without someone becoming very, very upset. Yet, we need to talk about it.

So, we're going to talk about it. We're going to look at what Scripture says, talk a bit about what the culture says, and then hopefully determine together, as the people of God, to respond properly to racism.

For the foundation, let's read Galatians 3:23-29:

> *Now before faith came, we were held captive under the law, imprisoned until the coming faith would be revealed. So then, the law was our guardian until Christ came, in order that we might be justified by faith. But now that faith has come, we are no longer under a guardian, for in Christ Jesus you are all sons of God, through faith. For as many of you as were baptized into Christ have put on Christ. There is neither Jew nor*

Greek, there is neither slave nor free, there is no male and female, for you are all one in Christ Jesus. And if you are Christ's, then you are Abraham's offspring, heirs according to promise.

Before we get to the heart of the biblical text you've just read, let me point out something that is foundational for a discussion of racism and sexism.

Humankind was created for God, not for division.

I'm indebted to Owen Strachan of Midwestern Baptist Theological Seminary in Kansas City, Missouri, for including this concept in his contribution to *A Biblical Answer for Racial Unity*.[1] He highlights the truth that Genesis 1-2 lay the foundation for humanity's existence. And that existence was not created for the purpose of experiencing all the division we have experienced, are experiencing, and have yet to experience as human beings.

As Strachan notes, "There's nothing, in fact, in the original creation that is supposed to be a problem for us."[2]

In the original plan, we were created to worship God, not worship self. In the Book of Genesis, it is recorded that the way mankind worshiped God was simply by obeying God.[3] That is the Christian worldview. But that is very different from what the world system embraces.

Genesis 1 and 2 (which, for the record, we believe to be the Word of God) makes it clear that God didn't create a scientific process whereby human beings would later come into existence. No. He did it himself. He created us himself. Make no mistake here: This is what the Bible says about our coming into existence. We are created by the very hand of God in real time, not by the hand of God through epochs of time, and that distinction matters.

And God said, "Let us make man in our image, after our likeness. And let them have dominion over the fish of the sea and over the birds of the heavens and over the livestock and over all the earth and over every creeping thing that creeps on the earth." So God created man in his own

image, in the image of God he created him; male and female he created
them (Gen. 1:26-27).

There's much we could say about all this. Please notice there is
purpose in our existence; we're to exercise dominion and have stewardship over God's creation.

And then notice that we are created in the very image of God.
Every human being has been created in the image of God. That
includes the ones our culture says aren't quite "right" — not good-
looking enough, smart enough, strong enough, or powerful enough
to make a contribution to society.

Every human being is an image-bearer of God. That is true for the
wanted child as well as the unwanted child. That is true for the
planned pregnancy and the unplanned pregnancy. That is true for
the child of two parents married and in love, as well as the child of
rape or incest. There are no accidental children.

The principles don't change. Either life begins at conception or it
doesn't. My denomination's confessional statement, *The Baptist Faith*
& Message 2000, reminds us we believe life begins at conception. It
says, "Children, from the moment of conception, are a blessing and
heritage from the Lord."[4] No qualifiers included!

So, painful as it is in certain cases — and I'm doing my best to be
loving, caring, and sensitive here — listen: life is sacred, regardless of
the circumstances surrounding its beginning. The little saying many
of us learned as kids is true: Two wrongs don't make a right. Taking
the life of innocent children because of how they were conceived
doesn't help anything or anyone.

Now the truth is, if our culture got this, that would take care of the
bulk of our problems. If we believed every person is an image-bearer
of God, that would fix both racism and sexism (and there would be at
least one less chapter in this book), and it would most certainly shut
down the abortion industry.

All people are created in the image of God. Like we sang when I
was a kid (and I know it's politically incorrect, but its premise is true),

"Red and yellow, black and white, they are precious in his sight. Jesus loves the little children of the world." He does. And so should we.

There is no primordial ooze from which we came. Please don't miss this fact. As Strachan clearly states, "The ground of our unity is the fact that we are made by God — and he made us for himself."[5]

RACISM EXISTS

I know I'm stating the obvious, but sometimes the obvious needs stating. The fact that racism is a thing, that it exists, is an issue in our day and time. It was an issue in Paul's day, as well, as he makes clear in Galatians 3:28: *"There is neither Jew nor Greek..."* This is pretty much the main text we'll use, but we'll be looking at it with some varying angles. Notice the context as Paul continues. He writes, *"There is neither Jew nor Greek, there is neither slave nor free, there is no male and female, for you are all one in Christ Jesus."*

It's important that we clarify something here: Recognizing our differences as human beings is not racism. Persons born in certain parts of the world are lighter or darker in skin tone than others. It's okay to say that. That's not racist; that's a fact. And the fact that we've become so sensitive about saying anything demonstrates what a big issue this really is.

In fact, there are differences among us. That's okay; that's how God created us. Some ethnicities prefer certain kinds of music. That's not racist to say it.

Tony Cobbins is a good friend. Tony was a student of mine at Midwestern Seminary and earned his doctorate there. He pastors a wonderful church in Kansas City. A few years ago, my wife and I went to worship at Tony's church, Canaan Worship Center. All I can say is that I've never been treated so well in all my life. You would have thought I was someone important! A few months later, I invited Tony to preach at the church I pastor. And preach he did!

Tony and I have lunch and talk periodically. He's a wonderful guy. When Tony preached in our church, the stained-glass windows rattled. He's a big man with a big voice, and from the minute he steps into the pulpit and starts preaching, he is full throttle. Now for the record, Tony is African-American. But I didn't invite him to preach in our church because he's black. I invited him to preach because he's a great preacher. He's also a great pastor. He's very likeable. He's my friend. Plus, I thought after all the years of listening to me, our church could use some good preaching for a change!

Tony invited me to preach at his church, and I'm going to do it sometime. But I told him, "Tony, are you sure?"

He said, "Of course, professor! I want my people to hear you preach."

And I said, "Are you sure you're not just inviting me so you'll look so much better the next week?"

And he said, "No, sir, Dr. Parker, I want you to preach to my people."

And I said, "Tony, I'm white."

He said, "I know" (as if I didn't know that he knew).

I said, "And the way I talk, I'm afraid your congregants will fall asleep before I get through my first point."

Now, listen. What I've just said isn't racist against Tony or me. We're just different. Our preaching time is different. When I'm about to land the plane, Tony is just taking off. Tony's church worships for a couple of hours and then feels cheated adjourning so soon. We have some differences. But please don't miss this: That's okay! And it's not racist at all to recognize the differences. In fact, I think it speaks volumes about the beauty of God's creativity.

Paul isn't saying there aren't any differences among these groups. He's saying that old divisions, and the wrong way people looked at each other with an air of superiority, are abolished. The equality and unity spoken of is spiritual in nature; it is *because* of Christ and it is *in* Christ.

The Jew has no advantage over the Gentile, and vice versa. Men aren't better than women in matters pertaining to faith. For believers, we're all one in Christ. This doesn't mean that differences of nationality, status, and gender cease to exist. It means that having become one with God, Christians now belong to each other, and the differences that formerly divided us are not supposed to divide us any longer.

Racism existed in Paul's day. That's why he addressed this the way he did. For all the grief that postmodernism puts on Paul, he's really a Renaissance man. He was way ahead of his time in calling for all people to be treated with dignity and respect, regardless of race, gender, or standing in society.

RACISM SHOULD NOT EXIST, ESPECIALLY AMONG KINGDOM PEOPLE

There is neither Jew nor Greek ... (Gal. 3:28).

At some level, Paul is describing the ideal world, the perfect horizon, the level playing field.

Race is the first example Paul mentions. He says there is neither Jew nor Greek. At that time, there was great division between Jews and Greeks. It was certainly a national division, but it was also a religious division. Jews viewed Gentiles as uncircumcised, so not as children of Abraham. The Gentiles didn't have the law, the ceremonies of Judaism, or the covenants of Jewish faith.

Just as many Gentiles would look down on Jews, Jews were looking down on Gentiles. Paul says this barrier must be broken down in Christ. Again, it's one thing to simply recognize, and perhaps even talk about, our differences (whatever they may be); it's quite another thing to make these basic human differences fodder for ceasing fellowship.

Some of you may be familiar with Steve Brown. He is a former pastor and has a Christian ministry called Key Life. I love and respect Steve greatly. And he's the real deal, by the way. When he's in the room, I promise he's the smartest guy there. He speaks with a voice that sounds like God's, has a white beard, and smokes a pipe (but only when he's breathing). He's Presbyterian, so the pipe is no big deal!

As a side note, I once told him I was going to send him pipe tobacco for Christmas. He said, "Ken, you can't do that. I'm a Presbyterian, so it doesn't matter. But you're a Baptist. If you buy pipe tobacco for me, you'll go to hell."

Anyway, as far as preaching goes, all I can say is he has impacted me more than any other preacher. He spends more time talking about grace (the right way) than anyone I've ever heard. I've been listening to him since I was a college kid, and he has made a tremendous impact on my life.

So, I invited Steve to preach at the church I pastor, and he accepted. So, he is preaching as a Presbyterian in a Baptist church, and he says a bunch of nice things about us. And then he says something like this: "If I lived in the Kansas City area, I'd join your church. This is a wonderful church. I'd become a Baptist. I'm a Presbyterian, you know (long pause). I'm not saying you have to be Presbyterian to get into Heaven ... but why take a chance?"

Do you see what he did? He pointed out some of the differences between us, but put everybody at ease by saying, "It's okay." And it is! We don't have to always highlight the differences, but it's fine to notice them. But don't let them cause a gulf between you and another group. And this is certainly the case when it comes to race.

In Paul's day, there was division over race. That hasn't changed, but believers today have to do all we can to eradicate racism from the ranks. This barrier must be broken down in Christ. Let me tell you what that means, and what it doesn't. It means we love each other and treat each other with respect and dignity. It means we do what we can to avoid hurting people who are different. It means standing up for people who are different than we are when someone is disparaging them. But it doesn't mean we don't have our differences. And it doesn't mean these differences are necessarily in prejudicial conflict.

Think about this in the context of the local church. If one ethnicity typically likes longer services and louder preaching, does that mean they should give up their preferences in order to finish worship earlier and with more of a subdued atmosphere? Are you crazy? If one ethnicity typically likes shorter services and more conversational preaching, they don't have to suddenly shift perspectives, either, do they?

Neither is right or wrong; they're just *different*.

In fact, one of God's special gifts to us is the people who are different than we are that he allows us to befriend or even marry. Parenthetically, Paul's words about being unequally yoked aren't about race. You cannot make a case from Scripture for banning the marriage of one race to another. One of the ways we fight racism is to be friends with people of other races, to get to know them, to hear their stories, to learn of their heart. There will be differences, but there are differences between spouses, and God uses that for his glory. So, why not use differences between races for his glory?

Have you ever heard Tony Evans preach? You can learn a lot about how to celebrate in worship from Tony Evans and the church he pastors. Have you ever been to the home of someone from a different race? I would say, as a white guy (and it's okay that I say that; I *am* white after all), that typically we can learn a lot about hospitality from people of other ethnicities.

I've never liked *kimchi*. I wouldn't like cabbage if you put peanut butter all over it and dipped it in hot fudge. But in the first church I served, we had a partnership with a Korean church. I dearly loved those people, and this kind of experience was very new to me. They were so kind, so hospitable, and so very gracious, and I learned how to fellowship across ethnic lines *pretending* I liked kimchi. I learned more about how to cherish the Word of God by worshiping with those precious people, and they worshiped somewhat differently than I did.

Within the body of Christ — the church universal — there have always been some different perspectives. That's okay. Where it's not okay is if we don't like each other *because* of our differences, or if we think one group is less important because of their differences. One of the early marks of Christian maturity (maybe even maturity in general) is the recognition that not everybody has to see it the way you see it in order to be right.

RACISM CAN BE NULLIFIED BY THE GRACE OF GOD

There is neither Jew nor Greek ... (Gal. 3:28).

Paul says racism can be nullified by the grace of God. In the economy of God, those walls of division are gone. With the grace of God as the backdrop, the things that divide the rest of the world shouldn't be allowed to divide the people of God.

Is God's grace operative in your life? If so, then when you meet people who are different, while you may not change and they may not change, you'll learn to accept and love each other.

I live just north of Kansas City in the picturesque community of Kearney. There's a lot of history here. One of the things Kearney is most famous for is being the hometown of outlaw Jesse James. In fact, James was a member of the church I pastor and is even buried in our church cemetery. For the record, he was a member here long before my time, so I'm not taking responsibility for his lifestyle choices!

At any rate, I love our community, but it is about 96 percent white. It is what it is. I'm not saying there's a negative issue there, and I can tell you as far as the church I pastor is concerned, everybody from any ethnicity is always welcome. I'm just saying that living in a community without a lot of different ethnicities makes it harder to understand people who are different than we are.

One of the joys of my life has been getting to know some younger African-American pastors. Some of them are from the Ferguson, Missouri, region, so you know some of the story they've been living. When I served as president of the Missouri Baptist Convention, we started meeting periodically with no agenda other than just learning to understand one another, getting to know each other, and building relationships with each other.

Of course, it helps that they're all St. Louis Cardinals fans (my team since childhood), but even besides that, we're friends. We're Christians. We're brothers. And there's a bond between Christians when we do it right that is bigger than any barrier race could ever erect. I don't want racism to hurt those guys; they're my family, and I've grown to love them deeply.

In fact, one night we were eating together and, due to the nature of the meeting, I was picking up the tab. Now, there's three white guys and four black guys, and the waitress said, "How would you like the check divided?" And my young friends said, "Just put it all together; Dad is getting it tonight," as they pointed at me. You should have seen her face!

So, what can we do to help eradicate racism? Grieve when someone is targeted because of race. Don't let the proverbial racial slur or joke pass without calling someone out on it. Befriend people who are different than you are. Talk to one another. Get to know why people think the way they do or see things the way they do. Listen to their story. Life is a big beautiful tapestry of variations to be enjoyed if we're open to it.

Let's have honest conversations about race. And we have to see people as more than the color of their skin.

I was happy a few years ago when Fred Luter, pastor of Franklin Avenue Baptist Church in New Orleans, was elected president of the Southern Baptist Convention. Fred's church was all but decimated when hurricane Katrina hit. They had people from their church that relocated all over the country. Long story short, the church worked hard to come back together, but a lot of people didn't come back.

But the church still grew. It's safe to say God used Fred to grow his church twice.

I got to spend the day with Fred a few years ago. He invited Lori and me to New Orleans and promised to show us around and take us to his wife's favorite restaurant. It was a big deal because Fred was the first African-American elected president of our denomination — a denomination that, at its founding, was on the wrong side of the slavery issue in America.

But I can't begin to tell you how tired I grew of hearing people say, "This is Dr. Fred Luter. He's a great African-American leader in our denomination." He and I even talked about it that day. I finally told some people, "How about we celebrate the fact that Dr. Luter is a great leader who just happens to be black instead of acting like the biggest deal is that he's black?" His ministry and his leadership are about so much more than the color of his skin.

And isn't that what Martin Luther King Jr. had in mind when he dreamed of the day people would be judged by the content of their character, not by the color of their skin? I get that it was a big deal that an African-American was elected SBC president. It was. And as much as a white guy can get it, I get that Fred had to overcome a lot to get to that point. But I'm not drawn to Fred's leadership because he's black. It's not his skin color that impresses me; it's his heart!

THERE IS NO RACISM IN HEAVEN

Paul introduces this concept (that there is neither Jew nor Greek) as the way forward. Moving ahead from the time of trusting in Christ, this is the way that it is; no superiority, no arrogance, no racism, no sexism.

Imagine the difference if Christians started living like kingdom people now, especially with regard to standing up against racism. Think of how the world would be changed. Think of the difference we could make. Think of how the lives of our brothers and sisters could be changed.

In his autobiography, Mahatma Gandhi wrote that during his student days he read the Gospels seriously and considered converting to Christianity. He believed that in the teachings of Jesus he could find the solution to the caste system that was dividing the people of India.

So, one Sunday he decided to attend services at a nearby church and talk to the minister about becoming a Christian. When he entered the sanctuary, however, the usher refused to give him a seat and suggested that he go worship with his own people. Gandhi left the church and never returned. "If Christians have caste differences also," he said, "I might as well remain a Hindu."[6] That usher's prejudice not only betrayed Jesus, it turned a person away from trusting him as Savior. I can only imagine the difference there might have been in the world if Gandhi been led to Christ that day.

Racism is one issue, but sexism is another. Although there are sad similarities, it's important to note again that this type of behavior, this kind of prejudice, has no place within the people of God.

Franklin Pierce University student CeCe Telfer won the women's 400-meter hurdles a few years ago. Telfer is the first student-athlete in the university's history to collect an individual national title. Telfer previously ran a variety of events for the university's men's team. CeCe, formerly known as Craig, is biologically a male, running female races. Telfer's story is one of a growing number of incidents in which a male athlete who has identified as transgender has won a female athletic competition.

Can you imagine if I showed up at a local hospital and said that I chose to identify, not as a pastor, but as a brain surgeon? The logic is the same. There have been times I've awakened in the morning feeling like I was twenty-five years old. Then I look in the mirror. The fact is I'm not twenty-five (or even thirty-five; I'll stop there). Would a restaurant let me eat for free if I identified as a child under the "Tuesday night kids eat free" promotion?

The reason I'm bringing up these ridiculous notions is to remind us that the world in which we live is not the world from which we should glean our morals and our thinking. As someone said, "We live in a society where homosexuals lecture us on morals, transvestites lecture us on human biology, and abortion providers lecture us on human rights."

It's a messed-up world. But we still have to do what we can to influence whatever parts of our world we can. So, there are some things we need to properly understand. Put on your thinking caps for what we're about to tackle.

Imagine: Two apples in a tree are looking down on the world. The first apple says, "Look at all those people fighting, robbing, rioting; no one seems willing to get along with his fellow man. Someday we apples will be the only ones left. Then we'll rule the world." To which the second apple replies, "Which of us — the reds or the greens?"

The reds and the greens both matter. Blacks and whites (and all other skin tones) matter. Men and women matter. The challenge, however, is when we talk about racism or sexism. Even having an opinion about something related to race is now considered "racist," or having an opinion about something related to gender is now labeled "sexist."

If I say (and this is a general statement), "I think women are more detail-oriented than men," someone will say I'm speaking negatively of men. I'm not. I am a man, and my experience has taught me that statement is generally true. Of course there are exceptions. Men who are engineers or architects are extremely detail-oriented.

If I say (and this is a general statement), "I think men are typically physically stronger than women," someone will say I'm speaking negatively of women. I'm not. It's just that my experience has taught me that statement is generally true. Of course there are exceptions. Women who are body builders are likely stronger than many men.

So, what exactly is sexism? Sexism, by definition, is "prejudice, stereotyping, or discrimination, typically against women, on the basis of sex."

Essentially, what we've said about racism thus far can also be said about sexism. Sexism exists. Sexism shouldn't exist among kingdom people. Sexism can be nullified by the grace of God. There is no sexism in Heaven. You could quit reading this chapter now, but please continue. I spent a lot of time working on the last few pages!

THERE IS NO PLACE FOR SEXISM AMONG BELIEVERS

There is neither Jew nor Greek, there is nether slave nor free, there is no male and female, for you are all one in Christ Jesus (Gal. 3:28).

So God created man in his own image, in the image of God he created him; male and female he created them (Gen. 1:27).

Do not rebuke an older man but encourage him as you would a father, younger men as brothers, older women as mothers, younger women as sisters, in all purity (1 Tim. 5:1-2).

We're all image-bearers of God, and we're to always treat one another with the utmost respect. Even as we talk about sexism, I want to be clear: We can't dissolve the differences between genders, nor should we! No one can be a woman nearly as well as a woman, and the same is true for being a man. The reason? Because that's how God created us. We believe, in fact, that gender is a gift from God.

All the way back in Genesis 1, remember what the Scripture says? Both are equally image-bearers of God. We are created as God wanted us to be created. Within the church, just like within the home, just like within creation, men and women are of equal value. But we also have different functions. And recognizing our differences — and certainly our different functions — is in no way sexist.

We need to say some things about the culture, and yet there is little we can actually do about the culture at large, unless or until the culture buys into what we buy into, and people are not going to do that until they become followers of Jesus.

Here's what I mean. Men and women should learn basic manners that don't necessarily rise to the standard of Scripture — although, in some cases, I think you can connect the dots to get to a biblical foundation.

For example, when a woman comes to the table, I was taught to stand.

Back in the old days, when pastors sat on the platform in worship, we stood whenever a woman approached the platform. There's not a chapter and verse that tells us to do that, but that was, and is, at some level an outgrowth of Paul's words in Romans 12:10 to *"outdo one another in showing honor."* It was and is our way of honoring women.

It's the same for opening doors. The Bible doesn't say that a man should open a door for a woman. But our culture generally says it's a sign of respect. So, I do that.

But here's part of the problem in the culture, and then I'll get back to the church. In our culture, we're sending mixed signals about gender and sexuality. In fact, we're very messed up. Sometimes a woman feels as if these gestures are demeaning to her autonomy, and so she says or thinks, "I'll get it myself." She doesn't want a man to open the door or pick up the tab at a restaurant. Maybe she's dating someone. She likes the guy. They date, then marry, and she's surprised when he still doesn't offer to do those things. And yet the pattern was already set.

I would hate to be a kid growing up now. People are amped up about things related to the sexes as perhaps never before. If you open the door for women, some look at you as if you're being condescending. No, that's just being nice. In fact, for the most part, I open doors for everybody. It's called *respect*.

When I was sixteen years old and went someplace with a girl (the movies or McDonald's), I paid. The Bible doesn't say to do or not do that, right? It's a cultural thing, but I think it's indicative of patterns that develop. Certainly, the Bible says something about a male taking responsibility for his own family. And I know that while you're dating, you're not family, but patterns are hard to change. So, it's quite likely if, during the first year of your relationship, your date doesn't pick up the tab for McDonald's, he's not going to pick up the tab for the mortgage, either.

Some of this may seem more like a soapbox than a sermon, so let me rein in my dialogue. As Christians, we're to treat one another with respect. And most certainly, we Christian men are to treat women with respect — utmost respect — in all purity. So, we men are to look at the opposite sex without impure thoughts in our minds and impure words on our tongues.

Paul reminds us in other places how we're to speak:

Let no corrupting talk come out of your mouths, but only such as is good for building up, as fits the occasion, that it may give grace to those who hear (Eph. 4:29).

Let there be no filthiness nor foolish talk nor crude joking, which are out of place, but instead let there be thanksgiving (Eph. 5:4).

So, there's no place for a Christian to ever objectify another person, to speak crudely or in a way that doesn't build up the other person. Simply put, treat one another with all purity.

There is a place for differences among believers:

So the LORD God caused a deep sleep to fall upon the man, and while he slept took one of his ribs and closed up its place with flesh. And the rib that the LORD God had taken from the man he made into a woman and brought her to the man. Then the man said, "This at last is bone of my bones and flesh of my flesh; she shall be called Woman, because she was taken out of a Man" (Gen. 2:21-23).

When it comes to gender, it's important to recognize that, while there's no place for sexism, there *is* a place for differences. The problem, at some level, is that there are people who say even recognizing differences is sexist. With all due respect, I don't believe that's the case. There is order in creation, and I believe (and I'm not alone in this) that the order of creation is meant to be reflected in the home and in the church, as well.

There are two terms that I have to mention here: *complementarianism* and *egalitarianism*.

Complementarianism essentially states that, though there may be gifts both men and women possess, there are biblically designated roles for each of the sexes.

For example, both men and women can balance the checkbook, serve as ushers in worship, help the kids with homework, and work on the church's landscaping. But complementarians would say a woman is not to serve as an elder (*pastor* and *elder* are interchangeable terms) because we believe Scripture (1 Timothy 3) prohibits her from doing so.

Egalitarians teach that men and women are both fully qualified in every area of service within the church, including the role of pastor.

My church, and Southern Baptist churches in general, believe the complementarian concept to be proper. Our churches believe that the office of pastor is reserved for men — not because men are better, but because of what Scripture says.

Neither of these positions draws conclusions out of thin air; both say they're biblical. The complementarians simply say they're following Scripture as it is; egalitarians say the Scriptures dealing with male headship are culturally conditioned and are not universal requirements.

I think it's important to remember that the man was created first in the Old Testament and possesses what the New Testament calls *headship* over his wife, and that certainly appears to be universal in scope.

As Owen Strachan noted a few years ago in a *Patheos* article:

Adam is constituted as the leader of his home; he is given authority in it, authority that is shaped in a Christlike way as the biblical story unfolds. According to the apostle Paul, a godly husband does not lord his role over his wife, but rather sees his headship in cruciform terms. He dies to himself over and over in order to love his wife and children well (Eph. 5:22-23) ...

Men are called to provide spiritual leadership and protection of the church (1 Tim. 2:9-15). Elders preach, teach, and shepherd the flock of God; only men are called to the office of elder, and only men who excel as heads of their wives and children are to be considered possible candidates for eldership (1 Tim. 3:1-7; Tit. 1:5-9).[7]

Look at Paul's words in 1 Timothy 2:12-14:

I do not permit a woman to teach or to exercise authority over a man; rather she is to remain quiet. For Adam was formed first, then Eve; and

Adam was not deceived, but the woman was deceived and became a transgressor.

In some ways, this is the linchpin to the complementarian argument. People say of Paul's words, "What is cultural and what's universal?" I believe the issue in 1 Timothy 2 is universal from the perspective that Paul takes us back to the beginning of humanity; it's the foundation for relationships in the culture, the home, and within the church.

It's important to note that the subordinate role of the wife was not a result of the fall. God established these roles this way from the beginning. God made the woman to be a suitable helper for the man. Now I know a lot of people don't like that. But I'm going to have etched on my tombstone: IT IS WHAT IT IS.

This is not about keeping women down in the workplace. No one should ever say a woman shouldn't make as much money as a man in business. This is not about men being superior in any way, and it's certainly not about men taking advantage of their position as leaders in the home. The picture here is of Paul forbidding a woman from exercising authority over men in the church assembly. The elders, according to 1 Timothy 5:17, are those who are supposed to rule the church, and 1 Timothy 3 indicates the elders/pastors are to be men.

Now, let me pause for some of you to catch your breath. The reason I believe what I believe, and the reason the church I lead functions as it does, is not because we're in any way seeking to squelch the leadership of women in our midst. We have some of the godliest, most-gifted, capable, kind, intelligent, and compassionate women on the planet. I'll say the same thing here as I've said about gay marriage, cohabitation, abortion, and other hot-button issues ... I don't have the luxury of changing the biblical text.

Like it or not, men historically have played, and are to continue to play, a crucial role in the church. Jesus chose twelve men to be his disciples. Early-church pastors were all (without exception) men. The Scriptures were written by men (some may debate that point). I'm not saying men are better, but for whatever reason, this is the way God has done what he has done, and if gender is a gift from God (which it is), then we should learn to accept that truth and function accordingly.

I promise you, the ladies that have worked on my staff and have served as volunteers in my church will tell you they've had a seat at the table. I would never want to denigrate the importance of a woman's role within the church. Having said that, the position of elder, which carries with it the responsibility of teaching the whole church, is reserved for male leadership.

And this is the case, not because men are better, but because of God's proverbial flowchart. Now, I recognize there are single-mom and single-dad homes. God bless all of you who are doing the work (literally) of two parents. This is not an indictment on you at all. But in a home with both a husband and wife present, who is supposed to lead the home? The husband. And we've seen the result, too often, of homes in which men have abdicated their leadership responsibility. If that's the case in the physical family, why would that not be the case in the spiritual family (as in the church)?

One of the many problems with all of this today is how lightly some people take the role of manhood and womanhood. We're tinkering with the created order. In fact, much of the positive concepts about the family and about sexuality, as I'm sure you've noticed, are vanishing from our society. And in the words of the famous television therapist, Dr. Phil, "How's that workin' for ya?" It's not — at least not well.

Abraham Kuyper, a theologian, journalist, and prime minister of the Netherlands from 1901-1905, said, "Modernism, which denies and abolishes every difference, cannot rest until it has made woman man and man woman, and putting every distinction on a common level, kills life by placing it under the ban of uniformity."[8]

Kuyper made that statement more than a hundred years ago. Can you imagine what he would say now? The point, however, is that God established the family, the church, and the culture as a whole for the holiness of his people. So again, while I know people today think they have a better way than the biblical way, I would simply say with all due respect, I disagree.

In a Gospel Coalition article from 2012, Mary Kassian wrote:

> Complementarians believe that God created male and female as complementary expressions of the image of God — male and female are counterparts in reflecting his glory. Having two sexes expands the view. Though both sexes bear God's image fully on their own, each does so in a unique and distinct way. Male and female in relationship reflects truths about Jesus that aren't reflected by male alone or female alone ... Complementarians stand against the oppression of women. We want to see women flourish, and we believe they do so when men and women together live according to God's Word.[9]

I couldn't agree more.

THERE IS NO PLACE FOR DENIGRATING ANYONE AT ANY POINT

Love one another with brotherly affection. Outdo one another in showing honor (Rom. 12:10).

Remember Rodney King? Back in 1992, in the midst of rioting across Los Angeles, he famously said, "Can we all get along?" Contrary to what has been reported, King didn't say, "Can't we all get along?" He said, "Can we all get along?" Well, the truth is, we can't. And the reason we can't is because people with differences won't allow themselves to be friends with, be nice to, or even tolerate those of a different mindset.

I recognize there are varying opinions about this topic, but I want you to know that regardless of what differences exist, as followers of Jesus, we're supposed to treat others with proper respect. I'm going to give you a personal insight that may prove helpful. I determined a long time ago not to get rattled with people when they disagree with me, even when they're ugly about it. And here's why: I can win the battle and lose the war. If my deportment and response to others who differ with me is less than Christ-like, I lose credibility, even if I'm right. And I don't want to do that.

In fact, I'll tell you that I'm as committed to the concept of honoring others as I am to the doctrinal positions I hold that might be the very point of conflict between us. I hold to that practice whether I'm talking face-to-face with someone, or even if I'm being lampooned by a keyboard warrior in his parents' basement. Don't stoop to being ugly!

When it comes to our faith, there is great comfort in knowing where you stand and with whom you stand. So, somebody disagrees. Okay. So, they're ugly about it. Okay. So, they think I'm ugly and my mother dresses me funny. Okay. I have a beautiful wife and three grandkids that are better than all of yours. I pastor an absolutely wonderful and growing church. I get to get up tomorrow and go to an office where people generally like me, where I'm surrounded by my books and I sit in a really comfortable leather chair, and where I can drink all the coffee I want. Then, on Sunday, I get to teach the Bible to people who are part of my family serving the God I love.

And one day, when the sun sets on my life and my voice grows silent, I get to live somewhere forever that is more beautiful than Augusta National Golf Club during Masters Week. Where's the downside? What I believe got me here! So no, I'm not going to let people get me rattled because of what I believe. And last time I checked, God still knows more than anyone else.

QUESTIONS FOR PERSONAL OR GROUP STUDY

1. In what ways are racism and sexism still propagated and even accepted in our current culture?
2. What are some instances of racism and sexism you've witnessed?

3. How can we ensure that our own blind spots regarding racism and sexism are brought to our attention?
4. How does what the Bible says about "Jews and Greeks" and "male and female" influence what you believe about racism and sexism?
5. What are some ways Christians can work together to end racism and sexism?

ALCOHOL AND MARIJUANA

WHAT IS THE "WISE THING" WHEN IT COMES
TO GRAY AREAS?

One of the many fine deacons with whom I have the privilege
of serving is Kent Hill. Recently, Kent and I scheduled a
meeting to look over some paperwork related to a church project. I
consider Kent a friend; he also happens to be our chairman of
deacons. At our meeting, Kent was apologetic about all the paperwork because it featured little more than one boring line after
another. However, it's the kind of detail to which someone in my position must pay careful attention.

So, Kent said to me, "Pastor, I'm so sorry that you have to read
through this. It's so boring."

Thinking I would be funny, I said, "Oh, you mean like a sermon?"

Kent replied, "No, it's not that bad!"

Seldom does someone "get me," but he did!

I doubt you'll be bored reading this chapter; at least I hope not.
But I also know some people won't be happy, either. I knew from the
beginning of this project that, in some ways, I would look forward to
this chapter and dread it at the same time. There are lots of reasons
for my feelings in this regard. First of all, I don't want people to write
me off, and I certainly don't want anyone to get angry. So, don't do
either of those and we'll be fine!

It might sound harsh to say this, but I also know that some people approach this subject with less than an open mind. In other words, they have their opinions already solidified (for many reasons), and the mindset is often, "Don't confuse me with the truth." So, the pro-drinking crowd is mad if we get to the point of saying we think it's best for Christians to leave it alone. The no-drinking crowd is mad if we don't consign social drinkers to hell by the time we're finished. So, I can tell you, nobody is likely to be happy.

I recognize at this point (although it is likely to change in a generation) most of the people in churches today are not in favor of marijuana for recreational use. I suspect there's a little debate about medicinal use. But probably nobody who reads this is going to say, "Look, my friends and I get together and we smoke weed socially. Nobody gets hurt. It doesn't harm my witness for Christ. I only do it at home. I've been doing it for years and it hasn't affected me."

But a lot of people use that same line of thinking when it comes to alcohol. They say, "It hasn't hurt me. My friends and I drink socially. I only drink at home. It doesn't harm my witness for Christ." In one of my previous pastorates, I had people say with a bit of a self-righteous edge, "Pastor, haven't you read where Jesus turned the water into wine?" And, of course, I replied, "No way! Is that in the Bible?"

But it's like the way unbelievers quote Scripture to me. They say — and it's always in King James English — *"Judge not, lest ye be judged."*

That's usually when I say, "Have you read 1 Corinthians 2:15: *'The spiritual person judges all things, but is himself to be judged by no one'?"* As you can imagine, that gets me invited to a lot of dinner parties.

So, someone says, "Haven't you read where Jesus turned water into wine?"

And I say, "Haven't you read what the writer of Proverbs says in 20:1, *'Wine is a mocker, strong drink a brawler, and whoever is led astray by it is not wise'?"*

The truth is, we all have some biases when it comes to most subjects, and certainly the subject of alcohol and marijuana is no exception. I readily admit I have biases related to this. I'm glad we got that out on the table, aren't you? It's likely a lot of you reading this chapter have a fairly permissive view about alcohol. Some of that is related to your age; some of that is related to your family background; some of that is related to your religious heritage (or lack thereof). The days of Christians (and specifically Baptists) holding to a "teetotaler" (abstinence) view are quickly fading. Interestingly enough, we're not as open to recreational marijuana use, even though the rationale for such use is the same as it is for alcohol.

Let me share some statistics related to alcohol and marijuana from Addictioncenter.com:

- About 30-40 million Americans smoke marijuana every year.
- About 43 percent of American adults admit to trying marijuana.
- In 2017, 1.2 million Americans between the ages of 12 and 17, and 525,000 Americans over the age of 26, used marijuana for the first time.
- In 2018, 13 percent of 8th graders, 27 percent of 10th graders, and 35 percent of 12th graders had used marijuana at least once in the past year. Fewer than 1 percent of 8th graders, about 3 percent of 10th graders, and about 5 percent of 12th graders reported using it every day.
- About 30 percent of people who regularly use marijuana have a marijuana use disorder.
- The average batch of marijuana in 1990 contained less than 4 percent THC, but that percentage has since risen to more than 12 percent. The average batch of marijuana has become more powerful.
- Drug overdose deaths have more than tripled since 1990.
- From 1999 to 2017, more than 700,000 Americans died from overdosing on a drug.
- Alcohol and drug addiction costs the U.S. economy more than $600 billion every year.

- In 2017, 34.2 million Americans were caught driving under the influence — 21.4 million under the influence of alcohol and 12.8 million under the influence of drugs.
- About 20 percent of Americans who have depression or an anxiety disorder also have a substance-use disorder.
- More than 90 percent of people who have an addiction started to drink alcohol or use drugs before they were 18 years old.
- Americans between the ages of 18 and 25 are most likely to use addictive drugs.
- About 28 percent of all traffic fatalities involve alcohol.

These statistics are sobering (pun intended). And in many ways, they ought to be convincing for us. But there's more that needs to be said, especially from the Word of God itself. Just a few thoughts, but I'll try not to share so much that it drives you to drink.

Let's look first at the Scripture:

Therefore let us not pass judgment on one another any longer, but rather decide never to put a stumbling block or hindrance in the way of a brother. I know and am persuaded in the Lord Jesus that nothing is unclean in itself, but it is unclean for anyone who thinks it unclean. For if your brother is grieved by what you eat, you are no longer walking in love. By what you eat, do not destroy the one for whom Christ died. So do not let what you regard as good be spoken of as evil. For the kingdom of God is not a matter of eating and drinking but of righteousness and peace and joy in the Holy Spirit. Whoever thus serves Christ is acceptable to God and approved by men.

So then let us pursue what makes for peace and for mutual upbuilding. Do not, for the sake of food, destroy the work of God. Everything is indeed clean, but it is wrong for anyone to make another stumble by what he eats. It is good not to eat meat or drink wine or do anything that causes your brother to stumble. The faith that you have, keep between yourself and God. Blessed is the one who has no reason to pass judgment on himself for what he approves. But whoever has doubts is condemned if he eats, because the eating is not from faith. For whatever does not proceed from faith is sin (Rom. 14:13-23).

Well, it looks like we've got our work cut out for us here, don't we?

SOME GRAY AREAS BECOME LESS "GRAY" WHEN ALL THE FACTS ARE KNOWN

In context, we realize Paul is addressing issues related to whether believers should be forced to abide by certain Jewish food laws. He's going to be dealing with those who are strong in their faith and those who are weaker in their faith. And guess what? So are we! Every day, it's likely we rub shoulders with people who are very strong in their faith and some who are one communion cup away from the exit.

To Paul's point, he and other believers had complete freedom to eat what they wanted. But they also were to be cognizant of how their freedom affected others, and it was important not to allow their freedom to become a stumbling block in any way.

So, what about Christians and alcohol and marijuana use? We have to ask ourselves the hard question: Are these substances in any way possible stumbling blocks, or hindrances, that we might put in the way of a brother? Many Christians are quick to condemn the recreational use of marijuana. Their main argument is that it's illegal for the most part, and because of that, the government does not regulate it.

But what if the recreational use of marijuana is legalized — as it has been in nearly a dozen states? Are we only opposed to something just because it's illegal? The argument we use for alcohol thus becomes the standard for marijuana: "It's legal. I don't overindulge; I just have one with my meal. It helps me relax. And doesn't the Bible say something about God has given us *'everything to enjoy'* (1 Tim. 6:17)?"

You recognize, I trust, that the Drug Enforcement Administration (DEA) has classified marijuana as a *Schedule 1 Substance*, the most dangerous class of drugs with "a high potential for abuse."[1] Schedule 1 substances pose a great risk of potentially severe psychological and/or physical dependence. Other Schedule 1 drugs include heroin, ecstasy, peyote, and LSD.[2]

Do you see the logic (or lack thereof) in the way our country deals with these kinds of issues? Public schools monitor Twinkie consumption because Twinkies are considered a threat to our children's health. But as a culture, we're now saying that at the age of twenty-one, alcohol and marijuana should be available. What exactly are we missing with this logic?

You see, there are some things that many in our culture and many Christians would say are not *necessarily* problematic, only *potentially* problematic. One thing that makes something problematic, at least for a Christian, is how other people might perceive what we're doing.

Paul makes it clear that we have to be careful about putting a stumbling block before others. In other words, we have to be cautious that our behavior won't negatively impact others, even if we feel the freedom to do what we're doing. And if someone takes offense over what we're doing, Paul essentially says we're not loving our brother or our sister well.

Contextually, it's important to note the issue of the *weaker brother*. I think it's more than just someone we might influence to do something that ends up becoming a spiritual (or other) problem for him or her. "When Paul spoke of the weaker brother (the one likely to stumble), he was not thinking of a person who might be led to take up drink, and so experience a sad fall. He actually had in mind a brother who was weak because he believed that if he ate or drank certain things he would somehow be defiled and made unclean in God's sight."[3]

I recognize this seems *somewhat* gray. But let's consider the facts. Let's recall those statistics from a moment ago. An estimated 10 to 16 million children under eighteen years of age in the United States have to grow up in a home negatively affected by alcohol. When someone drinks alcohol, his or her rational faculty is distorted, and the baser part of human nature is released.

To make matters worse, there's not a one-size-fits-all point at which smoking marijuana or drinking alcohol moves from *use* to *abuse*. I weigh more than two hundred pounds. It's very likely I could drink more alcohol than a lot of people who weigh less and still maintain control. But how do we know? When is the line crossed from simply drinking to actual drunkenness? We know that from the first sip, things began to change in our brain. If we continue drinking, we know it leads to the point of impaired cognition. Statistical data vary, but we know a significant number of people who begin drinking become problem drinkers. It's also important to point out that no one can become a problem drinker if they never drink.

So, while one may feel more relaxed after a drink or two, the mind is being dulled. As Peter Masters notes, people drink because "they want the mind, the seat of their anxieties, to be dulled. They want the lower instincts to be free. They want their feelings to be affected, and their cares to be slightly anaesthetized." This is "a drug ... being directed against God's highest gift, the reason."[4]

In other words, alcohol causes us to give up, for recreational purposes, one of God's most important gifts: our ability to reason, to be sober-minded, to think clearly. I could offer more statistics, but typically statistical data doesn't move us. Instead, I want you to think about your own circle, your personal sphere of influence, and the people you know. With them in mind, ask the following questions and see what families, faces, and situations come to mind:

- Do you realize the number of sexual assaults that never would have happened without alcohol?
- Do you have any idea how many car accidents never would have happened without alcohol?
- How many affairs wouldn't have happened?
- How many fights wouldn't have happened?
- How much money would still be in the bank if alcohol were not involved?

So, you have to ask yourself, "Is alcohol consumption really something in which I can participate, knowing the potential negatives, and fully experience the blessing of God?" I'm asking this question about alcohol because that's the drug more Christians are willing to use and defend. Most Christ-followers aren't ready to argue for recreational marijuana use — although again, I would point out that the arguments are very similar, which I think (and hope) might lead us to examine our stance in a somewhat different, perhaps even more informed, light.

Let's also appeal to Paul's words in 1 Corinthians 6:12: *"'All things are lawful for me,' but not all things are helpful. 'All things are lawful for me,' but I will not be dominated by anything."* Referring to activities that were not obviously immoral, Paul sets forth some boundaries for our behavior.

He notes in 1 Corinthians 10 that we need to see if something edifies (or builds up) others. Does the activity have positive benefits?

> *"All things are lawful," but not all things are helpful. "All things are lawful," but not all things build up. Let no one seek his own good, but the good of his neighbor* (1 Cor. 10:23).

So, when it comes to alcohol, which is legal, and marijuana, which is quickly becoming legal and more socially acceptable, we have to ask, "Does this help others? Does this have the potential to dominate me? Is this something that builds up others? Does my doing this bring good to my neighbor?"

In 1 Thessalonians 5:22, Paul writes, *"Abstain from every form of evil."* For various reasons, some translators render this as, *"Abstain from all appearance of evil."* The Greek word translated *evil* means "harmful" or "damaging." So, let's connect the dots. Is alcohol harmful? Is alcohol damaging? What do you think?

Again, I'm not going to fill these pages with statistical data. Instead, let me offer some perspective from experience. Granted, my experience perhaps differs from yours. I've been in a "helping profession," so to speak, for almost four decades. I've lived in three states and served six churches (two of these churches for almost thirty years). Ministry-wise, given there are various ways to say it, let me simply note that I've been a pastor, a Bible teacher, a professor, and a counselor. In these roles, I've worked with dozens of individuals and families that have sought counsel from me because their health, relationships, jobs, careers, income, economic stability, reputation, and Christian witness were being harmed because of alcohol use.

And bear in mind, these people would often say they did not *abuse* alcohol; they only *used* it (their words). How do we know when *use* will become *abuse*? Further, many of these scenarios occurred prior to the cosmic shift among American Christians that now view alcohol use in moderation as completely acceptable for church members — and even for church leaders.

While it's only conjecture on my part at this point, I believe time will tell what a terrible negative influence the acceptance of alcohol use is having on the future of the church. Think about how bad things have been related to alcohol use when the church was leading the way toward abstinence. With that wall being chipped away, I can't help but wonder how much worse it will get.

Again, anecdotally (not statistically), I want you to think about how many of the high-profile Christian "superstars" we've seen flame out in the last ten to twenty years. In many cases, one of the activities that has been foundational in their journey toward marital infidelity, gambling, serial sexual hookups, pornography use, embezzlement, and so forth, has been alcohol use.

And alcohol use has often been the gateway to marijuana use, which has also been the gateway to the use of other drugs. To deal with the stress of their celebrity status, they turned to something that might help dull the pain, ease the tension, or (allegedly) clear the mind. They self-medicate, and far too often they self-medicate until they spiral out of control.

AH YES... BUT WHAT ABOUT WINE IN THE BIBLE?

"But doesn't the Bible speak of drinking wine?" Of course it does. I'm not denying that for a second. But we need to recognize that some things that may *not* have been as harmful in other times may be *very harmful* in these days. Let's face it: Among other things, nobody in biblical times was going to the corner bar, having a few glasses of wine, and getting behind the wheel of a two-ton killing machine we call an automobile, right? Worst-case scenario, traffic-wise, in biblical times would be letting your donkey veer to the other side of the road and into the path of oncoming, slow-moving ox carts. And who would that have hurt?

Let me be clear: This is not backwoods, anti-intellectual grasping at straws, trying to control your life. I have neither the energy nor the inclination to do that. If I didn't believe what I'm saying to be true, I wouldn't be saying it. All I stand to gain by writing about this is grief. I want you to be protected. I want your life and your family's life and your reputation to be protected, so I'm appealing to Scripture, to history, and to logic to help you see this.

Historically, for example, the highest achievable alcohol content of wines produced through ordinary fermentation (the *only* process in biblical times) was around 14 percent. In those days, wine normally wasn't even fermented to that degree because of the unpleasant taste produced by bacteria that primitive technology couldn't eliminate.[5]

Andre Bustanoby, in his book *The Wrath of Grapes*, gives a detailed examination of the ancient process of making wine. He concludes that alcohol abuse was not a widespread problem for ordinary people living in ancient times because stronger wines were more expensive, and the common wine was poor-quality and of low-alcohol content. Indeed, much of it never became true wine at all. According to Bustanoby, "It was just aerobically fermented must."[6]

So, what is "must"? I'm glad you asked. It is the juice of the grape that begins to ferment as soon as it is pressed from the grape. The must was left in open jars or vats to undergo aerobic fermentation (in Palestine, that would be only a few days).

The next stage was anaerobic fermentation. That's when the must was shut off from air or oxygen. This was hard to do in antiquity because of porous containers and poor stoppers. So, the cheaply produced ordinary wines were stunted in development, sometimes lacking any anaerobic fermentation.

Until the juice of the grape undergoes anaerobic fermentation, according to Bustanoby, it isn't really wine. It is *new* wine; that is, it has a low alcohol content.

Now, that's not to say one couldn't get drunk on it. As Peter Masters notes, "The common wine of ancient Palestine was certainly fermented and no doubt intoxicating in quantity, but it was an exceptionally weak product by today's standards, estimated at being between 2% to 6% in strength."[7] With that as the background, I think it's safe to say Jesus wasn't serving his disciples the equivalent of today's MD ("Mad Dog") 20/20. For the record, I hope you don't know what that is.

It's not until the process of distillation in the Middle Ages that the previous top theoretical limit of some 14-percent alcohol would immediately increase.[8] These days, gins, rums, brandies, and whiskies possess 40-45 percent alcohol by volume. Think about the difference between that and the 2-6 percent alcohol content in much of the wine from biblical times. So yes, we're dealing with some significant distinctions, don't you think?

The process of distillation also led to the making of so-called "fortified wines." These wines are further strengthened in alcohol content by the addition of distilled alcohol. While I wouldn't argue that wine mentioned in the Bible couldn't make one drunk, I think it's foolish not to recognize the difference between the intoxicating ability of wine then and fortified wines today.

I could go on and on with this, but you get the point. It's not that people couldn't get drunk with cheap wine; they most certainly could. It's just that, by comparison to today's highly fortified alcoholic drinks, it really is a night-and-day comparison. So, for someone to say, "The people in Bible times were okay with drinking wine, therefore we should be, too," is like saying, "The Model T was great transportation and so is a Corvette." They're kind of the same but not really.

While biblical writers may have noted some virtue in imbibing low-fortified wines, I suspect these same writers would look at our alcohol-drenched culture today and say to believers, "Steer clear." It's also important to recognize the many biblical texts that issue a warning related to what wine and strong drink could do.

I think you would agree that the Bible most certainly condemns drunkenness. And often, people say, "Drunkenness is the only thing the Bible speaks against related to wine and strong drink." Well, it's true; it does have a lot to say against these. Noah got drunk (Gen. 9:20-29) and that led to a family crisis (the cursing of one son's offspring). Lot got drunk (Gen. 19:30-38) and ended up having sexual intercourse with his own daughters. It's not out of the realm of possibility that Isaac's wine consumption (Gen. 27:25) was used to trick him into offering his blessing to Jacob that rightfully belonged to Esau.

Those who would be special servants of Yahweh (Aaron and his sons, for example) were to be especially careful related to wine and strong drink usage. Consider Leviticus 10:9: *"Drink no wine or strong drink, you or your sons with you, when you go into the tent of meeting, lest you die. It shall be a statute forever throughout your generations."* And Proverbs 20:1 reminds us, *"Wine is a mocker, strong drink (NIV renders strong drink as 'beer') a brawler, and whoever is led astray by it is not wise."*

Proverbs 23:29-35 gives an apt description of one who imbibes too much:

> *Who has woe? Who has sorrow?*
>   *Who has strife? Who has complaining?*
> *Who has wounds without cause?*
>   *Who has redness of eyes?*
> *Those who tarry long over wine;*
>   *those who go to try mixed wine.*
> *Do not look at wine when it is red,*
>   *when it sparkles in the cup*
>   *and goes down smoothly.*
> *In the end it bites like a serpent*
>   *and stings like an adder.*
> *Your eyes will see strange things,*
>   *and your heart utter perverse things.*

You will be like one who lies down in the midst of the sea,
    like one who lies on the top of a mast.
"They struck me," you will say, "but I was not hurt;
    they beat me, but I did not feel it.
When shall I awake?
    I must have another drink."

We already know that some two thousand years ago the biblical writers said to abstain from every form of evil. If the word *evil* can mean "harmful" or "damaging," and if alcohol at some level is harmful or damaging, don't you think they would have something to say to the people of God about this today?

THERE IS MORE AT STAKE THAN JUST EXERCISING YOUR FREEDOM

At this point, many Christians play the "freedom card," and I get it. I'm not trying to add anything to the gospel of Jesus (believe it or not, I have read Galatians and I know that story line). But I think we have to be careful, even in our exercise of freedom, that we don't engage in behavior that in some way might be off-putting to others.

Let me jump ahead of you. Here's where people say, "But what about overweight church leaders?" I agree, it's a problem. "What about gluttony?" Yes, that's a problem. "What about Christians who flaunt their wealth?" True, that's problematic. No argument with any of these arguments. I agree we need to be consistent. We need to do whatever we can, within reason, to ensure that our behavior doesn't *"make another stumble."*

Even as we talk about what makes others stumble, we shouldn't ignore the fact that we would all rather face someone driving toward us at seventy miles per hour who just ate a half-dozen Krispy Kreme donuts as opposed to someone who just polished off a six-pack of Michelob Lite. Yes, we should be careful not to make others stumble. I think that includes taking into consideration how other people are affected by how we look, how we dress, the homes we live in, the cars we drive, the jewelry we wear, the restaurants we frequent, and so on.

Her name was Carol and she was a part of the first church I pastored. Back in those days, the choir entered from the back of the worship center, along with the ministers leading in worship. Since I've been preaching, I've always used a leather notebook to hold my sermon notes. Call it a pet peeve or OCD (in fact I'm so OCD that I have to spell it CDO, but I digress), but I've always used a nice leather notebook.

One day after worship, Carol approached me, obviously frustrated with me about something. Then she spilled the beans. She said, "Pastor, you greatly offended me this morning when you entered the worship center at the beginning of morning worship."

Now bear in mind, I dress up (I think cufflinks are biblical). I preach in a suit and tie. I have matching pocket squares. My shoes are always shined. I know that a man's belt and shoes are supposed to match. The bottom of a man's tie is supposed to correspond with the bottom of his belt buckle. When my Bible shows much wear, I get a new one from which to preach. I get my hair cut every twenty-one days like clockwork. I'm either clean shaven, or if I wear a Van Dyke (that's a mustache and goatee combo with all the hair on one's cheeks shaved, for those of you who don't know) it's all kept very neat. In fact, I brush it ... every morning. I work hard at avoiding any improper grammar in my preaching. I try not to end a sentence with a preposition. You say, "What's that all about?" And I say, "Never mind!" (Okay, sorry if you don't get that.) So, I thought, "What's Carol's beef with me?"

She said, "Pastor, I was greatly offended this morning because when you came into worship you were carrying your notebook *on top* of your Bible."

Now, I wanted to say, "Lady, is that the best you can do? I mean, I could give you some real dirt if you're out to get me. Talk to my wife. I'm like in the kingdom, but barely! Is that all you've got?" But I didn't. You know what I did? I said, "Carol, I'm really sorry. I didn't mean anything by carrying my notebook on top of my Bible. But if that's something that in some way offends you, I'll try not to do it anymore."

That was a long, long time ago. And if you come to hear me preach anytime soon, you might just notice the way I carry my Bible and notebook. I never carry the notebook on top of my Bible. Carol would be pleased. More to the point, Carol wouldn't be offended, and as painful as that may seem to some of us, *that really might matter.*

1 Peter 4:3 says, *"For the time that is past suffices for doing what the Gentiles want to do, living in sensuality, passions, drunkenness, orgies, drinking parties, and lawless idolatry."* Granted, it's unlikely the drinking parties most Christians attend end in orgies and lawless idolatry. But they might. Simon Peter is noting that followers of Jesus are to be different than the rest of the world. In fact, a commentary on this text notes that the "lives of unbelievers have not fundamentally changed from the first century to the twenty-first; believers should have nothing to do with such behavior, even when their nonparticipation means that others will malign them."[9]

Look again at Paul's words:

> For the kingdom of God is not a matter of eating and drinking but of righteousness and peace and joy in the Holy Spirit. Whoever thus serves Christ is acceptable to God and approved by men. So then let us pursue what makes for peace and for mutual upbuilding. Do not, for the sake of food, destroy the work of God. Everything is indeed clean, but it is wrong for anyone to make another stumble by what he eats (Rom. 14:17-20).

Let's be blunt. Does smoking weed or drinking beer make for peace? Does smoking weed or drinking wine lead to edifying others? Let's land this plane ...

WHAT IS THE WISE THING TO DO?

As I noted at the start of this chapter, alcohol may be a gray area to you, and I'm not going to argue the point. I know it's not a gray area for me. In fact, I would be *"condemned if I"* drink (to use wordplay on

Paul's words in Rom. 14:23) because I have *"doubts"* and because my drinking would not be *"from faith... For whatever does not proceed from faith is sin."*

Even with the little time we've spent looking at this issue, let me ask — in our context, with all the knowledge we possess, with all the havoc we know it wreaks upon our brothers and sisters and those yet to believe — can we honestly say we think recreational alcohol or marijuana use is a completely "gray" area?

Some gray areas become less "gray" when all the facts are known. Not one time in all my years of ministry has someone approached me and said, "Ken, I just want you to know how very much alcohol has positively impacted my life and my family." Not once.

Let me be clear: Obviously I agree with the apostle Paul when he says, *"For the kingdom of God is not a matter of eating and drinking but of righteousness and peace and joy in the Holy Spirit."* So, I'm not a big fan of division within the body of Christ, and I'm certainly not trying to cause any division with my writing. There are a lot of people who differ with my conclusions, and I'm fine with that. We still can love and serve the same Jesus.

But I think it behooves us to ask, "What is the wise thing to do?" I'm not a big fan of abandoning tradition or long-held convictions. I think we do well to consider why our forebears thought the way they thought. Think about this: Even the lost people in your circle of friends have an inherent sense that alcohol use is duplicitous with the Christian faith. I can't tell you how many people through the years have said to me, "But you Christians don't believe in drinking." Lost people have a check in their gut about us doing it. Why don't *we* have that same check?

Why is it (and I know this is changing some) that when some Christians run into other Christians (such as church leaders), they try to hide the alcohol in their grocery cart? I don't mean to offend here, but we've all heard the old joke that says, "What's the difference between Catholics and Baptists? Catholics talk to each other in the liquor store!" With all due respect to our Catholic friends, they're at least "owning" what they practice in this regard.

I'm loathe to become legalistic. I'm not denying that we're free in Christ. I am saying we need to be careful in Christ. I know things have changed in our modern era. But I don't think all the changes are good. Peter Masters notes, "For the last 150 years the overwhelming majority of Bible-believing Christians world-wide have been firmly committed to the practice of total abstention from alcohol. Only a relatively small proportion of evangelicals have demurred, reserving the right to drink in moderation."[10]

That's food for thought. Or maybe I should say drink for thought.

So, to close, let me appeal to a great theological platform for dialogue: Facebook. And I think you'll understand my consternation about this subject. This puts it in perspective on many levels. Someone once posted: "The early church wanted to know 'What must I do to be saved?' Today's church is asking, 'What can I do and still be saved?'"

QUESTIONS FOR PERSONAL OR GROUP STUDY

1. How has the use of alcohol or marijuana (or another drug) impacted your family, friends, and acquaintances?
2. What statistics quoted in this chapter take you by surprise? How do these stats impact your view of the recreational use of alcohol and/or marijuana?
3. Have you ever been made aware that some Christian's use of alcohol or marijuana is a stumbling block to an unbeliever? A believer?
4. Do you think the alcohol in biblical times was at least somewhat different than what we might find in the corner liquor store? If so, in what way?
5. In what ways would abstinence be the "safer" route for believers?

WHAT'S WRONG WITH GAMBLING?

WHEN A "HARMLESS" PURSUIT
BECOMES A DEVASTATING SIN.

Not very many people in America gamble. Wanna bet? According to a 2016 Gallup poll, nearly two-thirds of American adults (64 percent) admit they have gambled in the last year.

Certainly, most Americans would say gambling is a problematic behavior. Wanna bet? Gallup's poll from that same year revealed that 67 percent of Americans feel gambling is "largely morally acceptable." Bear in mind, these are likely the same people who say they don't eat, drink, or spend too much.

Families aren't affected by gambling. Wanna bet? According to Robert Custer, who started the first inpatient treatment program for compulsive gambling at the Veteran's Administration Medical Center in 1972, gamblers moving into the desperation phase feel more guilt due to their gambling and tend to blame others, thus alienating their family and friends.[1] Other studies have noted that families of pathological gamblers often have members who "gamble excessively, suffer from depressive or anxiety disorders, and misuse alcohol, drugs, or both."[2]

Children don't get hurt because of gambling. Wanna bet? I've kept a story in my files for more than twenty years about a seven-year-old girl in Nevada who was raped and strangled in a casino bathroom while her father gambled at 3:48 a.m. Sadly, I doubt that's the only time something like that has happened.

But gambling is a sound method to raise revenue. Wanna bet? In a 2014 documentary, John Oliver shares an important point. On his show, *Last Week Tonight*, he notes that state lotteries are sold to us as charitable foundations, but he finds little evidence that they have any positive impact on most Americans' lives. In fact, most of the $59.5 billion spent on state lotteries in 2012 ended up as prize money. That's a whole lot of money that did not go toward public education, even though that's where we're often told it goes.

But even if a lot of money *did* go to good causes, like public education, we have to think about the greater cost to society. You see, a lot of activities can raise money. That doesn't make them healthy, noble, or in any other way positive, right? Especially as Christians, we have to see the bigger picture of how things affect our world — economically, morally, emotionally, and, of course, spiritually.

Gambling doesn't affect the crime rate in a local community. Wanna bet? Melissa Kearney, an economist at the University of Maryland, demonstrated that casinos, in addition to bringing jobs to a community, also bring their share of negative consequences. These include increased substance abuse, mental illness and suicide, violent crime, auto theft and larceny, and bankruptcy.[3]

But hey, it's only a slot machine. It can't really hurt anybody. Wanna bet? Slot machines, which account for a high percentage of a casino's revenue, are considered highly addictive to players. Rob Hunter was a Las Vegas psychologist who at one time ran the nation's largest inpatient clinic for problem gamblers. He noted that treatment for problem gamblers (including those addicted to playing slot machines in casinos) is similar to that for those addicted to drugs or alcohol.[4]

As we turn our attention toward the issue of gambling, I want to say a couple of things before we go to the Scripture. As with a lot of subjects, we have to sometimes connect the dots from Scripture in order to make a case for or against something. For example, we talk about godly wisdom when we talk about abortion. There's not a verse in Scripture that says, "In twenty-first century America, you shall not continue abortion." But there are a lot of verses that really do connect the dots and point to the sinfulness of taking the lives of unborn children.

I'm going to take a risk; I'm going to gamble a bit myself (pun intended) that once we walk through a few Scriptures and connect the dots, you might see gambling in a different light. That is, at some level, my hope. I'm betting on it.

WHAT'S WRONG WITH GAMBLING?

You shall not covet your neighbor's house; you shall not covet your neighbor's wife, or his male servant, or his female servant, or his ox, or his donkey, or anything that is your neighbor's (Exod. 20:17).

I introduce this text as the foundation because, in the ultimate sense, wanting something you don't have at the cost of someone else really is the issue behind gambling. At some level, gambling is an issue of coveting — that is, wanting something that doesn't rightfully belong to you, so much so that you risk significant loss in order to experience gain.

People think gambling won't hurt them. According to statistics shared by the website nogamblingaddiction.com, there are twice as many addicted gamblers in the U.S. than cancer patients. Americans that live within fifty miles of a casino are twice as likely to become addicted. Each compulsive gambler in the U.S. costs the economy approximately $16,000 per year. Twenty-five percent of addicted gamblers have tried to commit suicide, and Nevada has been the center of such attempts for the last several years.[5]

The bottom line is this: Somebody is paying for all those beautiful buildings in Las Vegas, right? Somebody is footing the bill for the boats that dot the riverbanks around the nation. And, as so many people have told me through the years, the casinos have great food at low prices. Listen to me: *Somebody* is paying for all that food, even if you're not.

The challenge with talking about things like this is when people say, "Why do you make such a big deal about _____ (fill in the blank)?" Well, it's not that we always make a big deal about them. We know the gospel of Jesus is the biggest deal of all. The gospel is that *"Christ died for our sins in accordance with the Scriptures, that he was buried, that he was raised on the third day in accordance with the Scriptures"* (1 Cor. 15:3). So, whether you're a compulsive gambler, adulterer, thief, or anything else, the gospel makes it clear you can be forgiven. That is the biggest deal.

But we have to recognize that the gospel has ramifications for *how* we live. Sadly, in our day and time, there are so many people, even within the church, who just don't understand the inherent dangers found in certain behaviors. I know that we're free in Christ. And the last thing I want to do is become a legalist. I'd rather hang out with liberals than legalists, but that's a subject for another chapter! Having said that, what we do in the body after we've given our lives to Christ really does matter; holiness has outward manifestations, too.

So, first and foremost, let me remind us we're all sinners. We all need forgiveness. And the only way we experience forgiveness from God is by repentance from sin and faith in Jesus. That's the biggest deal, and if you get nothing else from this chapter, that's enough. But I would be remiss if I didn't remind us that once we believe in Christ, once we're forgiven, once we're saved, we have to exercise wisdom so that we live the righteous way.

I'm indebted to Chuck Pourciau, a pastor who helped me understand how to connect the dots between gambling and the violation of biblical principles. Let me share just a few of the principles that Chuck helped me see in Scripture that relate to gambling.

GAMBLING VIOLATES THE LOVE PRINCIPLE OF THE BIBLE

And he said to him, "You shall love the Lord your God with all your heart and with all your soul and with all your mind. This is the great and first commandment. And a second is like it: You shall love your neighbor as yourself" (Matt. 22:37-39).

Jesus offers a simple principle: We should refuse to engage in actions that exploit or mistreat other people. When pleasure or profit is gained at the cost of potentially hurting other people, we violate this biblical principle.

Some twenty years ago, as casinos were being built all around the nation, do you know what the leading new business industry was at the time? Pawn shops. People were pawning their personal possessions in order to gamble or pay off gambling debts.

I went back and checked a statistic from 1997, which was the first time I spoke as a pastor about gambling. According to that statistic, the number of pawn shops in Kansas City had increased from four to thirty-eight since casinos first came to town. Do you think perhaps there's a correlation?

So, whether it's buying a lottery ticket, playing a roulette wheel, or putting money in a slot machine, what are we actually admitting when we do that? At some level, whether we're even aware of it, we're saying we're not contented with what we have. Further, we're eager to get what we can even at the expense of others who may not be able to afford it.

Some people say the Bible doesn't really address gambling, or trusting in luck. Wanna bet? Look at Isaiah 65:11-12:

> *But you who forsake the LORD, who forget my holy mountain, who set a table for Fortune and fill cups of mixed wine for Destiny, I will destine you to the sword, and all of you shall bow down to the slaughter, because, when I called, you did not answer; when I spoke, you did not listen, but you did what was evil in my eyes and chose what I did not delight in.*

The Israelites who set a table for Fortune and filled cups of mixed wine for Destiny are involved in pagan rituals invoking good luck. And God says that in so doing, they're forsaking him. He is saying they're doing what is evil in his eyes and choosing things in which he does not take delight. They are trusting in luck instead of God, so the prophet Isaiah links trusting in luck in that sense with forsaking God.

GAMBLING VIOLATES THE STEWARDSHIP PRINCIPLE OF THE BIBLE

The earth is the LORD's and the fullness thereof, the world and those who dwell therein ... (Ps. 24:1).

Does everything you have belong to God? Is your money *your* money, or is it actually *God's* money? Here's the problem: If you say, "It's my money," then you don't understand that every good thing you have in life has come from God. James says that's the truth. If you say, "It's God's money," and you choose to gamble, you're not risking your money, you're gambling God's money. Regardless of what you may or may not realize, it *is* God's; all of it!

It is one thing to invest wisely for the kingdom of God as the parable of the talents in Matthew 25 instructs us. It is quite a different thing altogether to foolishly squander even a dime of God's money. Would you agree?

Gambling, in its most basic form, communicates greed and lust for material possessions. Proverbs 15:27 reminds us, *"Whoever is greedy for unjust gain troubles his own household ..."*

Again, we have to appeal to wisdom. James 3:17 states, *"But the wisdom from above is first pure, then peaceable, gentle, open to reason, full of mercy and good fruits, impartial and sincere."* Does any form of gambling fit that profile? Is gambling pure? Is it peaceable? Does it bear good fruit? You get the picture.

Some people might assume I'm overreacting a bit to the issue of gambling. Without betraying any confidences, let me simply say that through the years, while pastoring four churches in two states, I have counseled church members and former church members who have come to the church office and asked for money. The reason they have needed help is because they gambled away their money. These are real-life people who sat in worship services and then visited my office because they gambled away their money and couldn't pay their bills. This is not theoretical to me, and so in my mind it begs the question, "Is gambling the wise thing to do?" Is gambling really harmless?

GAMBLING VIOLATES THE WORK PRINCIPLE OF THE BIBLE

Whatever you do, work heartily, as for the Lord and not for men, knowing that from the Lord you will receive the inheritance as your reward. You are serving the Lord Christ (Col. 3:23-24).

Whether you're a pastor, teacher, car dealer, or construction worker, the principle is the same: Whatever you do, work heartily as for the Lord. Agreed? And if you cannot do what you do and give the glory to God, then in good conscience, you can't keep doing what you're doing.

So you can work at a factory or push a broom for the glory of God. But can you, in good conscience, be involved in a get-rich-quick scheme that takes money from people without actually giving the vast majority of them anything in return? This may sound harsh, but let me ask, "Can you roll the dice at a casino to the glory of God, knowing the money you're likely to lose belongs to God in the first place?"

You see, all through Scripture, work is viewed as a positive use of one's time. In fact, it is good stewardship to be a good worker. But when we seek to get something for nothing, we are violating the work principle of the Bible.

Nowhere have I seen this more keenly illustrated than in the January 26, 1997, edition of the *Kansas City Star*. According to a story in the *Star*, there was a lottery poster in Massachusetts that read:

HOW TO MAKE MILLIONS. PLAN A — START STUDYING WHEN YOU ARE ABOUT SEVEN YEARS OLD, REAL HARD.

THEN GROW UP AND GET A GOOD JOB. FROM THEN ON, GET UP AT DAWN EVERY DAY ... DO THIS EVERY DAY FOR THIRTY YEARS, HOLIDAYS AND WEEKENDS INCLUDED. PLAN B — (a picture of two lottery tickets).

Whatever someone wins at gambling is won through someone else's loss; it costs someone something. It might be a paycheck. It might be a child's milk money. It might be a pair of shoes or an elderly person's medication. We certainly can't trace all this completely. But we can say with certainty about gambling: Only by some people losing do some other people win.

Joseph Conrad once wrote, "All ambitions are lawful except those which climb upward on the miseries of mankind."[6] That's about as apt a description of gambling as I've ever read.

GAMBLING VIOLATES THE CONTENTMENT PRINCIPLE OF THE BIBLE

You shall not covet your neighbor's house; you shall not covet your neighbor's wife, or his male servant, or his female servant, or his ox, or his donkey, or anything that is your neighbor's (Exod. 20:17).

So when the woman saw that the tree was good for food, and that it was a delight to the eyes, and that the tree was to be desired to make one wise, she took of its fruit and ate, and she also gave some to her husband who was with her, and he ate (Gen. 3:6).

Exodus 20:17 reminds us we should not set our hearts on something that belongs to someone else. Genesis 3:6 details the incident in which Adam and Eve demonstrated their dissatisfaction with God's provision.

Let that sink in. At some level, sin came into the world because two people were not content with what God had given them. Aren't we glad that's the only time that's ever happened?

The truth is, gambling often represents the same attitude Adam and Eve exhibited. It is an affront to God and his blessings if we're gambling because we're not content with what we have. God gives us what we need. He knows the place in life he wants for us. Remember what the apostle Paul said, *"But godliness with contentment is great gain"* (1 Tim. 6:6).

Now before we close this chapter, let's be clear, because somebody is probably going to write me off about this, thinking I'm overly zealous or legalistic. The reason some might write me off is because they're thinking about playing a card game with their buddies where they might win or lose five dollars in the course of an evening. This is not an indictment against you if you play a round of golf and the loser buys chocolate shakes for the group.

I don't know where the line is, but here's the difference. A few bucks out of pocket buying a shake for a couple of guys you've golfed with isn't the same as spending your kids' food money on lottery tickets. Now, if you don't have the few bucks to buy shakes, you shouldn't buy shakes, but that's a subject for another day.

The problem is, there are far too many people who are gambling away things they need to make it for another day. So please recognize the biblical principles gambling violates.

GAMBLING VIOLATES THE WITNESS PRINCIPLE OF THE BIBLE

Do not, for the sake of food, destroy the work of God. Everything is indeed clean, but it is wrong for anyone to make another stumble by what he eats. It is good not to eat meat or drink wine or do anything that causes your brother to stumble (Rom. 14:20-21).

"... or do anything." That's a pretty tall order, isn't it? It is, but we have to take it seriously. Paul reminds Christians that we have to take into account how our actions impact those around us. In many cities in America, shuttle buses that run between communities and casinos

have darkened windows. Do you know why? Because the industry wants to protect the anonymity of the gamblers. They recognize there are still people who view gambling as a negative influence on society. If the world sees gambling as a negative, how much more cautious should Christians be about it?

The bottom line is that gambling, even what many would see as innocent, has a negative impact on the witness of the church of Jesus. Let me share a story that illustrates my point.

This happened many years ago, but I'll never forget it. I have purchased one lottery ticket in my life. It was at a store in my hometown of Cahokia, Illinois. I was only 17 years old. I was working at the Cahokia McDonald's as a senior in high school. I don't remember exactly the level to which the lottery's total had risen, but it was astronomical — several million dollars. Everybody was talking about it. It became the big conversation around the water cooler. I don't (and didn't) have a penchant for any financial risk-taking, but for some reason, I decided I'd get a ticket.

So, I'm a high school kid working at McDonald's. I bought just one ticket. I didn't think I would win. And while I don't remember how much the ticket cost me, and while it wasn't a good use of the money, it didn't create an economic hardship for me in any way. Innocent enough, right?

So, I bought the ticket. I turned and left the counter, and I'm on my way out of the store. As I walked toward the door, my supervisor from McDonald's (who had never indicated any kind of faith background to any of us), saw me and said, "Ken, I thought you were a Christian."

What's wrong with gambling? Even pagans recognize that Christians shouldn't do it.

QUESTIONS FOR PERSONAL OR GROUP STUDY

1. What are some biblical principles that gambling violates?
2. How might gambling in any form affect your view of God's provision and your stewardship of resources?
3. What impact might gambling have on your witness for Christ?
4. Overall, do you have a positive or negative view of gambling? Do any of the points shared in this chapter cause you to think differently about those views?
5. Have you ever purchased lottery tickets? Why is this a harmful way to spend a few bucks?

8

DEPRESSION HURTS

IT'S REAL, AND IT'S NO RESPECTER OF PERSONS.
BUT IT'S NOT SINFUL.

Winston Churchill, Abraham Lincoln, Isaac Newton, Vincent Van Gogh, Ludwig Von Beethoven, Jane Pauley, Terry Bradshaw, and Mike Wallace. What do these famous people have in common? They all suffered from depression.

The term *depression* covers a variety of negative moods and behavioral changes. Sometimes these are normal mood fluctuations, and sometimes they rise to the level of clinical problems — meaning, they're significantly interfering with day-to-day functioning. The mood change can be brief or long-lasting. A person might have just a tinge of a melancholy disposition or a foreboding sense of darkness that just won't lift.[1]

For women, the risk for the first episode of any degree of depression is highest between the ages of 20-29. For men, the similar risk period is between the ages of 40-49. Women are at least twice as likely as men to experience all types of depression.[2] We could offer lots of facts and figures about depression at this point. There is chronic low-grade depression, persistent depressive disorder (dysthymia), major depressive disorder, major depressive disorder episode with psychotic features, bipolar disorder, postpartum depression, and on and on. There is even a condition known as *seasonal affective disorder*, which typically begins in early autumn and lasts throughout the winter. It is a real condition that affects some 5 percent of the population.[3]

We could talk about the correlation between anxiety and depression, and there most certainly is one. But much of what might apply to depression, and a good response to it, applies to other moods with which people struggle that have a negative effect on their functionality. We could talk about various ways people are treated for depression and what the causes are.

In case you're wondering, sometimes there are biological factors in play. Suffice it to say, it is reasonable to note that to some degree, these issues "run in families," so to speak.[4] So if my mom and dad suffered from depression or anxiety, there's a higher probability that I will, too, simply based on biological factors. And that's to say nothing of circumstances — meaning, if I lose my job or face a major illness, I might end up anxious and depressed, and even as a man of faith, understandably so.

It's one thing, perhaps, to mention celebrities who have dealt with depression. It's quite another to mention our heroes who have suffered from depression — or at the very least, from what we can tell, demonstrated symptoms connected to depression.

What about depression and very wise people? What about depression and righteous people? Does living a life of faith exempt one from the shroud of this type of darkness? The answer is "no." So, we're going to look to Scripture and gain some understanding into this condition that affects so many people, including Christians.

DEPRESSION IS A REAL CONDITION

So I turned about and gave my heart up to despair over all the toil of my labors under the sun (Eccles. 2:20).

Ecclesiastes is technically penned by an anonymous (or pseudonymous) author; that is, he never reveals his name in the text. Having said that, traditional Jewish and Christian scholarship has ascribed authorship to Solomon, since the book describes the author as the "son of David, king in Jerusalem."[5] There also are a lot of reasons scholars question Solomon's authorship. In fact, entire volumes have been written about whether Solomon is the writer of Ecclesiastes.

We know the writer was the son of David, king in Jerusalem. But, as many people note, that could be indicative of a lot of people.[6] We also know he was a man of great wisdom. Debating the authorship of the book is a little out of the purview of this chapter, so allow me to skirt the debate and simply refer to the author as "the Preacher" (see Eccles. 1:1). The author refers to himself with this title and, in doing so, simply references himself as one who assembles groups.

So, the Preacher gives his heart to despair. Now, for the record, he has good reasons to do so. He's thinking about how he has worked his whole life, and now he has to leave all he's earned to someone who didn't toil for it. Because of this and other worries, the author says all his days are "full of sorrow." May I simply tell you that at some level, in my little sphere of influence, what the Preacher says resonates with me.

I remember making great strides in one particular church where I served as pastor. We grew spiritually and numerically. Receipts were up, and we were baptizing a lot of people. We completed a major renovation. Everything was going well. It was a very fruitful time of ministry, but it was not to last. I left to pastor another church. And in time, the search committee from my previous church called to tell me about the man they felt led to call as my successor. Weeping over the phone, one member of the committee said, "We believe this is the man who is going to take what you've done here and continue moving us in the right direction to even greater ministry."

I thought that was awesome. They called the man as pastor. Then they observed his interaction with his wife and were disappointed. Then the staff worked with him for a while and were disappointed. The congregation tried to work with him, but they, too, were disappointed. They witnessed everything from improper language to sloth.

The new pastor "grew" the church to about half the size it was before he came. And frankly, it almost killed me. I thought about all the Fridays I hadn't taken off and worked instead. I thought about all the money we spent for renovation. I thought about all the people we had baptized and the programs we had begun, and then this guy comes out of nowhere and messes it all up. I know that sounds a little harsh, but that's how I felt at the time. Obviously, I know now it was more complicated than that.

It really bothered me and made me sorrowful. Perhaps you've had that same kind of experience. You worked so hard to build something up only to see it torn down. It fills your days with sorrow, doesn't it? Most people face some down days, but normally those days don't linger.

The mental health community makes a distinction between *Major Depressive Disorder* and *Dysthymic Disorder*.[7] Dysthymia is defined as "a condition characterized by mild and chronic depressive symptoms."[8] Major Depressive Disorder is a little different, in that the person experiencing this disorder has had "one or more major depressive episodes without ever experiencing a manic or hypomanic episode."[9]

Estimates vary as to how many people in the United States currently deal with some form of depression. I've read that it affects anywhere from ten to fifteen million American adults. For what it's worth, I think the percentage is higher than that. And often, people deal with more than one type of mental challenge. Let me share a few symptoms of depression:[10]

- A depressed mood most of the day (feeling sad, empty, hopeless, or on the verge of tears)
- Loss of interest or pleasure in activities you once enjoyed (including sex)
- Extreme irritability over seemingly minor things
- Fixation on the past or on things that have gone wrong
- Weight loss (even when not on a diet) or, sometimes, weight gain; decrease and increase in appetite
- Difficulty sleeping or being overly tired
- Restlessness or feeling slowed down

- Fatigue or loss of energy
- Feeling worthless or guilty
- Lack of concentration or difficulty making decisions
- Thoughts of death or suicide

There's no single cause of depression. Brain chemistry, hormones, and genetics certainly play a role, as do the following:[11]

- Low self-esteem
- Anxiety disorder, borderline personality disorder, post-traumatic stress disorder
- Physical or sexual abuse
- Chronic diseases like diabetes, multiple sclerosis, or cancer
- Alcohol or drug use

Let me be extremely careful how I say these next sentences. I think it's important to recognize that sometimes our choices lead to depression. Please understand, I'm not saying sin always is the culprit of one's depression. At the same time, we can't rule out that possibility. When I know what to do and don't do it, or I do what I know I shouldn't do, that puts a strain on my relationships with God, my family, and my friends. It even changes my self-image. Now, make sure you know what I am *not* saying: I'm not saying depression is always a result of sin. Got it? That is simply not the case.

As Jonathan Holmes notes, "What we do is driven by what is in our hearts."[12] If we allow ongoing secret sin in our hearts, that undoubtedly has a negative effect on "what we do," right? And then doing what we shouldn't, or not doing what we should, can most certainly produce a depressed effect.

I suspect most everyone reading these pages has either known someone who struggled with depression or has suffered it themselves. It's real.

In many ways, I think depression might be even more pervasive today than in the past. I can't prove it, but I think this is the case because of technology. We're never "off." People are always "on call;" there's never a break in the action. Loved ones are scattered across the country so there's not always a close-at-hand support system. Family members used to live much closer to one another, so face-to-face communication and support were daily occurrences.

Expectations are vastly different today, as well. People have to be ten different places at the same time. So, we're frazzled. Fatigue is a constant companion in many cases. Unfortunately, we don't always apply the principle of Sabbath rest, which further exacerbates the problem. Also, while our forebears were well-acquainted with fatigue, they had more physical activity day in and day out. While I'm sure their physical labor caused stress of its own, in many ways that kind of work was also a stress reliever.

Depression is real. I know it sounds peculiar to have to say it, but it's true. I'm reminded of the book and then the major motion picture *Heaven Is For Real*. For the record, I don't believe the little boy died and then came back to life. If you know Scripture, that is no real surprise to you. But the statement is still true: Heaven is for real. So is depression.

DEPRESSION IS NO RESPECTER OF PERSONS

We've already noted that the Preacher in Ecclesiastes likely was depressed. But he's not the only biblical character whose disposition and behavior fit the mold. Look at the prophet Elijah.

> But he himself [Elijah] *went a day's journey into the wilderness and came and sat down under a broom tree. And he asked that he might die, saying, "It is enough; now, O LORD, take away my life, for I am no better than my fathers"* (1 Kings 19:4).

Isn't that amazing? Here's a man of God who has just stared down the prophets of Baal in a very public setting in which Yahweh proves himself the one true God. And the next thing you know, Jezebel is after Elijah and he wants to die. Please understand: Elijah is an extraordinary man. In 2 Kings 2 the Scripture records that Elijah is taken to heaven in a whirlwind.

Elijah is an exceptional character, a real "man's man." This is *Braveheart's* Mel Gibson, *Die Hard's* Bruce Willis, *Rocky's* Sylvester Stallone, and *Fast Five's* The Rock all rolled into one ... only sanctified! And he wants to die!

Are you familiar with the story of Jonah? Jonah gets so mad at God — because the Ninevites repented at his preaching — that he travels east of the city and makes a little booth for himself. God, in his grace, causes a plant to come up over Jonah to shade him. This makes Jonah happy. Then God sends a worm to attack the plant, and it withers. Finally, God causes the sun to rise along with a scorching east wind. Jonah grows faint and he tells God, *"It is better for me to die than to live"* (Jon. 4:8).

I don't have any way of reading Jonah's medical chart, but I have a strong suspicion he is depressed. So, the Preacher in Ecclesiastes is depressed. Elijah is depressed. It certainly looks as if Jonah is depressed. My hunch is Noah's drunken stupor may have been brought about by depression, too; all that time on an ark with a bunch of animals — and your family! Okay, maybe that wasn't the reason, but I'm sure he had his reasons.

Depression is no respecter of persons. Charles Spurgeon, arguably one of the greatest preachers who ever lived, battled depression fiercely throughout much of his life. Listen to how Spurgeon articulated what he felt. Depressions of various kinds, he said, make us like those who "traverse" the "howling desert." We endure "winters." We are "bruised as a cluster, trodden in the wine-press," and we enter the "foggy day," amid storms like those "caught in a hurricane."[13]

Spurgeon knew what he was talking about. He said, "The waters roll continually wave upon wave" over the tops of us. We are like those "haunted with dread," in the "dark dungeon," or "sitting in a chimney-corner under an accumulation of pains, and weaknesses, and sorrows." We "sit in darkness, like one who is chilled and benumbed, and over whom death is slowly creeping." We are "panting warriors" and "poor fainting soldiers," in need of relief from this "long fight of affliction."[14]

His words resonate with some of you. I'm so sorry; but it's okay. I want you to know, it's okay. You are not alone.

The point is, in biblical days, being a righteous person didn't preclude someone from becoming depressed. It didn't then, and it doesn't now. Phillips Brooks is credited as saying, "Christianity helps us face the music even when we don't like the tune." Righteous people throughout the ages have dealt with the darkness of depression, too. It is no respecter of persons.

DEPRESSION IS NOT SINFUL

And he [Jesus] withdrew from them about a stone's throw, and knelt down and prayed, saying "Father, if you are willing, remove this cup from me. Nevertheless, not my will, but yours, be done." And there appeared to him an angel from heaven, strengthening him. And being in agony he prayed more earnestly; and his sweat became like great drops of blood falling down to the ground. And when he rose from prayer, he came to the disciples and found them sleeping for sorrow, and he said to them, "Why are you sleeping? Rise and pray that you may not enter into temptation." (Luke 22:41-46).

Verse 45 records Jesus' disciples are "sleeping for sorrow." That sounds like depression to me. And yet their grief isn't sin. Jesus is asking the heavenly Father to provide another way. He's sweating blood in agony, crying out to God. Why do we have such a hard time thinking Jesus might have been depressed? I'll tell you why ... because we've been hardwired wrongly to think there is something inherently bad in us if we're depressed. And that's simply not right.

The reason I say we've been hardwired wrongly this way is because of the way many Christians treat depression and other mental maladies. We need to lift the veil on these and help our brothers and sisters understand that, most often, it's not their fault. Depression isn't sin.

Although sin can *sometimes* lead to depression, it is not *necessarily* a cause. Tomorrow, if I cheat on my wife, lose my job, lose my income, lose my house, lose my relationship with my sons and grandchildren and so forth, I am certain to become depressed. In that case, my sin is at the root of it all. In that case, the most significant part of the cure *is* repentance from sin and faith in Jesus. As Bryan Chapell writes, "Christ's victory on the cross provides freedom both from the guilt and the power of sin."[15] But there are a lot of people who are depressed because of genetics; some who are depressed because of circumstances over which they've had little or no control. Many are depressed and there's absolutely *no link* between their depression and their own personal sin.

Cancer isn't a sin, right? There should be no shame in cancer. Why do we let people feel shame or guilt because of depression or anxiety? It's not right! I don't think we even mean to. Again, we need to lift the veil and bring this into the light. People are hurting. People are even dying because of it, and in most cases, it is simply *not* their fault.

BECAUSE OF JESUS, THERE IS ALWAYS HOPE

Hearkening back to Joshua 1:5, the writer of Hebrews offers some concluding encouragement to his letter. As recorded in Hebrews 13:5-6, he says of the Lord, *"I will never leave you nor forsake you, so we can confidently say, 'The LORD is my helper; I will not fear; what can man do to me?'"*

There are a lot of different ways to address depression: meeting with others, enriching activities, individual and group counseling, strategizing how to deal with one's problems, and sometimes medication. All of these can be good, and they can be used by God to help. You're not weak or sinful if you need to talk with someone. You're not weak or sinful if you have to take medicine that helps your brain function properly. We don't think cancer patients on chemo are weak or sinful. So, if you're on medication for anxiety or depression, it's not because you're weak or sinful, either.

I realize that in some cases, medication is viewed as the "quick fix," without making allowances for other ways to help. But as Zach Eswine notes, "... taking medicine is a wise act of faith, not of unfaith."[16] He goes on to quote Spurgeon about this issue. Spurgeon said, "It would not be wise to live by a supposed faith, and cast off the physician and his medicines, any more than to discharge the butcher, and the tailor, and expect to be fed and clothed by faith."[17]

But here's the good news. Just like with any illness, Jesus is always there. If you've believed in him, you belong to Jesus and Jesus belongs to you. Regardless of what you might endure, Jesus will never leave nor forsake you. He may not take you around the pain, but he will most certainly walk with you through it.

QUESTIONS FOR PERSONAL OR GROUP STUDY

1. What are some signs of depression?
2. Think about how you would respond if someone says, "People of faith shouldn't be depressed. Depression demonstrates their lack of trust in God."
3. In what ways is it helpful to know that people we consider giants of our faith have struggled with depression?
4. What role might faith play in helping someone with depression?
5. What role might medication play in helping someone with depression?

THE SANCTITY OF LIFE
ABORTION, EMBRYONIC STEM CELL RESEARCH, CLONING,
AND EUTHANASIA.

A little boy was watching his father, who happened to be a pastor. The dad was very busy preparing his message. The little boy said, "Daddy, how do you know what to preach? How do you know what to say?"

The father responded, "God tells me what to say, son."

The little boy said, "Then why are you scratching so much of it out?"

The truth is, many people in the world, and even some in the church, might wish to scratch the topic of the sanctity of life from serious discussion. In fact, I can't think of anything that tends to cause people more consternation than this issue.

The term *sanctity* simply means "sacred." We're talking about the sacredness of life. According to Webster, *sacred* simply means "set apart," "dedicated," or "entitled to receive respect." We believe human life is deserving of respect. Christians believe life is sacred; it is a gift from God.

Why should Christians talk about the sanctity of life? After all, Roe v. Wade is already on the books. The U.S. Supreme Court cemented the "Constitutional right" to abortion in 1973. So, there's really nothing we can do, right? Not exactly! We still need to talk about it because we still need to do whatever we can to help foster a culture that values life.

Not everyone understands from a biblical perspective what the sanctity of life — that is, respecting life — really means. I have heard people say the church should be silent regarding this issue because we're all on the same page, or because it's only a political thing. But Christians aren't all on the same page. One reason we're not on the same page is because in a lot of churches the sanctity of life isn't discussed.

I was 29 years old before I recalled hearing a message on the sanctity of life in my local church. And I heard it that day because I preached it during the first month of my tenure as a senior pastor. While there's little doubt this subject lends itself to being politicized, the reality is we can talk about it without ever mentioning Democrats or Republicans.

I'm afraid too often the church views abortion like starving children on TV. We want to change channels so the problem goes away, or at least escapes our line of sight. But we cannot ignore it. If I am silent on this issue, I communicate indifference at the very least. As the church largely was silent while millions of Jews were exterminated in Nazi concentration camps, I believe we are held accountable before God when we do not speak on behalf of those who have no voice.

I believe on this issue we must speak the truth in love, yet still speak the truth. We must confront our culture. Amos was an example of a prophet of justice. Amos 5:24 reads, *"But let justice roll down like waters, and righteousness like an ever-flowing stream."* Our call to righteousness, rightness before God, compels us to speak the truth about this issue.

Let me also clarify God's forgiveness at this point. Violation of the sanctity of life is not the unpardonable sin. I'm sure many who read this have been touched by this issue. The goal is not to heap guilt on anyone. I certainly don't wish to construct a hierarchy of sins. Mainly, I want to clarify and articulate a biblical position on the issues surrounding the sacredness of human life. Just as the church should be redemptive concerning any sin, we should also warn against the pain that accompanies it.

Please understand, I want to be informative and redemptive. If you've fumbled the ball regarding this issue, your sin is no greater than my sin, whatever it might be. But every woman I've spoken with through the years who has had an abortion, or every man who has participated in some way facilitating one, has articulated they wished someone would have told them about the residual effects that would appear later.

MANY ISSUES, ONE OVERARCHING PRINCIPLE

When we talk about the sanctity of life, it includes many subjects: abortion, cloning, embryonic stem cell research, euthanasia, and valuing the elderly. In all of these, there is one overall principle: Prosperity and the blessing of a nation are found in choosing life. Deuteronomy 30:19-20 says:

> *I call heaven and earth to witness against you today, that I have set before you life and death, blessing and curse. Therefore choose life, that you and your offspring may live, loving the LORD your God, obeying his voice and holding fast to him, for he is your life and length of days, that you may dwell in the land that the LORD swore to your fathers, to Abraham, to Isaac, and to Jacob, to give them.*

Granted, appealing to an Old Testament text to convince people that life is sacred likely won't win your debate. But if we're talking with other believers, obviously the Bible should be the starting point for our understanding, right? And throughout both testaments, it's clear that in the sight of God (yes, even with all the bloody wars fought throughout the Old Testament) life is sacred.

While obviously I would have some significant theological differences with her, Mother Teresa articulated something significant about this issue. She once said, "Any country that accepts abortion is not teaching the people to love, but to use violence to get what they want. That is why the greatest destroyer of love and peace is abortion."[1]

True, the context of Scripture in Deuteronomy is not strictly addressing our world, much less our nation in the 21st century. But it is addressing life. Even in Old Testament times there were rules in place to govern human behavior. There were ancient rules about the consequences if a man strikes a woman carrying a baby and the baby dies. Obviously, the life of the unborn mattered to God. I don't think that has changed.

ABORTION

Let's ask a few questions about these issues. First of all, we have to ask, "Why oppose abortion?" After all, the arguments these days favoring abortion permeate the culture. I think the arguments of the self-proclaimed "pro-choice" crowd are greatly flawed. Let's look at some of them.

Often, we'll hear this: "A woman's body belongs strictly to her." Let's talk logic for a minute, okay? Webster defines *woman* as "a female human being." Webster defines *human* as "having human form or attributes." Since probably close to fifty percent of those aborted are female human beings, not every woman has the right to control her own body because some young women in the making do not have that choice.

Let me also clarify: A good number of medical persons as well as pro-abortion activists no longer argue whether or not the so-called fetus to be aborted is a human being.[2] Many of them readily admit the fetus constitutes a human life. The point for them is determining whether or not the mother has control over her own life to the degree that she can terminate the pregnancy if it is deemed "unwanted."

Logically and legally, no one has absolute control over his or her body. Society doesn't allow us to take just any drug. Every state has a limit on how much alcohol a person can consume and still legally drive. A body covered with chicken pox is not allowed in the school classroom. When I was just a kid, streakers found the argument about the "right to control their own bodies" ineffective as a defense with regard to their public nudity.

Pro-abortion advocates say, "Control your own body." As Christians, we're to follow the Scripture. The Word of God says in 1 Corinthians 6:19b-20: *"You are not your own, for you were bought with a price. So glorify God in your body."*

The next argument often leveled against the pro-life crowd is this: Every child should be a wanted child. I agree. Every child *should* be a wanted child. Think back to Jesus' interaction with children. Jesus wants them even when others don't. This argument is an obvious appeal to emotions. Who should decide which child is wanted? What if the child cannot contribute to society (like Helen Keller was once labeled)? What if a child has less mental capacity or is not athletic? What if a couple wants a girl but discovers they're going to have a boy? Who decides the parameters?

As believers, we recognize what Scripture teaches about the prerogative of giving life. Genesis 1:27 records, *"So God created man in his own image, in the image of God he created him; male and female he created them."* We believe all people (every shade of color, male and female, highly intelligent and intellectually challenged, short and tall, thin and heavy, etc.) are created in God's image. We don't believe it's our right to determine from conception who lives and who dies. The writer of Ecclesiastes reminds us there is *"a time to be born, and a time to die"* (3:2). It's our contention that those times should be left up to God.

We never get very far into this discussion without someone saying, "Well, I understand abortion isn't the best bet, but surely there needs to be an opportunity to end a pregnancy if a child is going to be deformed or if the pregnancy is due to rape." As tragic as both scenarios are, is it the child's fault? Should a baby that is the product of rape not be allowed to live because of the sin of the biological father?

Again, I realize the Bible won't matter to someone who doesn't believe, but for those of us who do, we should take it into consideration. Deuteronomy 24:16 says, *"Fathers shall not be put to death because of their children, nor shall children be put to death because of their fathers ...*" In context, this is dealing with various laws, and it ends with the notion that people are put to death for their own sins.

A child that is a product of rape is an image-bearer of God. One's beginning (terrible as the scenario of rape is) doesn't determine one's worth. You perhaps have seen the social media exchange between the pro-abortion and pro-life ladies. It went as follows:

Alexis: "Ending abortion will bring nothing but pain. Not only for women, but for children. Children will be born to parents who can't afford them, parents who aren't ready, or they will live their lives in foster care. More poor kids, more abused kids, more traumatized kids."

Sarah: "I was terribly abused and grew up in a single-parent welfare home. Stop using lives like mine for validation because I like my life, warts and all. You know what would've helped when I was a child? If pro-choice people stopped insisting people like me were better off dead."

The point is, we're made in God's image, fashioned with attributes of God's character. There are no accidental children. Every child is created in God's image. But what about a baby born with disabilities? We've all known people who have been given a warning about this. Let me remind us again what the Bible says. Exodus 4:11 reads, *"Then the LORD said to him, 'Who has made man's mouth? Who makes him mute, or deaf, or seeing, or blind? Is it not I, the LORD?'"*

There are no accidents in the economy of God. Even if a child is born with disabilities, God is still the one who created that child in his image. If God had only allowed perfect people to live, who would Jesus have healed? Who would Jesus have forgiven?

There are those who say it is unfair for an unmarried woman to face the difficulty of an unwanted pregnancy. Here's the principle we need to grasp at this point: One person's difficult circumstances do not justify violating the rights of another person. It's unfortunate for someone to lose a job. But this difficult situation would not justify that person breaking into your home and robbing your family, right? We need to find workable solutions that treat what the world calls "crisis pregnancy" situations with a view to redemption. That includes love, acceptance, and encouragement.

A lot of people may say, "It's not a child; it's just a fetus." One big argument many have tried to raise is deciding when a so-called fetus becomes a human being. Think about this logically. Even if one has doubt concerning when this takes place, wouldn't it be better and even wiser to err on the side of caution? Shouldn't we give the benefit of the doubt to the side of preserving what all people would admit is at the very least potentially a human being?

I believe human life begins at conception. I'm a part of a denomination (the Southern Baptist Convention) that believes that, as well.[3] When we think of conception, this newly fertilized egg contains a staggering amount of genetic information, sufficient to control the individual's growth and development for an entire lifetime. A single thread of DNA from a human cell contains information equivalent to a library of one thousand volumes, or six hundred thousand printed pages with five hundred words on a page.

According to John J. Davis in *Abortion and the Christian*:

> It is a well-established fact that a genetically distinct human being is brought into existence at conception. Once fertilization takes place, the zygote is its own entity, genetically distinct from both mother and father. The newly conceived individual possesses all the necessary information for a self-directed development and will proceed to grow in the usual human fashion, given time and nourishment. It is simply untrue that the unborn child is merely "part of the mother's body." In addition to being genetically distinct from the time of conception, the unborn possesses separate circulatory, nervous, and endocrine systems.[4]

I have heard the objection from some in the Christian community who say, "You cannot find a verse to justify your position that life begins that early."

Really? Well, what about Matthew 1:18:

Now the birth of Jesus Christ took place in this way. When his mother Mary had been betrothed to Joseph, before they came together she was found to be with child from the Holy Spirit.

Or how about Luke 2:4-5:

And Joseph also went up from Galilee, from the town of Nazareth, to Judea, to the city of David, which is called Bethlehem, because he was of the house and lineage of David, to be registered with Mary, his betrothed, who was with child.

Obviously, the child in question is Jesus. But remember Jesus was fully God and fully man. I know this is an argument only Christians who accept the Bible embrace, but you never find any translation of Scripture that does not attribute personhood, or doesn't recognize Mary is carrying a baby human being. These little ones have human characteristics, which is at least the partial definition of being human.

Let me tell you some of this baby's characteristics: (1) His heart has been beating since he was eighteen to twenty-five days old; (2) brainwaves are recorded at forty days; (3) he squints, swallows, and can make a fist at less than twelve weeks.[5]

Now, why shouldn't these little ones be protected? There are elderly people who cannot make a cup of coffee for themselves, but shouldn't they be protected and cared for? In terms of viable life, useful life, we should not value life in any age group more than another. Yet, we as a society have legalized treating the helpless — the unborn and the very old — in ways we would never treat a middle-aged adult.

A professor in a world-acclaimed medical school once posed this medical situation — and ethical problem — to his students:

"Here's the family history: The father has syphilis. The mother has TB. They already have had four children. The first is blind. The second had died. The third is deaf. The fourth has TB. Now the mother is pregnant again. The parents come to you for advice. They are willing to have an abortion, if you decide they should. What do you say?"

The students offered various opinions, and then the professor asked them to break into small groups for "consultation." All of the groups came back to report that they would recommend abortion.

The professor then said, "You just took the life of Beethoven!"[6]

All of human life is sacred. Christians believe every one of us is put on the planet for the purpose of glorifying God. And we glorify God in the way we live our lives. The Apostle Paul said in Ephesians 2:10: *"For we are his workmanship, created in Christ Jesus for good works, which God prepared beforehand, that we should walk in them."*

EMBRYONIC STEM CELL RESEARCH

But when it comes to the sanctity of life, abortion is just one area we need to address. What about issues like human embryo stem cell research? You may have noticed in an attempt to soften the blow about this, analysts began referring to this as "early stem cell research." Call it what you will, but it is still human embryos being destroyed.

Embryonic cells are the earliest cells from which the body's organs are developed and have the ability to grow into the 210 types of tissue in the human body. What's the problem with this research? In order for scientists to isolate and culture embryonic stem cells, a living human embryo must be destroyed.

It is never morally or ethically justified to destroy one human being in order to benefit another. By requiring the destruction of embryos, the tiniest human beings, embryonic stem cell research violates the medical ethic of "Do No Harm." Opposing the willful destruction of human embryos for medical research does not mean that stem cell research cannot proceed. Science should continue to explore stem cells found in adult tissues, bone marrow, and umbilical cord blood, and this may be done without the destruction of human embryos.

CLONING

What about cloning? Is that even possible? In simplistic terms, clones are a group of cells descended from a single cell. In this sense, identical twins are clones of a single zygote. For the purposes of current scientific debate, *cloning* refers to a "duplication of genetic material from one organism to the next." Cloning intentionally copies the genetic code of one person in order to create another with the same genetic material.

The method employed for cloning is called *nuclear transfer* and results in the creation of a new organism by way of fusion, as opposed to fertilization. Nuclear transfer consists of removing the nucleus of an unfertilized egg and replacing it with the nucleus of a somatic cell from the donor to be cloned. A somatic cell, such as skin or a white blood cell, contains the donor's DNA or genetic code. Instead of fertilization, a small electric pulse is applied to stimulate the newly constructed cell into the division process, thus beginning the development of the newly cloned human being.

Why should we be opposed to this? Cloning is an unsafe process that sacrifices human life for scientific gain. The technology to clone humans and animals is essentially the same. You may remember Dolly, the cloned sheep, from many years ago. The creation of Dolly required 277 sheep embryos before the nuclear fusion process was successful.[7] That many sheep embryos either failed to develop or were destroyed. Experimenting or destroying human embryos can never be considered ethical. Life is a gift from God and not a mere industrial product. Cloning violates two values God bestows upon each human being at conception: pricelessness and uniqueness.

EUTHANASIA

What about euthanasia, or as the culture refers to it, "mercy killing"? Euthanasia involves the intentional killing of a patient by direct intervention of a physician or another party, supposedly for the good of the patient or others. The most common form of euthanasia is lethal injection. For several years, I served on the Ethics Committee of St. John's Mercy Hospital in Washington, Missouri. I heard so many of the emotions and the arguments about some of these issues.

I do believe in helping people die with dignity. I stayed at the bedside of my mother for many days while we made her comfortable and allowed God to take her home in his time. I was fortunate enough to be able to do the same with my father. The point is, true "death with dignity" should involve more pain management, spiritual and emotional support, and less pressure to end a life prematurely.

The arguments many use to sell mercy killing sound soothing. People want to alleviate pain. Quality of life considerations sound logical, but who determines what constitutes quality? Even the phrase *mercy killing* sounds compassionate to some. So why oppose it? We oppose it because it sends a message that some lives aren't worth living. It communicates that disabled and dependent citizens are not valuable.

The worth of a life, any life, has already been determined. It was determined by God and should never be determined by mere mortals. At the risk of sounding overly simplistic, the verse many of us learned as children reinforces this point of the worth of all lives. In John 3:16, the Bible says, *"God so loved the world."* It doesn't say he loves only the healthy, only those with keen intellect, only those who can make a notable contribution to society. He loves all people, period.

What other problems are present with euthanasia? It creates a duty to die. Escalating health-care costs and a growing elderly population set the stage for an American culture eager to embrace alternatives to expensive, long-term medical care. *Right to die* is a phrase not too far removed from the concept of *duty to die.* Our seniors, and disabled and depressed family members, feel the financial pressures

of their relatives. As the culture pushes this notion, they might begin
believing it is their duty to die, thus alleviating financial burdens.
Look already at the power of insurance companies to dictate healthcare decisions.

The people of the Netherlands have legally practiced physician-
assisted suicide for several years. One study reported by Tony
Sheldon showed that in 2001, "just over half of doctors in the Netherlands fulfilled their legal responsibility to report their actions
concerning euthanasia."[8] So even as ghastly as the statistics might be,
the number of euthanasia cases is even larger than reported.

Further:

> The study shows that since 1996 reporting of cases of euthanasia
> cases increased from 41% to 54% of cases. The researchers
> estimated that overall 3500 cases of euthanasia occurred in 2001,
> 2.5% of all deaths. This compares with 3200 (2.4%) in 1995. The
> number of assisted suicides fell from 400 in 1995 to 300 in 2001. The
> total number of requests for euthanasia remained the same, at
> about 9700. Of these 39% were accepted by the doctor in 2001, a
> similar percentage to that in 1995. The number of cases where a
> doctor ended a patient's life without an explicit request, which have
> caused controversy in the past, also remained the same, at around
> 900.[9]

That's a very significant number, don't you think? Nine hundred
people! It's especially significant if it's you or your family member
whose life has been ended without permission. This simply demonstrates the unbelievably slippery slope of this process.

The practice of euthanasia there now even includes "psychiatric
euthanasia."[10] People who report psychiatric disorders are legally
euthanized. How would you feel if your depression made ending
your life a legal viable option to the culture in which you lived?
According to today's statistics about depression, that would eliminate
a significant portion of the population. I don't want to downplay
depression, but most often, it gets better. But we would miss that

resolution if our lives were taken in the midst of our personal darkness.

In 2020 in the Netherlands, according to the *NL Times*, Health Minister Hugo de Jonge told parliament that "even the youngest individuals in society — individuals who aren't in a place to make decisions for themselves — will soon be able to be put to death."[11] But let's face it, in American culture, what has occurred since 1973 with the Roe v. Wade decision, and the way our culture has continued to further push the limits of abortion, is certainly not much different.

MADE IN GOD'S IMAGE AND CREATED FOR GOOD WORKS

Why is life sacred? Remember Genesis 1:27, *"So God created man in His own image ..."* In Psalm 139:13-14, perhaps the most often quoted biblical text about this issue, the psalmist writes, *"For you formed my inward parts; you knitted me together in my mother's womb. I praise you, for I am fearfully and wonderfully made."*

Being created in the image of God means more than having certain abilities. It means that humans bear the image of God their creator, regardless of personal abilities. Abortion, cloning, embryonic stem cell research, and euthanasia are symptoms of a much greater problem. Our culture no longer recognizes the sacredness or value of human life.

School violence, from Columbine to this very day, shows that a generation without regard for human life ultimately takes human life. The statistical data on school shootings is almost unbelievable. Part of the problem is that we've grown so complacent about this that we've come to accept it as part of the modern landscape. But that wasn't always the case. Is there any doubt that this kind of violence is allowed to freely grow among those who have grown up without being taught life is sacred?

So, all this is the bad news. As Christ-followers, what can we do to help? Love people! Show the redemptive nature of Christ in the way you treat others. Share Jesus with everyone you can. If you shake your fist at a young lady about to have an abortion, what are you communicating? Have you ever really wondered how she ended up there? Does that gesture give her the impetus to ask for your help, counsel, and support?

You see, in many ways we communicate she's in a no-win situation. For far too long, Christians have judged her if she's pregnant without being married, and then we judge her if she tries to hide that by having an abortion. In most cases, she doesn't need us to tell her something has been done that's wrong. She needs us to offer compassion, support, and acceptance. I wonder if she's overwhelmed with shame and guilt because she didn't feel she could ever be accepted by the church.

So, she chooses to have an abortion. If that's the case, the shame belongs to the church. Let me remind us again through the ministry of church, people learn about grace. Every local church is supposed to be a "grace place." We're in the business of taking tough situations and helping people turn them into bearable situations. Forgiveness is our business.

What else can we do? Support crisis pregnancy centers. It's likely you have some in your area. Addresses are available. Volunteer to help. Give money. Give your time. Recommend them. Counsel someone with a crisis pregnancy to visit such a center. Take them and show them Christ's love as they wade through their rough waters. Offer to help with supplies for the new infant. Maybe your church could band together to help pay for childcare.

While not strictly a political statement, I do think it's important that Christians support pro-life leaders. That's one way we flesh out our faith. Encourage people from all walks of life, regardless of what positions they occupy, to take a stand for life.

Communicate to your family how you value life. Lori and I have advanced medical directives. I would encourage you to do the same. These directives let those in authority know our views about how we wish to be cared for medically. These directives can keep you from forcing people you love to make difficult, if not impossible, decisions during high-stress times.

Restore the elderly to their place as pillars of society! Don't allow disabilities and tragic illnesses like Alzheimer's to take away the honorable place of the aged. There is a biblical admonition to honor those whose heads are crowned with gray. It is nothing short of a crime in our society today that the aged among us must sometimes choose between medication and food. The reason this is the case has less to do with politics and more to do with our views concerning the sanctity of life.

Many years ago, I read about someone sending a letter of support to their aging parents; I borrowed some of the language from what I read. Lori and I sent a letter to our parents about this in an attempt to relieve them of feeling responsible for their declining health. While my parents are both in heaven now, I'm grateful we were able to let them know they would never be a burden or an unwanted obligation to us. We valued and loved our parents. Here's what I included in the correspondence:

It's hard to believe you're in what society calls the "golden years." It's our wish that you will always feel spry and healthy. We hope these years will be golden, full of warmth, good health, and immense pleasure for you.

We know that over time our lives change and under certain circumstances you may become less able to do things for yourselves and more in need of a helping hand from others. We want to assure you we will be there to give you a helping hand. We promise to care for you physically, emotionally, and spiritually. We pledge to support and care for you as your children and now your friends.

We write this letter to assure you that regardless of what the future brings, you have been created in God's image and you're of immeasurable worth to him and to us. Your abilities or disabilities will never determine your value to us; your value is unchangeable, based on the fact that you are precious to God and to us. It will be a privilege and honor to care for you. You will never be a burden to us.

We realize we can never repay you for the sacrifices you've made because of your love for us. We love you and want you to know that it will be an honor to serve you as you have served us.

— Ken & Lori

Let me finish where we started:

I call heaven and earth to witness against you today, that I have set before you life and death, blessing and curse. Therefore choose life, that you and your offspring may live, loving the LORD your God, obeying his voice and holding fast to him, for he is your life and length of days, that you may dwell in the land that the LORD swore to your fathers, to Abraham, to Isaac, and to Jacob, to give them (Deut. 30:19-20).

In a world that often, for various reasons, chooses death ... choose life!

QUESTIONS FOR PERSONAL OR GROUP STUDY

1. What are several sanctity-of-life issues in addition to abortion?
2. In what ways has this chapter opened your eyes to the many issues related to the sanctity of life?
3. How can you talk about sanctity-of-life issues without it turning into a political conversation?
4. What can you, as an individual, do to communicate your personal views about the sanctity of life as it relates to your own care as you age or, perhaps, become incapacitated?
5. What can you, your family, or your church do to tangibly demonstrate your belief in the sanctity of life that offers hope and help to others?

MARRIAGE

SCRIPTURE CLARIFIES THE MISUNDERSTANDINGS
OF MATRIMONY.

No matter how hard we try, sometimes what we're trying to communicate is misunderstood. You may have heard about the man who decides to leave work just a little early and go home to tell his wife how much he loves her. Before he leaves work, he showers, shaves, and puts on his best cologne. Then he stops by the florist and picks up some flowers. He goes to the front door of his house and knocks.

His wife answers the door, sees him standing there, and says, "Are you kidding me? This has been a terrible day. I had to take Billy to the emergency room for stitches, your mother called and she's coming to visit for two weeks, the dog ran away, the washing machine broke, and now you've come home drunk!"

There are a lot of ideas about what marriage is. And sadly, a lot of the ideas are wrong. This can be because the purpose of marriage is misunderstood. It might be youthful naiveté. It might be due to only having seen poor examples. Let's go to the source, to the creator of marriage, to see some of what he says about it:

Then the LORD God said, "It is not good that the man should be alone; I
will make him a helper fit for him" ... So the LORD God caused a deep

sleep to fall upon the man, and while he slept took one of his ribs and closed up its place with flesh. And the rib that the LORD God had taken from the man he made into a woman and brought her to the man. Then the man said, "This at last is bone of my bones and flesh of my flesh; she shall be called Woman, because she was taken out of Man." Therefore man shall leave his father and his mother and hold fast to his wife, and they shall become one flesh (Gen. 2:18, 21-24).

MARRIAGE IS MISUNDERSTOOD

If you ask fifty people what they think about marriage, you're liable to get a hundred wrong concepts, along with a few right ones. Even among people who don't believe in God — that is, those who live life without seeking to understand biblical concepts — you used to be able to hear at least a somewhat coherent definition that resembled a biblical worldview. Granted, they would not necessarily understand all the nuances of love and marriage (who does?), but they would understand some of the basics.

About how to understand marriage, Andreas Köstenberger writes, "For the first time in its history, Western civilization is confronted with the need to define the terms marriage and family."[1] Isn't that true? The basic terms now have to be defined. For centuries, the idea of marriage was clearly understood to be between a man and a woman, and family was clearly understood to involve a parent or parents and a child or children. Much of that is out the proverbial window, at least in America today. Today marriage is greatly misunderstood.

Since I am a pastor, my primary audience is typically comprised of Christians. So, in my teaching and preaching, I appeal to what we believe is a sacred book. I don't live in a fantasy world that makes me believe for one moment that people not committed to Jesus, or at least to a portion of a Judeo-Christian ethic, actually care what I think or say, or what the Bible has to say for that matter.

But for those who claim to be followers of Jesus, what we see in Scripture matters to us. Now the truth is, it matters to everybody; it's just that not everybody recognizes that *yet*. Marriage is misunderstood. People think it's an invention of man; it's not. In fact, the entirety of the text from Genesis we read at the beginning of this chapter reminds us that marriage is God's idea, not man's.

Further, one of the main misunderstandings about marriage is found in what unbelievers think we believe. You'll hear them talking about how terrible it is for a woman to be in a marriage to a Christian because she's under his thumb and doesn't get to be her own person or pursue her dreams, and so forth. Nothing is further from the truth!

A Christian woman is free to be her own person, pursue her dreams, and, dare I say it, even make her own mistakes at times. You may have heard about the man who tells his wife that she should just embrace her mistakes. So ... she reaches out and hugs him!

Scripture makes it clear how husbands and wives are to function. As Köstenberger states:

> Genesis 1-3 centers on at least three very important clusters of principles: (1) the man and the woman are created in God's image to rule the earth for God; (2) the man is created first and is given ultimate responsibility for the marriage relationship, while the woman is placed alongside the man as his "suitable helper;" and (3) the fall of humanity entails negative consequences for both the man and the woman.[2]

One misunderstanding centers on the variations of the roles of men and women. The idea of submission that Scripture addresses in marriage is greatly misunderstood. While the woman is given to man as his *helper* (that's biblical language, right?), and therefore is placed under his overall loving charge, she is his partner in *ruling the earth for God*.

However, the Bible indicates there will be a problem with this arrangement. We see this in a biblical text that is often misunderstood. In Genesis 3, after the Fall, God tells Eve that things have changed. She will have much more pain in childbirth, and God says to her, *"Your desire shall be contrary to your husband, but he shall rule over you*" (3:16). Many translations render this, "Your desire shall be for your husband" or "toward your husband."

The word some versions translate "for" can also be translated "against." The idea is that, after the Fall, sometimes the inclination of a woman is going to be toward usurping her husband's authority and responsibility in the home. I would imagine you've seen this in action. The wife takes on the role of main leader in the home. The husband is not viewed as an equal partner, much less as the leader. He is emasculated. He will not be the leader in his own home, much less the spiritual leader in the home.

Where that's the case, you can mark it down, not only is there great dysfunction between a husband and wife, but the children pay an exorbitant price for this faulty practice. The spouse pays the price. The children pay the price. And it spills over into the church, as well.

But let me offer a clarification here. The idea of submission is not a direct result of the Fall. Eve was to submit to Adam *before* they sinned. It's just that after they sinned, after the Fall, there would be a further tendency for her to desire to wear the proverbial pants in the family. The man is created first and is given ultimate responsibility for the marriage relationship. The authoritative position of the man is a function of God's sovereign plan. This is not an afterthought on God's part. God determined that someone would be responsible for the family in the ultimate sense, and he said it was the man.

I recognize some people may not like that. Even so, what matters is not what *we* like but what *God* said. There are functional differences between men and women, and that's by God's design. It's not that one is more important than the other. No! In a marriage, both partners are of *equal value*. So where does submission come in? What does the Bible really say about that? "Surely that's not a concept for us to follow today," some will say.

Submission. The word is actually in the Bible. I know Gloria Steinem doesn't want it to be there, but it's there. Now, take a deep breath. I know some people want us to neglect this concept, and I suspect some people in the church would like that, as well. But the main reason anyone would want us to neglect the concept of biblical submission in marriage is because: (a) they don't understand what it really means, or (b) they choose to disregard God's Word.

We're living in a day where people strive to disregard the importance of gender distinctions. When we read Paul's words in the New Testament (and I know some people want Paul to go away, too, but there's this pesky little thing known as Scripture that gives him a place), we discover the importance of biblical submission. Bear in mind, Paul is writing to Christian men and women.

Let's look at what he writes in Ephesians 5:22-25:

> *Wives, submit to your own husbands, as to the Lord. For the husband is the head of the wife even as Christ is the head of the church, his body, and is himself its Savior. Now as the church submits to Christ, so also wives should submit in everything to their husbands.*
>
> *Husbands, love your wives, as Christ loved the church and gave himself up for her ... In the same way husbands should love their wives as their own bodies.*

A man loves his wife like Jesus loves the church. A woman submits to her husband (who has loved her like Jesus) like the church submits to Christ. Is it any wonder the feminists despise the church? You see, they hate this beautiful picture. And let's be clear, this is not a picture of *subservience* but rather *submission*. This is not anything ugly; it is something quite beautiful. We'll come back to that in a moment.

The world, frankly, has messed up the concept of submission. They make it out to be something ugly and restraining, something they think will rob us of our creativity and ability to find our place in the world. That's not biblical submission at all. Biblical submission robs us of nothing bad, but instead, it liberates us to be exactly who we were created to be.

But the world doesn't want that anymore. The world doesn't want us to be who we were created to be. We're telling little girls to be little boys and little boys to be little girls. Babies are becoming *theybies* because parents in our day aren't willing to admit that little boys and girls are born with body parts that define them as male and female. While we Christians certainly recognize gender as God's gift (Gen. 1:27), one doesn't have to have any kind of religious leanings to recognize gender.

Biblical submission is just that ... it's *biblical* and it is *submission*, but it's not what many people think. What the Bible teaches about marriage was (and is) radical. Those who see the Bible as a textbook, making allowances for female subjugation and so forth, simply demonstrate their ignorance of the Bible.[3]

We need an accurate way of describing marital roles. The idea of biblical submission is not like *slavery*. A husband doesn't own a wife. It's not *subservience*, as Köstenberger notes, where one person is doing the bidding of another without intelligent input or interaction. And it's not even hierarchical, which is like a top-down militaristic chain of command. It's much more beautiful than that.[4]

Stay with me here. We believe in what we call the *Trinity*. That's the Father, Son, and Holy Spirit, right? Each person of the Trinity is of equal nature and worth. Jesus submitted to his heavenly Father. If Jesus chose to submit to God the Father, and he was equal to God the Father, then doesn't it stand to reason that God would design a human relationship where one party is to submit to another, and yet each party is equal in nature and worth? So, submission doesn't imply one party matters more. It certainly grants no cause for one to mistreat the other. It really implies love and response to love.

A lot of people have the idea that being married will make them happy. Certainly, it is a great gift God gives us when, in our lives as married couples, we experience happiness. But the overarching picture we get in Scripture is that God's concern is not mainly with our happiness (although it matters), but rather, our holiness. Marriage, by design, should help make us more holy as opposed to simply happier. I think it's safe to say, marriage is *misunderstood*.

MARRIAGE IS EMBLEMATIC

"Therefore a man shall leave his father and mother and hold fast to his wife, and the two shall become one flesh." This mystery is profound, and I am saying that it refers to Christ and the church (Eph. 5:31-32).

After Paul has given his beautiful words about husband-and-wife relationships, he says it's all a picture. It's symbolic. It is emblematic or prototypical of Christ and the church. The beauty in the marriage relationship mirrors the beauty in the relationship between Christ (the groom) and the church (his bride). The wife submits to her husband, who loves her sacrificially. The church submits to the Lord, who loves her sacrificially. I know it's a mystery, but it is a beautiful one. The husband-and-wife relationship offers a glimpse into the relationship between Christ and the church.

We realize that marriage is a "common grace" notion; that is, God's design is for men and women to marry, even though not all men and women are followers of Jesus. Marriage is one of God's good gifts to all people; it just takes on added meaning as we contemplate what it represents for Christians. Remember, we're talking about two Christians, a husband who is a believer and a wife who is a believer. The husband should never ask his wife to submit to anything that is demeaning, demoralizing, illegal, unethical, or even uncomfortable. But as a husband loves his wife in the same way Christ loves the church, submission is a beautiful response.

After worship one Sunday, when I had preached on this topic, one of our men said, "I have a funny story to tell you." Now, I'm going to change this just a bit so I don't give away his identity, even though he gave me permission to tell this. He said he was in a training session for his work, and the guy leading the session was explaining something about how to turn in expense reports. He had it all up on a big screen, I suppose, and was explaining, "Do this, do that, check this, check that. And then when you're finished," he said, "Just hit SUBMIT."

And my friend in our church said he couldn't help himself. He said to the group, "I wish my wife had a submit button like that."

People have a lot of mixed-up ideas about marriage, don't they? The way people in our country view marriage continues to change, doesn't it? I attended a wedding in the last few years of two people who both claimed to be Christians. It was officiated by a lady who never mentioned God, didn't pray, and never quoted Scripture. And when it came time for the vows, she said something like, "Do you promise to live together as husband and wife as long as you so choose?" *As long as you so choose?* Wow! Never mind the idea of "till death do us part." Things have changed regarding what people believe about marriage.

There are people who believe that same-sex marriage is acceptable. Granted, I understand it is acceptable in the eyes of the law, but in the sight of God, same-sex marriage is not an acceptable lifestyle choice. With all due respect to those who struggle with same-sex attraction, giving in to one's feelings in that regard isn't the answer. Just because I have an urge, or a bent, or a proclivity toward something doesn't mean that's the best thing, the right thing, or the righteous thing. We don't have to give in to our every feeling. Reason is one of the many things that sets us apart from the animal world.

The truth of the matter is — and this is the kind of thing no one likes to say, much less hear — a good number of people, single and married, have been attracted to someone other than their girlfriend or boyfriend or husband or wife, even *after* they've made a commitment to them. But since we can reason and have a conscience, we can choose not to dwell on that attraction and certainly not to give in to that attraction. We're image-bearers of God, so we don't give in to every feeling or inclination we may have!

So, what else is marriage?

MARRIAGE IS OPTIONAL

Now as a concession, not a command, I say this. I wish that all were as I myself am. But each has his own gift from God, one of one kind and one of another (1 Cor. 7:6-7).

Marriage isn't for everybody. Just a verse earlier, Paul says:

Do not deprive one another, except perhaps by agreement for a limited time, that you may devote yourselves to prayer; but then come together again, so that Satan may not tempt you because of your lack of self-control (1 Cor. 7:5).

Paul is talking to the church about matters of sexuality. Some thought that in order to be fully committed to Christ, one had to abstain from sexual activity, even if married. Suffice it to say, Paul is saying that if you're married, you don't have to abstain, but if you choose to abstain, make sure it's only for a brief period of time agreed upon by both husband and wife, and for the purpose of spiritual pursuit.

Then in the verses at hand, he is saying both marriage and celibacy are gifts. Being married is a gift; being single is a gift. Even if you can't wait to have grandchildren, don't push your kids toward marriage. By God's design, it's not for everybody!

Marriage may be God's plan for your kids, or it may be that singleness is God's plan for them. In both instances, we recognize they're a gift. Being married allows you to share the joys and sorrows of life as a Christ-follower with someone you trust completely and is with you in the day-in and day-out of life's experiences. Being single allows you the opportunity to dedicate even more of your time and effort to the kingdom of God because you don't have marital responsibilities.

Granted, that looked somewhat different in Paul's day than in ours, but the principle is the same. A married person has to provide for others, cook, clean, put food on the table, and in many cases take care of extracurricular activities with the kids and so forth; a single person doesn't. We do a tremendous disservice to singles in the church if or when we imply that only marriage brings about the kind of life God desires for each of us. That's simply not true!

I certainly do not want to act as if I know more than I do, but let me just offer an encouraging word, having made it through some five decades on the planet. Take Paul's words to heart. Both singleness and married life are good. And what's best is whatever station in life God calls you to embrace. In other words, better to marry if that's God's plan, even with the inherent challenges married life brings. And it's better to remain single, if that's God's plan, than to end up in a relationship that you shouldn't be part of in the first place. Marriage is *optional*.

MARRIAGE IS COVENANT

> *So you will be delivered from the forbidden woman, from the adulteress with her smooth words, who forsakes the companion of her youth and forgets the covenant of her God ...* (Prov. 2:16-17).

This is just one case among many where explicit biblical terminology of covenant is utilized in describing the marriage relationship.

> *Because the LORD was witness between you and the wife of your youth, to whom you have been faithless, though she is your companion and your wife by covenant* (Mal. 2:14).

I'm attempting to explain what we Christians believe about marriage. There are a lot of differing ideas about it, even among Christ-followers. Let me clarify. We're going to talk about marriage as *sacrament*, a term our Roman Catholic friends utilize. Then we're going to talk about marriage as *contract*, which really is not a good biblical picture at all. And we'll talk about marriage as *covenant*.[5] But in the first and third concepts (sacrament and covenant) we agree: marriage is one man with one woman for life.

In fact, let me offer a definition of marriage, the covenantal understanding, if you will, by John Stott, based on Genesis 2:24, which we've already read. The covenantal view holds that "marriage is an exclusive heterosexual covenant between one man and one woman, ordained and sealed by God, preceded by a public leaving of parents, consummated in sexual union, issuing in a permanent mutually supportive partnership, and normally crowned by the gift of children."[6]

So, there are three views: sacrament, contract, and covenant. The view of marriage as sacrament finds its roots in Scripture but mainly, as it is understood today, is a product of church tradition. The word *sacramentum* is the Latin term Jerome used in the fourth century to translate the Greek expression meaning *mystery*, which clarifies the analogy between marriage and the joining of Christ and the church, as we noted previously in Ephesians 5:32. The sacramental model is rooted in the writings of Augustine. He was trying to articulate that marriage creates a "holy, permanent bond between a man and a woman, which depicts Christ's union with the church."[7]

That certainly sounds good, but the problem was when the Roman Catholic Church recast Augustine's concept of marriage and developed a sacramental theology of the seven sacraments dispensed by the church. Therefore, marriage came to be seen as a sacrament, meaning that by participating in marriage under the authority of the Catholic Church, grace is accumulated for the married couple. Granted, you may need a lot of grace in marriage, but you don't get it from just being married!

There are a lot of challenges to this view. First, there's nothing in Scripture that demonstrates being married mystically dispenses grace. Secondly, as Köstenberger reminds us, this approach to marriage doesn't fit with biblical teaching on marriage as a whole because the "Creator designed marriage for creating new physical life, not as a mechanism for attaining spiritual life."[8] Lastly, it subjects the husband-and-wife relationship to the control of the church.

So, some see marriage as a sacrament. Next, some see marriage as a contract. This is essentially the secular view of marriage, at least in the Western world. Marriage is seen as a contract that is voluntarily formed, maintained, and dissolved by two people.

Interestingly enough, Gary Chapman, in his work, *Covenant Marriage*, notes five characteristics of such contracts.[9] They are as follows:

1. They are typically made for a limited period of time.
2. They most often deal with specific actions.
3. They are conditioned upon the continual performance of contractual obligations by the other partner.
4. They are entered into for one's own benefit.
5. They are sometimes unspoken and implicit.

So, what's the problem with this view? It's inadequate. As we discuss marriage as a contract, this is not to say that a wedding performed by a justice of the peace is invalid. It's just that if you only hold to the contractual view of marriage, you're missing the mark of what the Scripture depicts about this most beautiful, mysterious relationship.

Marriage as a contract is rooted in the sufficiency of civil law. Because of that, it allows marriage to be defined by the whims of an ever-changing culture. This is where we are today. The definition of marriage is subject to change as the culture changes. These days, as we know, it isn't just a man and woman arrangement anymore. Now it's two men or two women. Someday it will likely include polygamy, incestuous relationships, as well as relationships between people and animals. That used to seem so far-fetched; that's not the case any longer.

That brings us to marriage as covenant. We get this from Genesis 2, Malachi 2, the Book of Proverbs, as well as other biblical texts. In this model, marriage is not just a contract between two people; it is a sacred bond between a husband and wife before God as a witness. According to *The New International Dictionary of the Bible*, the verbal root of *covenant* carries with it the idea of "to eat with," which signifies mutual obligation, or "to allot," which signifies a gracious disposition. In the Old Testament, the word identifies three different types of legal relationships, including a two-sided covenant between human parties who both voluntarily accept the terms of the agreement.[10]

As Christians, we understand the covenant of marriage can only occur between two professing Christians. I'm not talking about prohibiting a Baptist from marrying a Presbyterian or a Pentecostal from marrying a Methodist. What I'm saying is this: When Paul says in 2 Corinthians 6 not to be unequally joined together with unbelievers, we take that to mean, among other things, that the covenant of marriage is for two Christians.

So, what do you do if you're already married to an unbeliever? Don't change a thing! That's what Paul tells us in 1 Corinthians 7. Pray for your unbelieving spouse, treat him or her with grace and kindness, and see if he or she is ultimately led to repentance from sin and to faith in Jesus.

All of this is to say that marriage doesn't impart grace. It may take a lot of grace, but it doesn't increase your standing with Jesus or necessarily make you more like him. Marriage is certainly more than the equivalent of signing on the dotted line, as we do in a contract. It is a beautiful mystery in which we join ourselves to another human being for life with God as our witness, having been invited into all aspects of our relationships as he dwells within us through his Holy Spirit. Marriage is a big, big deal — even if not always in the eyes of man, most certainly in the eyes of God.

MARRIAGE IS INTIMATE

Therefore a man shall leave his father and his mother and hold fast to his wife, and they shall become one flesh (Gen. 2:24).

Adam and Eve became "one flesh." Marriage is the most intimate of all human relationships. A man and a woman are joined together by leaving their family of origin and cleaving to one another, steadfastly and faithfully clinging closely to each other. In marriage you are joined to your spouse. This is the establishment of a new family unit, a new home. It's a beautiful thing and reaches the pinnacle of beauty in what God has designed in terms of sexual intimacy.

For a beautiful picture of sexual expression in marriage, I would call your attention to the Song of Solomon. Properly read and understood, it is a detailed account of sexual intimacy between a husband and wife. Now I know some have said Song of Solomon is simply about Jesus and the church. Of course, the mystery concept of marriage being a picture of Jesus and the church is part of it, but as you read the Song of Solomon, don't miss the simple beauty God describes in the sexual expression between a man and a woman. We need to celebrate the beauty of that kind of union!

Of course, sex is for procreation. But sex is also for pleasure. We shouldn't blush when we talk about it. God knows what it is, right? After all, he created it! It is one of God's good gifts to his children. So sexual expression within marriage is a beautiful thing. It is to be enjoyed. If God wills, it is to yield children. And it is never to be experienced outside of marriage.

I know the culture scoffs at us as Christians. They think we're prudes and we don't enjoy our sexuality. Let me set the record straight on this. If you choose to love someone and you choose to be faithful for life, if you are loving and kind to one another and you meet one another's needs in life, you will also meet one another's needs in sexual expression. If you marry and you're committed to each other, that allows for the opportunity to have the best sex of your life.

Hollywood can't compete. They're always busy looking for the next partner. You already have yours! They're trying to figure out how they can get to the point of actually having sex; you don't have worry about all that, by God's design. It is yours for the sharing together. They're trying to figure out how to have so-called "safe sex." You don't have to worry about it because you're having *faithful* sex.

I'm convinced, if the rest of the world understood the magnitude of the beauty, enjoyment, and experience of the sexual expression between two committed Christians, they'd be knocking our doors down to figure it out. They're empty and longing and looking and waiting and hoping for the real thing, but until they're in a committed marriage, everything else is just a substitute. G. K. Chesterton, among others, has been credited with saying, "The young man who rings the bell at the brothel is unconsciously looking for God."

Some of you remember Paul Newman. He was a kind of Tom Cruise or Hugh Jackman back in the day. Newman famously had a wonderful marriage to Joanne Woodward. They once asked him why, with all the opportunities to stray, he had been faithful. He famously said, "Why go out for hamburger when I can stay home for steak!"

Everything else is a cheap substitute. It's one of the great tragedies of the liberal narrative today about homosexuality. The church is being blamed for the depression, anxiety, and in some cases, suicides of young gays and lesbians because we're not accepting of their life-style. That's ridiculous. Interview a young gay person, and you'll find they're not depressed because of what *we* think; they're depressed because of what *they* think. Deep down, they know. I'm not saying their temptations aren't real; I am saying their intuition is right. Sadly, they know they're missing something.

MARRIAGE IS PERMANENT

What therefore God has joined together, let not man separate (Matt. 19:6).

Don't read the word *permanent* as meaning eternal. It means "lasting a long time; not expected to change." Again, what a beautiful mystery connecting us to Christ and the church. Once we belong to a spouse, it's permanent. Once we belong to Christ, it's permanent. We die physically, of course, and our marriages end in death. But since Jesus doesn't die, our relationship with him lasts forever. I don't know anyone that hasn't been impacted by the tragedy of divorce. And, certainly, there are instances in which divorce is warranted, and I'm not going to pour salt in anyone's wounds about that. But the point is, marriage is *supposed to be* permanent. We don't fall out of love because we don't really fall in love. We choose to love, and we choose not to love. Marriage takes effort, patience, time, and maturity.

Love may result in a lot of outcomes, but in the grand scheme of things, above all, love is a decision.[11] We decide to love, and we decide not to love. Of course, there are countless circumstances that play into this decision before we're married — and after we're married. But love is not just a feeling; it's a decision, and the ultimate decision to marry and the responsibility to stay married belongs to only two people.

If you're married already, work hard at it. Give it your all. Do what you can to maintain your commitment if at all possible. If you're not married, then don't jump into a marriage. If you're going to chase anybody, chase someone who is running toward Jesus. That's your best bet.

A lot of people say, "Well, I just don't know about my spouse. Maybe we shouldn't have gotten married." One of my co-workers in ministry many years ago said he knew the moment he said, "I do," that he had made a mistake! Was that because he had rushed into marriage, or was that because he was looking for the opportunity to "explain away" what should have been a permanent commitment?

I love the story John Piper tells. As I recall, Piper said a lady came to him very upset. She said, "Pastor, I don't think I married the right man." You know what he told her? He said, "Go home and see whose name is on your marriage license. That is the right man."

QUESTIONS FOR PERSONAL OR GROUP STUDY

1. Why is it important to know the distinctions between marriage as sacrament, contract, and covenant?
2. How does the idea "Love is a decision" differ from the way our culture typically understands love? Why is this difference significant?

3. What are some common misunderstandings about marriage?
4. What are some important factors that play a role in a healthy marriage?
5. How can you help someone who says, "I don't think I married the right person"?

DIVORCE, REMARRIAGE, AND COHABITATION
SEEKING GOD'S PERMISSION, AND ACCEPTING HIS PROHIBITIONS.

One of the challenges of teaching the Bible is that the Bible doesn't say what a lot of Christians think it says. What is written in the Bible may not mean exactly what a particular Christian thinks it means or what that Christian *wants* it to mean. One of the banes of my existence as a preacher is that, periodically, I have to correct something that someone else has erroneously taught. You may not think that's a big deal, but if a beloved spiritual figure has posited the theological error, some people feel that disagreeing with that figure is tantamount to desecrating his grave.

Let me give you an example. I'm going to open a can of worms before I open an even bigger can of worms. And I'm not doing this because I'm a theological liberal or because I want you to get angry and stop reading. I'm doing this because I want you to know the truth.

I don't have any piercings or any tattoos. Let me tell you why. First, I don't like pain. Second, I don't like pain. Third, I like everything I wear to match. I wear monogrammed socks. Even at home, when nobody is going to see me, my shirt has to match my pajama pants. And when I die, if I have anything to do with it, I'll be sent out in cufflinks. It's the way I roll. So, the idea that I'd have green ink on my arm next to a pink shirt would send me over the edge. In fact, I might have a breakdown of sorts. I have friends, family members, and staff members who have tattoos. I don't do tattoos; they're just not my thing. Did I mention I don't like pain?

A lot of people like tattoos. But when a Christian doesn't like tattoos, he goes to Leviticus 19:28 — *"You shall not make any cuts on your body for the dead or tattoo yourselves: I am the LORD."* And then he'll use that verse to beat up a fellow believer because he or she got tatted. I never wanted to get tattoos. In my generation, they were symbols of rebellion, or time spent in the armed forces stationed far, far away (translation: where your parents couldn't see how much alcohol you drank). You had either been in the Marines or Hell's Angels; that was about it. Really. There were a lot more rebellious things that seemed more fun and less painful than getting my arm nailed with needles.

The only advice I can offer about tattoos and piercings is that you ought to think it through, and you ought to be old enough to understand the long-term relationship you're going to have with them. And you ought to recognize that some people, Christian and otherwise, will be judgmental. But that's it. And for the record, I don't care. Unless it's vulgar, or in some way draws attention to a part of your body that ought to be presented with more modesty, I don't care. In fact, I shouldn't care.

Now, here's where I open the can of worms based on Leviticus 19:28.

Of course, that text should give us pause. But unless you're cutting yourself, or getting a tattoo *for the dead* as part of a pagan ritual, we shouldn't say you're sinning if you get a tattoo. In the context of Leviticus, it was clearly a heathen practice. There may be some places where it still is, and of course that wouldn't be good. God wanted his people to be set apart and stand apart. Nowadays, I see guys with Scriptures all over their bodies. They're not doing that for the dead in some heathen ritual; at least I don't think they are.

But here's where this is tough. A lot of Christians *want the Bible to say tattoos are wrong* because they think they're wrong. And oftentimes they think tattoos are wrong because someone they respected taught them they were wrong. And this is where this can of worms gets opened even more.

We're going to look at what the Scripture says about three emotionally charged subjects: divorce, remarriage, and cohabitation. Christians want the Bible to say certain things about all three of these practices. A lot of people have strong feelings about all three of these. I do, too. But what I *feel* isn't nearly as important as what God *says*, right?

Even as we prepare to look at a lengthy biblical text, let me remind you of an important truth. We need to deal with these issues so that we know the truth, and so those who come behind us can know the truth as well. We want to do all we can to help people avoid living in disobedience and then regret. But no matter what has happened in your life — divorce, remarriage, or cohabitation — if you're in Christ, you're forgiven. If you're not a believer, and this is part of your current life or part of your past, then yes, you need to repent of your sins and trust in Jesus. When you do, there's no condemnation.

Listen to these words from Romans 8:1: *"There is therefore now no condemnation for those who are in Christ Jesus."* Let that sink in. So, none of what you're going to read is meant to be condemning, okay?

Let me draw your attention to 1 Corinthians 7:1-16 to set the stage as we deal with three subjects: divorce, remarriage, and cohabitation:

Now concerning the matters about which you wrote: "It is good for a man not to have sexual relations with a woman." But because of the temptation to sexual immorality, each man should have his own wife and each woman her own husband. The husband should give to his wife her conjugal rights, and likewise the wife to her husband. For the wife does not have authority over her own body, but the husband does. Likewise the husband does not have authority over his own body, but the wife does. Do not deprive one another, except perhaps by agreement for a limited time, that you may devote yourselves to prayer; but then come together again, so that Satan may not tempt you because of your lack of self-

control. Now as a concession, not a command, I say this. I wish that all were as I myself am. But each has his own gift from God, one of one kind and one of another.

To the unmarried and the widows I say that it is good for them to remain single, as I am. But if they cannot exercise self-control, they should marry. For it is better to marry than to burn with passion.

To the married I give this charge (not I, but the Lord): the wife should not separate from her husband (but if she does, she should remain unmarried or else be reconciled to her husband), and the husband should not divorce his wife. To the rest I say (I, not the Lord) that if any brother has a wife who is an unbeliever, and she consents to live with him, he should not divorce her. If any woman has a husband who is an unbeliever, and he consents to live with her, she should not divorce him. For the unbelieving husband is made holy because of his wife, and the unbelieving wife is made holy because of her husband. Otherwise your children would be unclean, but as it is, they are holy. But if the unbelieving partner separates, let it be so. In such cases the brother or sister is not enslaved. God has called you to peace. For how do you know, wife, whether you will save your husband? Or how do you know, husband, whether you will save your wife?

So, there are three subjects under the umbrella of two main perspectives. Based on what the Scripture records, we're going to see: 1) what is permitted; 2) what is forbidden.

MARRIAGE, UNDER CERTAIN CONDITIONS, IS PERMITTED

Now concerning the matters about which you wrote: "It is good for a man not to have sexual relations with a woman." But because of the temptation to sexual immorality, each man should have his own wife and each woman her own husband (1 Cor. 7:1-2).

Some in the church at Corinth had written Paul because, evidently, there were believers who had adopted the idea that sexual relations of any kind, even within marriage, would be wrong. If we're not careful, we'll misread what is said here and think Paul is saying it is simply good for a man not to have sexual relations with a woman at all, but that's not what he means.

Look at the text again. When Paul says, *"It is good for a man not to have sexual relations with a woman,"* he is referencing what some Christians at Corinth have written to him. Some have said this is advocating celibacy. It's more likely Paul is stressing that it would be wrong for men to use women for "mere sexual gratification."[1] He is advocating for sexual relations to occur only within the context of marriage, and this for "mutual sexual fulfillment."[2]

So, he's not saying that it's not good for men and women to have sexual relations, as it might appear on the surface. In fact, Paul quickly and quite clearly refutes that notion with what he says next.

But this doesn't mean marriage, under all circumstances, is necessarily permitted. In 2 Corinthians 6:14-15, Paul writes:

> *Do not be unequally yoked with unbelievers. For what partnership has righteousness with lawlessness? Or what fellowship has light with darkness? What accord has Christ with Belial? Or what portion does a believer share with an unbeliever?*

Obviously, Paul's words here are not a play-by-play about marriage only; you should apply these verses to countless situations in everyday life. If you go into business with a pagan, mark it down: You're not going to share the same *ethos* and *ethic,* and there is likely going to be trouble. But certainly, when it comes to choosing a spouse, being on the proverbial same page about many things (faith included) — that is, being equally-yoked — *is a big deal.*

Pretty clear, isn't it? Don't expect that man or woman you're dating, who is apathetic or even hostile to the things of God, to suddenly change for the better because he or she says, "I do." It *can* happen, but you can't count on it. And in all likelihood, it won't happen.

Further, some of what our country now calls marriage, God

doesn't recognize. God's plan is that one man marries one woman for life. I know that these days, in a lot of places, I would be viewed as narrow-minded and even mean-spirited to say such a thing. In some places, saying marriage is only for a man and a woman would be viewed as hate speech.

In March of 2019, Baptist Press shared a story about Gateway Seminary. Gateway, located in Ontario, California, is one of six Southern Baptist Convention seminaries. Facebook refused to boost a post from Gateway Seminary, which linked to a blog entry of the seminary president, Jeff Iorg. The entry simply described the Bible as the ultimate authority.[3] The article in question mentioned abortion, gender issues, and polygamy, and Facebook didn't boost it because, at the time, they had concerns Gateway Seminary was a hate group.[4]

The seminary's article was about how following the teachings of Scripture are important, and not doing so has a negative domino effect on our culture.

Can you imagine that? Because Christians still believe the kinds of principles upon which the United States of America was founded, we're potentially seen as a hate group. Nowhere is the rhetoric any hotter than in the debate over gay marriage. And even in churches today there are people who say, "The world has changed, and we have to change with it."

I'm a Southern Baptist, and yes, I know we have our share of challenges, so I'm not being judgmental here. I've watched our United Methodist friends debate this issue, and it has been deeply disturbing to me. At their General Conference in St. Louis in February of 2019, the church determined to stick with what they're calling *The Traditional Plan*.[5] The Traditional Plan reaffirms the Methodist view that "the practice of homosexuality is incompatible with Christian teaching."[6] It sharpened prohibitions of pastors from marrying same-sex couples and Methodist churches from hosting such unions. It indicates that United Methodists who are in same-sex marriages are in the wrong.

As I understand it, it was the delegates from Africa and other nations, not the United States, that tipped the vote toward affirming The Traditional Plan.

Adam Hamilton leads the United Methodist Church of the Resurrection in Leawood, Kansas. It is the largest United Methodist Church in America and has several campuses. Hamilton is bright, articulate, and obviously a leader with great ability. Sadly, on many occasions, he has been an outspoken critic of the United Methodist Church sticking to its biblical roots. Since the church is located in my general area, I often see his interviews on local television stations. Regarding the concept that same-sex couples shouldn't be married and that the church shouldn't host their weddings, Hamilton said, "This idea is repugnant."[7] In other words, he more closely aligns with cultural liberalism than with conservative Christianity.

It has been nothing short of painful watching Hamilton, a well-read, well-educated, eloquent speaker, jump through hermeneutical hoops attempting to amend what Scripture says about such an important topic. Rather than be grateful that his General Conference affirmed the Bible, he's been on a campaign to discredit those who made the decision. He said of the African delegation, who in my mind saved the Methodist Church for now, that the reason they're against homosexuality is because it's against the law in their countries.

I'll bet if you ask them, they'll tell you they're against it because it's against God's Law in the Scriptures. Part of Hamilton's rationalization for supporting same-sex unions is because he notes that 75 percent of millennials support same-sex marriage. Okay. With all due respect, millennials don't get the final vote; God does.

I'm not against Methodists at all; they're my brothers and sisters, and I'm not throwing stones. I am saying some of them are fooled into thinking that because the world is changing its views of morals, the church has to change its views as well. Listen carefully: No, we don't. In fact, we *cannot* change on biblical principles if we want to be right with God.

To be concise, let me simply say that gay marriage is not acceptable in the eyes of God. I'm not saying that we don't accept gay people as created in the image of God. Gay people are image-bearers of God. Gay people matter to God. Gay people are not "less than" in any way. But like any other ongoing, unrepentant sinful behavior (I'm talking here about those who engage in homosexual activity, not those who simply struggle with same-sex attraction), we have to love people enough to be truthful with them.

While we should be loving and caring toward all people, that doesn't equate to laying our biblical convictions on the altar of cultural conformity.

I love gay people, and I'm not attempting to be condescending when I say this: I feel sad for them. I feel sad for them because, first of all, same-sex attraction is not a temptation I've faced. I don't know how difficult it must be, but it obviously is quite difficult. Secondly, I feel sad for them because, if they give in to those temptations, they've bought the lie of the enemy and the lie of our current culture, as well. And that's very sad to me.

But lest you think this is yet another anti-gay rant from a conservative Christian, there's another lie people buy into: it's the idea of *serial monogamy*. They think if they marry someone of the opposite sex and they're faithful to them as long as they decide to stay married, that's enough. But it's not. Marriage isn't about being faithful for a time, and then moving on to be faithful with someone else for a time, and so forth. It's not just, "I'll be faithful to the wife I married until I choose to leave her and marry someone else to whom I will pledge faithfulness."

Some of you reading this book aren't believers, and I want you to know why we believe this. We're not being ugly or judgmental; we are just trying to help people be faithful to the Lord. That's it! When we make a big deal as believers about marriage, it's because we're just trying to help people follow the Bible. I'm not judging anybody. I don't dislike people who disagree with me. I'm just trying to help people and teach the Bible.

DIVORCE, UNDER CERTAIN CIRCUMSTANCES, IS PERMITTED

But if the unbelieving partner separates, let it be so. In such cases the brother or sister is not enslaved. God has called you to peace. For how do you know, wife, whether you will save your husband? Or how do you know, husband, whether you will save your wife? (1 Cor. 7:15-16)

Paul is talking about a situation in which a believer is married to an unbeliever, and he says if the unbeliever leaves, the believing partner isn't bound (*"is not enslaved"*). As we see in a moment, not only does that mean the believer doesn't have to stay married, but it indicates that he or she is free to remarry.[8]

So, what exactly are grounds for divorce? We know adultery is one. Jesus mentions in Matthew 19:9, *"And I say to you: whoever divorces his wife, except for sexual immorality, and marries another, commits adultery."* We'll get to the latter part of that verse in a moment, but since Jesus mentions sexual immorality as the exception clause, it is clear he's indicating divorce is permissible when sexual immorality has occurred.

Even if the marriage vow is broken, divorce is only an *option*; it's not a *requirement*. I have counseled many couples in the throes of infidelity. The majority have remained married and gone on to experience a tremendous marriage together. So, divorce is not a requirement, but it *is* an option.

If you're a Christian and your spouse is not a Christian, you are not bound to the marriage relationship if your spouse leaves. Desertion, then, also is grounds for biblically justified divorce. If you're a Christian married to an unbeliever, do your best to stay in the relationship. You might be the one to lead your spouse to Christ. But if your spouse leaves, I believe you're free.

It's important to note that some Christians disagree with my point of view. And I think it's wise to recognize differences of interpretation exist among conservative believers who hold to the inerrancy and infallibility of Scripture. For example, some church leaders for whom I have the utmost respect believe "Paul gives no support for the idea that in certain cases it is acceptable for a person to initiate a divorce."[9]

For some of you, what I'm about to say might seem like a slippery slope, but I feel it must be said. For the record, I think great caution must be issued here, so as not to make it seem anything and everything should be grounds for divorce. While I realize it is sometimes difficult to define abuse, if abuse is present, I don't believe an individual is bound to stay in a relationship. I know both men and women can be abusers, but for the sake of example, we'll say a man is the abuser for now.

In many cases, if a man is abusing his wife, he is breaking the law. I'm speaking here of physical or sexual abuse. I certainly believe emotional abuse is a real thing; it's just that it's more complex to unpack. I would tend to connect the dots in much the same way between ongoing emotional abuse and desertion (in the sense that the abuser is abandoning the marriage or breaking the marriage vows via emotional abuse).

Back to physical and sexual abuse and how they represent breaking the law: that law-breaking should cause an action whereby the abuser is removed from the home. If he is removed from the home because of his actions, he has most certainly deserted his wife by committing criminal acts and being punished for them. You are free to differ with my "connecting the dots" here, but I believe a case for interpreting desertion this way can be made.

Whether or not the law steps in and the abuser is removed from the home, I still believe, for all intents and purposes, he has deserted her; at the very least, he is breaking his marriage vow to love, honor, cherish, etc. Further, if one who is abused remains in a truly abusive relationship, it could be argued she is breaking a commandment of the Lord.

Mark 12:31 reads, "... *love your neighbor as yourself.*" One of the first tenets of loving self is self-preservation. You cannot take care of yourself, love yourself, and fulfill this command if you allow your husband to beat you. I say it curtly this way, not to further inflict harm on a spouse (that's the last thing I want to do), but to demonstrate the absurdity of thinking that one must stay in the home no matter what.

We've already noted that Paul encourages married couples to freely give conjugal rights to each other (1 Cor.7:3-5). In 1 Corinthians 7:32-34, as he's talking about freedom from anxiety about worldly things, Paul is referencing the need to provide food and clothing to a spouse. Look at the text:

> I want you to be free from anxieties. The unmarried man is anxious about the things of the Lord, how to please the Lord. But the married man is anxious about worldly things, how to please his wife, and his interests are divided. And the unmarried or betrothed woman is anxious about the things of the Lord, how to be holy in body and spirit. But the married woman is anxious about worldly things, how to please her husband.

Although Paul doesn't explicitly state it, many would say he is inferring that neglect through desertion, as well as neglect of sexual intimacy or failure to provide for a wife's basic needs, are potential grounds for divorce.

It's important to offer a caveat, however, and recognize that in some cases due to illness or disability, some partners may not be able to function sexually, or perhaps even provide for the basic needs of the other. Common sense and a broad-based biblical understanding dictate that Paul is talking about those who can but simply choose not to.

This concept hearkens back to Exodus 21:10-11. Look at what it says:

> If he takes another wife to himself, he shall not diminish her food, her clothing, or her marital rights. And if he does not do these three things for her, she shall go out for nothing, without payment of money.

It's a very different context, but it deals with the importance of providing food, clothing, and conjugal rights. Certainly, unfaithfulness would be easy to identify as grounds for divorce. But as you can imagine, the rabbis were loath to allow divorce on grounds of refusing conjugal activity. It's much more difficult to define. How often is often enough for sexual activity? And isn't the idea of conjugal or marital rights even more than simply sexual activity? If a man never shows his wife affection but has sex with her several times a week, is he really fulfilling *all* of her needs?

And what about the requirement for the man to provide for his wife's *necessities* (food and clothing, etc.)? How do you define necessities? A man could buy food and clothing for his wife and provide a place to live, but if the couple has enough money and he prohibits his wife from having dinner with her friends, or buying makeup, or having coffee out, is he really providing for her in the way he should?

Of course, the economic health of a married couple has to be taken into consideration here, and if you've been married more than a month, you know there are seasons to a couple's economic condition. What's more, there's a big difference between necessities and desires. Not every couple can afford the "average" or "above-average" home. That's not grounds for divorce. Not every husband can provide a luxury automobile for his wife. That's not grounds for divorce. Some of what I refer to as "sanctified common sense" has to be added to the mix at this point.

Burning the toast, or not giving in to every sexual whim of a spouse, would not be grounds for divorce. We have to be reasonable. Even in cases where terrible things have happened between spouses, I think it's wise to recognize that the couple didn't get into this difficulty overnight. So, there's usually no need to rush any process, especially toward severing the relationship via divorce. Obviously, if one is in physical danger, leaving the home — or having the one who is the aggressor leave the home, at least for a time — is the prudent thing to do immediately.

There are many factors to consider in bizarre behavior, not the least of which is the potential role of alcohol or other controlled substances in a spouse's behavior. It's also good to rule out biological issues. For example, people with brain tumors sometimes have bizarre episodes completely dissimilar to their normal behavior. Also, some people's functioning ability (in many different areas) may change throughout marriage. For example, through absolutely no fault of their own, people who have been sexually abused are often left with challenges related to sexual response. I don't believe for one minute that divorcing a spouse in the throes of that kind of challenge is permissible.

What about when a spouse ends up with dementia or Alzheimer's? Of course, they can't function as they used to (old age tends to diminish us, as well), but divorce is not an acceptable option for Christians in these situations. My point is: At the first sign of trouble, or when one spouse is clearly in decline physically or mentally, no one should run to a lawyer to file for divorce. Having said that, in some cases, as we noted earlier, divorce is *permissible*.

This is the part a lot of Christians don't like. I don't think this issue is cut and dried. Let me be clear: Well-meaning, Bible-believing, conservative Christians may see some of these things differently. As Andreas Köstenberger notes:

> Those with divergent interpretations of 1 Corinthians 7:15 should remember that those who do have freedom to remarry are not espousing a low view of marriage, nor are they acting contrary to the biblical text. Rather they are acting in accord with their understanding of Scripture.[10]

So, Paul says divorce, under certain conditions, is permitted. Moses, by the way, said the same thing.

Look at Mark 10:2-4:

> *And Pharisees came up and in order to test him asked, "Is it lawful for a man to divorce his wife?" He answered them, "What did Moses command you?" They said, "Moses allowed a man to write a certificate of divorce and to send her away."*

That's true. Moses did that very thing. Jesus goes on to say it was because of the hardness of their hearts that God made this concession (Mark 10:5). God did not want a woman to be left alone to fend for herself without any prospect for the future, so allowing divorce gives her a clean break, ostensibly in order that she might remarry.

Let me say to those of you who are divorced: You don't have to walk around with a red X on your forehead. *"There is therefore now no condemnation for those who are in Christ Jesus"* (Rom. 8:1). You're free! Someone else might try to keep you in bondage, but Jesus won't. You're free. I'm so sorry for what you've been through, and I'm certain there are some painful residuals, but you're free. Even if your divorce does not fall within biblical parameters, through repentance and faith, you're free.

REMARRIAGE, UNDER CERTAIN CONDITIONS, IS PERMITTED

To the unmarried and the widows I say that it is good for them to remain single, as I am. But if they cannot exercise self-control, they should marry. For it is better to marry than to burn with passion (1 Cor. 7:8-9).

Obviously, Paul makes an allowance for widows to remarry. He notes that for single people and widows who feel compelled to marry, it is permissible. It is important to note, however, that according to 1 Corinthians 7:39, those that remarry (and we've already noted this about those who marry) should do so *"in the Lord."*

A wife is bound to her husband as long as he lives. But if her husband dies, she is free to be married to whom she wishes, only in the Lord (I Cor. 7:39).

It might seem odd that Paul uses this phrase in verse 39. He is speaking to widows. He wants to assure Christian widows they do not have to follow the Jewish law of levirate marriage, which would have caused them to marry their brother-in-law if they were childless. We don't see levirate marriage carried over into the New Testament (I know some of you just whispered, "Amen.").

According to David Instone-Brewer in his book, *Divorce and Remarriage in the Church*, a divorce certificate was found belonging to a man named Joseph and a woman named Mary, and it was dated AD 72. Joseph was the second-most-popular male name at the time, and Mary was the most-popular female name. Please don't confuse this Joseph and Mary with the Joseph and Mary of the Gospel accounts in Scripture.

The ancient document followed the traditional wording, including the words that were compulsory in a Jewish divorce certificate. It read: "You are free to marry any Jewish man you wish."

According to Instone-Brewer, in the first century, most, if not all, believed that a divorcee had the right to remarry. The Romans had this right preserved in their law and didn't want any kind of restriction on it whatsoever. It doesn't appear that there were any Jewish parties in the first century that prohibited remarriage after divorce.[12]

In fact, Instone-Brewer notes:

> A Roman citizen who didn't remarry within eighteen months of a divorce (or within two years if their partner had died) could be prosecuted under a law that was enacted by Emperor Augustus in 18 B.C. He was concerned that many young men were divorcing the brides their parents had arranged for them to marry and then living carefree, licentious lives. He was also concerned that there were not enough children being born to Roman citizens, so he wanted these young men to get remarried and father children.[13]

Pious Jews were typically compelled to marry, which begs the question, "What about Paul?" There are all kinds of conjecture, none of which I would bank on. At any rate, Paul had an understanding of marriage, and he's not opposed to marriage at all, as many want to say. Look at 1 Corinthians 7:26 for a moment. Paul writes, *"I think that in view of the present distress it is good for a person to remain as he is."* His words to those contemplating marriage, encouraging them to wait until "the present distress" had passed, are likely referring to the famine that affected the region at that time.[14] So, it's not that Paul is anti-marriage. Obviously, babies often come with marriage, and it's not easy to care for a spouse, much less babies or toddlers, during a famine.

The biggest pushback related to remarriage, however, comes from the way many interpret Jesus' words in Matthew 19:9: *"And I say to you: whoever divorces his wife, except for sexual immorality, and marries another, commits adultery."*

Some have tried to say that Jesus is using hyperbole, overstating his case, to be convincing. He did that earlier, for example, when he said it's better to cut off your hand if it causes you to sin. As another example, perhaps Jesus' words about remarriage being adultery are similar to saying that looking at a woman with lust is committing adultery. Anyway, that's the argument some put forth to explain Jesus' words. I'm sure I don't know all Jesus is doing here, but I don't think that's the intended meaning.

Rather, I think Jesus is making three points:

First, he is ruling against polygamy. If a man is not free to marry another woman because he is still bound to his first wife, that means God permits him to have only one wife.

Second, Jesus is chipping away at the double standard of the day by referring to the husband's sexual relationship with the second woman as adulterous. By insisting that the man is committing adultery against his first wife, Jesus radically redefined the role of women in marriage. Put simply, he is elevating the wife's stature.

Third, Jesus' appeal to Deuteronomy 24 protected women from the capricious power of their husbands to divorce them at will.

There are those who say remarriage is permissible under *all* circumstances. Some say it's permissible under *no* circumstances, and some say it's permissible under *some* circumstances. I fall within the category that it is permissible under *some* circumstances, but I have grace toward those who do not share my views.

My conviction here is based on the fact that divorce is most certainly *not* an unpardonable sin. Further, the circumstances of divorce are not always as cut and dried as some people, Christians included, wish to make them.

By the same token, if a couple comes to me desiring to be married, and they've only been divorced a short time, I would conclude perhaps they've not had sufficient time to grieve the failure of their previous marriages. So, I would not advise entering into a new marriage covenant right away. I would potentially be in favor of it, depending on circumstances, after additional time passed.

While time is no guarantee healing will occur, it is necessary in order for healing to have a chance. If a couple comes to me desiring to be married, and this would be the fifth partner for one or both of them because of several divorces, I would not advise them to begin a new marriage. But typically, if divorce has occurred, and there has been adequate time for repentance where needed, along with reflection and healing, I'm not opposed to remarriage.

I don't want to soften the words of Jesus, but it's important to recognize that even if a relationship begins with adultery, that doesn't mean it continues as adultery. I think the bigger point here is that Jesus is simply highlighting the importance — the great significance — of marital fidelity.

And what are we to make of Paul's words again? He says in 1 Corinthians 7:9b, *"It is better to marry than to burn with passion."* He knows not everyone has the self-control to go through life without a marriage partner with whom we may experience sexual intimacy.

Again, for some people, singleness is a gift; for others, singleness is not their gift. And Paul says rather than living your life in continual frustration, you would do well to find a marriage partner, someone who is *"in the Lord,"* and get married.

COHABITATION, UNDER ALL CIRCUMSTANCES, IS FORBIDDEN

For the record, when I'm talking about cohabitation, I'm talking about couples living together and engaging in sexual intimacy without having been married — either in the eyes of God or the state. Obviously, what we're dealing with in the context of this book is slanted toward a biblical understanding or worldview. I'm not trying to convince unbelievers, although the principles would be helpful for them, as well.

According to lifestyle website thespruce.com, many studies conclude that couples who cohabitate prior to marriage are at a higher risk of divorce.[15] Remember, cohabitation doesn't just occur among young people. There are a lot of middle-aged and elderly people that choose to cohabit, as well.

Further, the number of young and middle-aged Americans who have cohabited has doubled in the past twenty-five years.[16] If you've done that, I'm not condemning you. But while I don't want to pour salt in anyone's wounds, neither do I want to miss an opportunity to teach truth that might prevent others from doing something wrong.

It's a different world now than it was even five years ago as far as sexual ethics are concerned. I can't tell you how many people have asked me through the years (with a bit of doubt in their tone), "You mean you and your wife didn't live together before you got married?" What once was viewed as somewhat abnormal, just plain wrong, or at least socially unacceptable, is now often seen as the norm. That's completely understandable when it comes to the non-Christian world. I mean, unbelievers act like unbelievers, right?

But the greater problem is that there are a lot of believers who see things the way unbelievers do. I can't tell you how many young couples I've known in the last twenty years that have been raised in an evangelical church, professed to be followers of Jesus, but seemed to ignore the sexual ethic of the New Testament when it came to their own relationships.

Simply put, the people of God — the church — should "toe the line" on this one. Just because there's pressure to cave doesn't mean we are obligated to do so. And we shouldn't. I imagine everybody reading this who claims to be a Christian knows that any sex before marriage, and any sex with someone besides your spouse after you're married, is wrong. The Bible is replete with warnings against such behavior. While I realize people have always sinned sexually, we're at a point — even in the so-called Christian subculture — that there's no shame related to sin anymore. In some cases, pagans are more discreet about their sin than Christians are.

Often, Christian couples say, "Well, we're living together, but we're not having sex." I am willing to offer them the Nobel Peace Prize for Self-Restraint if that truly is the case (no, I don't think there's such an award). But here's the thing: Even with the outside chance that is the case, aren't we Christians supposed to protect our witness? How do our actions potentially affect those around us? Would your neighbors really believe you if you said, "We're living together, but we're not having sex"?

Here's what the Bible says from Ephesians 5:3 that gives credence to my point: *"But sexual immorality and all impurity or covetousness must not even be named among you, as is proper among the saints."* Being *"named among you"* means "being hinted."

So, even if a couple living together isn't having sex, why take the chance to ruin one's ability to influence others for Jesus? Why take the chance that you'll give in to sexual sin? And why take the chance that you'll ruin your witness?

What I'm about to say is not meant to be crude but informative and encouraging. It runs contrary to what the world says. The culture tries to make you think everybody sleeps together prior to marriage. Listen to me: No, they don't. There are, in fact, a lot of people who recognize the sacred nature of sexual connection. And rather than just give in, they decide not to put themselves in high-risk situations. In fact, it might surprise you to know there are people with no religious affiliation or affection that believe sexual union is such a significant part of a committed relationship, they won't have sex prior to getting married, either.

I know what a lot of people think: "Well, we're going to get married. We'll just test the waters." Really? Are you sure you're going to marry each other? I can't tell you how many young ladies have thought that, and they've given themselves to the man they think is "Mr. Right," only to discover he was "Mr. I'll Use You for Sex Until I

Decide to Move On." And the same is true of young men looking for "Ms. Right."

So, protect your body. Protect your heart. Protect your faith. Protect your witness. Don't give in. Living together doesn't replicate marriage. It's not the same. And it doesn't help you prepare for marriage. In fact, as we noted earlier, statistical data show that couples who live together prior to marriage have a higher rate of divorce than those who do not. Cohabitation and marriage are two different things with different expectations and different results.

Just a few years ago, a study utilizing magnetic resonance imaging (MRI) examined the brain functioning of cohabitating and married women when facing stress. Researchers studying the subject administered a mild electric shock on the ankles of both cohabitating women and married women. The women had three choices of help and support during the experience: hold the hand of their partner, hold the hand of a stranger, or face the shock alone.

The study concludes:

> When a married woman held the hand of her spouse, she registered a deep sense of calm in the hypothalamus region of her brain as she prepared for the shock. Conversely, cohabitating women holding the hand of the live-in partner registered little to no calm. What surprised researchers is that while both sets of women stated that they felt commitment from the partners, the cohabitating women recorded the same level of calm as those holding the hand of a stranger. Researchers speculate that while cohabitating women say they feel commitment from the partner, doubt resides in the deepest part of their brains.[17]

And you know why? It's pretty simple, I think. God didn't intend for us to just have sex; he intended for us to marry.

I've written some tough truths in this chapter. But I want you to know that nobody living within the forgiveness of Christ should feel condemnation. Everybody reading this has sinned. I always want to be part of the process of healing, applying grace to the wounds of those who are hurting. And I want the same to be true of the church. As Christians, we're supposed to be people of grace.

Further, I think it's important to admit that not all Christians have identical convictions about these issues. Even so, we should all be committed to extending grace and forgiveness to those who have sinned and those who have been hurt. Grace is a theological verity; it's a reality. In the life of the church, however, grace also is an atmosphere. So, I encourage you to do everything you can to create and maintain an atmosphere of grace within your heart, your small group, and your whole church, because you never know the difference it might make.

The truth is, there is a place for all of us in the church — that is, for everybody who repents and believes in Jesus. We're always in need of God's grace. Like Steve Brown has said so often to Christians, "You don't have to pretend to be good anymore. You announced to the world when you joined the church you weren't."[18] That's not a negative statement; it's really pretty liberating, isn't it? I don't have it all together and neither does anyone else, but in this group we call "church," we want to help one another along the way until we get home to heaven. So, remember, in the church there should be room for all of us who repent and believe.

WALLACE'S STORY

His name was Wallace Ellis. He was a Christian. He had been raised in a Christian home, surrendered to Jesus as a child, and was baptized at the age of nine. He was smart and handsome, and he had a winsome personality. As a young man, he married. He and his wife were married just a few years, and, like a lot of young couples, they had their share of difficulties. Times were tough. The economy was difficult. And, to add to their stress, he was a soldier during a time of great conflict on the world stage.

Eventually, Wallace and his wife separated. In time, they got back together for a while, but things were still extremely difficult. Finally, they divorced. He didn't want the divorce, but it happened anyway. They had one child, a son.

Wallace went through a terrible time trying to adjust. In the midst of all of this pain and grief, he rededicated his life to Christ. He wanted to live his life for Jesus and, in some way, use his life to help others. He went to his pastor at the time and told him he wanted to do something in the church or do something for the church. He just wanted to be involved and help.

And do you know what the preacher said? He said, "I'm sorry, Wallace. There's no place for someone like you to serve here."

Frankly, I think the world would be better off without a "pastor" like that. So, the Sunday after Easter, about sixty-five years ago now, my twenty-six-year-old uncle, Wallace Ellis, went home and committed suicide. I never had the chance to meet him because he was told there was no place for people like him in the church.

I wish I could have known Wallace. I wish I could have talked with him. Do you know what I would have said? I would have said, "That's great, Wallace, because the church exists for people just like you!"

QUESTIONS FOR PERSONAL OR GROUP STUDY

1. What might the church do to help strengthen marriages, as well as help prepare couples for marriage?
2. What factors in our culture contribute to divorce?
3. What do you believe are biblical grounds for divorce?
4. Do you think remarriage is acceptable? If so, under what conditions?
5. How might the church help those who choose to live together understand that cohabitation is not a prelude to marriage?

THE PLAGUE OF PORNOGRAPHY

IT'S NOT A VICTIMLESS SIN.

Let's call him Chip.

I was his pastor in another city at another time in my life. I hadn't known him or his family very long before his secret came out. He and his wife, Susie, had been married for several years and had one child. They were active in the church and, by all accounts, demonstrated a solid marriage and a growing relationship with Christ. They were prominent church leaders. That is, until that Monday morning.

They both came to my office. It seems that Susie was going through the bills and found a cable bill where Chip had ordered a pornographic movie one weekend while Susie was out of town. She was devastated. And the truth is, she didn't know the half of it. I met with them that Monday, and again the next week and the next. I don't really remember now how long we met together, working through their problems. While I was willing to meet with them, I was more encouraged that they sought the help of a trusted Christian counselor.

As our time together went on, more truth came out. Chip hadn't just watched a movie. He had amassed a computer history that would make any person blush. And even that wasn't the end of it. It seems his computer sin had led to skin-on-skin sin — rendezvous with women in various cities around the country.

His wife was distraught, his child disappointed, his life in disarray. Chip had gone from a happily married Christian leader to a man asked to move out of his home and get tested for sexually transmitted diseases. He lost his high-paying job. Most tragically, he besmirched his formerly good reputation. His life was a mess.

And it all started with one click of the mouse; one *wrong* click. Over the following months, I learned his story. For the sake of time, let me fast forward a bit. Bear in mind that Chip was a Christian. A happily married man. A father and a church leader. And he told me that once he started watching pornography, he was hooked. It took more and more images — each darker and more deviant than the last — to have the same effect on his brain.

He said when he was "found out," he had already considered testing the waters of homosexuality, and he was convinced he would have been viewing child pornography within a few months.

But people say pornography doesn't hurt anyone. It hurt Chip, his wife, his child, his church, his company, and his witness. And please don't be so naïve as to think the people, usually women, who are the subject matter of pornography aren't being hurt in the process. Nobody sets out to spend their lives being used that way. The women and children exploited for pornography are trafficked, abused, beaten, and berated. It is not a victimless sin.

There's so much that needs to be said about this. Let's look to Scripture to set the stage.

Owe no one anything, except to love each other, for the one who loves another has fulfilled the law. For the commandments, "You shall not commit adultery, You shall not murder, You shall not steal, You shall not covet," and any other commandment, are summed up in this word: "You shall love your neighbor as yourself." Love does no wrong to a neighbor; therefore love is the fulfilling of the law.

Besides this you know the time, that the hour has come for you to wake from sleep. For salvation is nearer to us now than when we first believed. The night is far gone; the day is at hand. So then let us cast off the works of darkness and put on the armor of light. Let us walk properly as in the daytime, not in orgies and drunkenness, not in sexual immorality and sensuality, not in quarreling and jealousy. But put on the Lord Jesus Christ, and make no provision for the flesh, to gratify its desires (Rom. 13:8-14).

So, what's wrong with pornography? Who does it hurt? Why do people use it? What light does Scripture shed on the issue of sexuality gone astray? What do we know about the plague of pornography in our culture? How does it affect us?

Paul makes it clear that we're to *"make no provision for the flesh."* That is, don't make any allowance to gratify the flesh's sinful desires. "No provision" embodies the basic concept of planning ahead or giving forethought to something. Paul is saying: Don't plan ahead to gratify the desires of your sinful flesh.

Let's talk about men for just a moment, because while both men and women utilize pornography, it's commonly accepted that men generally use it more than women. There are a lot of things that take place in a man's heart that ultimately lead him to pornography. In his book, *Counsel for Couples*, Jonathan Holmes shares the following motivations for pornography use:

Anger — It is not a woman's fault (read that phrase again) that a man uses porn, but if a man finds his wife sexually indifferent, he may turn to pornography to satisfy his disappointment. Disappointment is the pathway to anger. In no way does this justify the use of porn, but it's offered as a way to understand what transpires on the path to pornography use.

Boredom – It's perhaps hard to believe, but this is sometimes the case. What starts as surfing the web ends up in a moral wipeout.

Reward/entitlement – Some men feel like they've worked hard and deserve some kind of pleasure, so they turn to pornography.

Escapism/fantasy – Many men are dissatisfied with their work life, home life, and sex life.

Fear of rejection – Many men have significant insecurities related to their sex lives. They may say they fear rejection from their wives and turn to pornography, where there is no chance of rejection.[1]

Please understand, none of these are justification for utilizing pornography. I want to stress that most *behavior* that is sinful begins with *thinking* that is sinful. Sinful behavior comes from sinful and lustful ideas we contemplate. Pornography, in our day, is a significant culprit in aiding people to sin. It really is that simple. And think how much more prevalent its use is these days because of the ease by which it is accessed. As Patrick Carnes has noted, "Computers provided new technology for our oldest obsession."[2] So, who and what do pornography negatively affect?

PORNOGRAPHY AFFECTS THE FAMILY

Keep Paul's words in mind as you read this chapter. That's the biblical foundation we're contemplating. Think about the imagery Paul uses: taking off something and putting on something. It is symbolic of thoughts and behaviors. *"Make no provision for the flesh."* Clothe yourselves with Christ.

We've all been dismayed in recent years — and rightfully so — at the countless reports of sexual misconduct by people from all walks of life. There is outrage against men who have used their power and money to take advantage of women and children. Women and children especially become objects to these kinds of people. And that should make us angry.

We could spend a lot of time conversing about the hypocrisy of Hollywood. They're angry at the men who objectify women but refuse to admit that their industry is a primary culprit in all of this. For just one example, we need look no further than the Super Bowl half-time shows from the last decade. Granted, recent shows may not have garnered the national attention the Janet Jackson "wardrobe malfunction" did in the 2004 Super Bowl half-time show, but most years the half-time show manages to push the boundaries with performances that previously would have been labeled "indecent," and certainly not acceptable for prime time. Scantily clad women and suggestive lyrics combine to lead viewers down a path that is prone to objectify women.

It's been reported, for example, that Super Bowl Sunday in the United States is the day that records the most cases of human trafficking each year.[3] So, guys are watching football, drinking till their inhibitions decline, or their anger rises. They get amped up watching scantily clothed women gyrating in sexual ways on their television screens, and they place an order for a sexual liaison. It all works together.

You can't even comfortably watch a half-time show as a family without being bombarded with pornographic images. Among the saddest things to me, besides performers having their children up on the stage, is that somewhere along the line, these women — no doubt very talented — have lost one of God's greatest gifts of common grace to humanity; they've lost their self-respect. They willingly allow themselves to be objectified, all in the name of sport. But if the demand wasn't there, marketers wouldn't deliver the "product."

Think how this affects our families. A dad, watching the half-time show, can't get that sexual imagery out of his brain. A mother knows she can't physically measure up to what the culture claims is the standard. Boys and young men experience warped thinking, believing this is the way most women want to be viewed. Daughters watch it all and ask, "Why would my dad think this is okay for family viewing?" And then parents wonder why their girl brings home the testosterone-overloaded brute that she does.

The writer of Hebrews clarifies the role of sexuality in marriage. He writes, as recorded in chapter 13, verse 4, *"Let marriage be held in honor among all, and let the marriage bed be undefiled, for God will judge the sexually immoral and adulterous."*

The word for "bed" used here is *koite*, which is connected to the Latin word *coition*, from which we get the word *coitus*. This simply describes the special relationship a married couple experiences in the marriage bed they share with one another. The point is (lest you think this is crude, it's straight from the Bible), sexual expression is reserved for married people together alone. It is a holy and sacred experience that God designed to be very good. But people everywhere continually work to distort it.

It is distorted through heterosexual adultery and fornication. It is distorted through any kind of homosexual relationship. It is distorted through pornography. When people view porn, they are connecting visually with someone else in a way reserved for connection with one's spouse. And it is not a victimless sin. Someone's wife, someone's daughter, someone's sister, is being treated with absolute ruthless contempt when she is objectified purely for sexual pleasure. Pornography is not a rite of passage; it is a sinful gateway to a lifetime of sexual dysfunction.

There are many reasons people choose to dabble in pornography, and many reasons people end up addicted. For some, they were exposed to it at a very young age, and it piqued their natural curiosity about sexuality. Some people turn to porn attempting to understand something unhealthy that has been done to them; they're victims of sexual or physical abuse. It's important to recognize that pornography use often leads to addiction. Let me clarify: "When discussing sexual addiction, it is necessary to recognize that not everyone who has a regrettable sexual experience is an addict."[4]

Space doesn't permit me to deal with all the sexual dysfunctions pornography may spark, but suffice it to say that the use of pornography sets one up for sexual dysfunction, failed relationships, and shame beyond imagination. Using pornography is giving in to a conscious or subconscious delusional thought process. As Carnes notes, "The addict substitutes a sick relationship to an event or a process for a healthy relationship with others. The addict's relationship with a mood-altering experience becomes central to his life."[5]

We know the family is the basic building block of our culture. So, our culture is not properly built if the building blocks we use are greatly damaged. Pornography affects the family, and the family affects the entire culture. The Holy Spirit knew this when he inspired the apostle Paul to write, *"But put on the Lord Jesus Christ, and make no provision for the flesh, to gratify its desires"* (Rom. 13:14). Pornography affects the family.

PORNOGRAPHY AFFECTS THE BRAIN

In Philippians 4:8, Paul the apostle writes:

> *Finally, brothers, whatever is true, whatever is honorable, whatever is just, whatever is pure, whatever is lovely, whatever is commendable, if there is any excellence, if there is anything worthy of praise, think about these things.*

These are the kinds of things we Christians are supposed to contemplate. Pornography doesn't fit these categories. In fact, focusing on pornographic images — using our minds that way — causes damage to how we function. With pornography use, specific pathways in the brain are triggered that prompt the same neurological response of pleasure and reward. These pathways are the same as those seen in drug addiction.[6] Testosterone, dopamine, and norepinephrine are key players in sexual arousal and response. Pornography use hijacks these. The need for satisfaction is met, not with a person of the opposite sex in a committed, monogamous marriage as God designed, but rather in a very unsuitable substitute.[7]

One of the greatest tragedies of the porn industry is the fact that it preys on adolescents. Puberty and pornography are a deadly mix. Sexual curiosity, which is a natural thing, is already present. The problem is that kids look to porn for answers, but what they get isn't true. This is one reason the church needs to be clear in its sexual ethic. We cannot shy away from talking about issues related to sexuality just because it might make someone uncomfortable.

When a young person is developing into manhood or womanhood, when hormones are surging and confusion is sometimes present about innumerable things, pornography is the wolf that enters the neighborhood with the sole purpose of blowing down the house.

Adolescence is hard enough without this kind of intruder.

Valerie Voon, a neuropsychiatrist at the University of Cambridge, is one of many researchers exploring the question of how to classify pornography use. Using brain scans, Voon studied whether subjects who viewed pornography showed the same brain activity as substance abusers. In a 2013 British documentary, *Porn on the Brain*, she concluded that the brain activity of habitual pornography users looks the same as those of alcoholics.[8]

Please understand, her findings are not predisposed toward a conclusion; she's not researching as a Christian healthcare professional. This is research from an organization that is not tied to any type of evangelical roots. And she is saying pornography use causes one's brain to resemble that of an alcoholic.

Make no mistake: pornography affects the brain.

PORNOGRAPHY AFFECTS THE HEART

Paul reminds Christians in Romans 12:10 that we are to *"outdo one another in showing honor."* Husbands and wives viewing porn are not honoring their spouses. They're denigrating them. Whether they mean to or not, viewing pornography communicates that their spouse isn't good enough, or can't meet their needs, or isn't worthy of sexual faithfulness.

Pornography negatively affects countless relationships. This leads many Christians to ask: "Does use of pornography constitute marital infidelity?" In other words, "If my spouse uses porn, is he or she cheating on me?" At the very least, it's hard to defend against the accusation of cheating if one is turning to someone or something other than a spouse to find sexual satisfaction.

Pornography affects the heart. Do you see that?

Juniper Research estimated that in 2017, a quarter of a billion people used their cell phones and tablets to access pornographic content. This statistic represents a more than 30 percent increase over 2013.[9]

The Barna Group conducted a survey in the United States in 2014, which demonstrated that 64 percent of self-identified Christian men and 15 percent of self-identified Christian women view pornography at least once a month. Some 37 percent of Christian men and 7 percent of Christian women view pornography at least several times a week.[10]

The sexting phenomenon has enabled people to send graphic sexual pictures and messages to practically anyone. These pictures and messages often are sent to people they know as well as people they don't. The Barna Research Group found that 62 percent of teenagers and young adults have received a sexually explicit image from someone, and 41 percent of those surveyed acknowledged they had not just received a sexting image but had sent one themselves.[11]

The battle against pornography is not easily won. It's not just an issue of behavior modification. The heart has to be changed. The only way the heart is changed is when we allow God to change it. Please understand, there is hope. My purpose is not to shame those of you who are dabbling in, or even addicted to, pornography. If the previously noted statistical data is true, it's a given that many who read this chapter are struggling with pornography use. My point is to highlight the sin but then point to the solution in Jesus.

There are many things that can be done. In addition to filters for electronic devices, there's anti-pornography software. There are sites such as covenanteyes.com or netnanny.com that can provide help. Don't just stay stuck.

Remember Chip from the beginning of the chapter? He lost his job, his reputation, and almost his wife. Today he's gainfully employed and serving Jesus through various ministries of his local church. He's respected. He and his wife have gotten through this "worse" portion of "for better, for worse." They're still together. He has a good relationship with his child, and he's even a grandfather now. For some twenty years, he has been leading groups in churches for men who are addicted to pornography.

He knows it's a day-to-day and moment-by-moment battle. But through the power of Christ, he's winning.

You can, too!

QUESTIONS FOR PERSONAL OR GROUP STUDY

1. Are the statistics about pornography use surprising to you in any way? If they are, how so?
2. Who does pornography negatively affect?
3. In what ways can we responsibly teach older children and young people about the dangers of pornography use?
4. How do you think the use of pornography affects a Christian's walk with God?
5. What are some practical steps you, your spouse, and your family can take to protect all of you against the subtle but dangerous threats of pornography use?

HEAVEN AND HELL

OUR LIVES ON EARTH PASS QUICKLY, BUT THEY'RE NOT
THE END OF US.

L ife goes quickly, doesn't it? One statement I make periodically
is that I'm more than halfway home these days. Like my friend
Steve Brown often says, "I'm at the age now where I'm cramming for
finals." I have more days behind me on this earth than I do ahead of
me. I don't feel old at all, and people say I'm moving toward middle
age, but statistically, true middle age is actually about thirty-eight, so
I'm a bit beyond that!

I went to Dick's Sporting Goods a couple of years ago because
there was a particular golf club I was considering purchasing. I had a
few questions, so I went to the young man at the counter and asked
him about the club. Then he said, "Do you want to hit it?"

I said, "Sure."

So, we walked into the hitting area, and he explained why this
club is so forgiving, easier to hit, and so forth. And I said, "That's
great. I need all the help I can get."

Then I added something like, "When you get even a little past
your prime, it really makes a difference."

And he said, "Well, I'm only twenty-one and in college, so it
doesn't matter to me."

I said, "I know. Just last week I was your age, Son. Now the socks I wear are older than you."

Life indeed goes fast, doesn't it? With that being the case, I think differently about heaven. I think differently about it every year. Heaven isn't just streets of gold and the river of the water of life. It's also where my parents are now. I have twin siblings in heaven. I have a lot of friends and relatives already living there.

An elderly man once said:

As a boy, I thought of heaven as a city with domes, spires, and beautiful streets, inhabited by angels. By and by, my little brother died, and I thought of heaven much as before, but with one inhabitant that I knew. Then another brother died, and then some of my acquaintances, so in time I began to think of heaven as containing several people that I knew. But it was not until one of my own little children died that I began to think I had treasure in heaven myself. Afterward, another went, and yet another. By that time, I had so many acquaintances and children in heaven that I no more thought of it as a city merely with streets of gold, but as a place full of inhabitants. Now there are so many loved ones there, I sometimes think I know more people in heaven than I do on earth. I'm ready to go!

I know that many of you have heard about heaven all your life. I also know that a lot of people have never heard *enough* about heaven in their lifetime. Something I think is so sad is how many people, even people of faith, don't talk about heaven and hell because they feel as if they'll be viewed as unsophisticated or intellectually stunted.

As Geoffrey Rowell notes on his study of hell:

Heaven, hell, death, and judgment are the traditional Four Last Things of Christian theology, but ... twentieth-century theologians have, for the most part, been embarrassed at saying much about any of them. In this they stand in sharp contrast to the majority of nineteenth-century divines, who ... regarded it as a central part of Christian teaching."[1]

For all the good that we've done in explaining to people that eternal life begins the moment they receive Christ, I'm afraid we've neglected to give them adequate truth about what's to come for those who believe in Christ and what's to come for those who reject him. Let's look at some of what Scripture says:

> *For God so loved the world, that he gave his only Son, that whoever believes in him should not perish but have eternal life. For God did not send his Son into the world to condemn the world, but in order that the world might be saved through him. Whoever believes in him is not condemned, but whoever does not believe is condemned already, because he has not believed in the name of the only Son of God. And this is the judgment: the light has come into the world, and people loved the darkness rather than the light because their works were evil. For everyone who does wicked things hates the light and does not come to the light, lest his works should be exposed. But whoever does what is true comes to the light, so that it may be clearly seen that his works have been carried out in God* (John 3:16-21).

So, what can we say about heaven and hell?

HEAVEN IS MADE POSSIBLE BECAUSE JESUS CAME

> *For God so loved the world, that he gave his only Son, that whoever believes in him should not perish but have eternal life* (John 3:16).

God gave Jesus. Jesus laid down his life for us, so that we might be able to live forever. This eternal life really has two components. While we take comfort in eternal life yet to come, it's important to understand that our eternal life begins the moment we believe in Jesus as our Savior. Eternal life is both *here* and then *hereafter*. We enjoy the relationship we have with Jesus now, but someday, when we go to heaven, we'll enjoy our eternal life with Jesus in the hereafter.

Depending on which surveys you read, sometimes the majority of people think heaven exists, and typically, there's an assumption that everybody is going there. Of course, there are always the naysayers who try to convince the world that the Christian faith is for imbeciles, and nobody with more than a first-grade education believes in Jesus anymore. While we don't have the space to deal with all of the statistical data, let me simply say that Christianity isn't in trouble. We're not all imbeciles. We're not going away. It's not about over.

In fact, a recent Harvard University study demonstrated just the opposite. According to a study by scholars at the university, as well as Indiana University at Bloomington, religious belief continues to enjoy "persistent and exceptional intensity" in America. These researchers contend that our nation "remains an exceptional outlier and potential counter example to the secularization thesis."[2] It's a good study. It puts to bed the ridiculous notion that the Christian faith is going away.

So, let's talk about this place called heaven, and then let's talk about the place called hell. There have long been major debates about where heaven is and, ultimately, where heaven *will be*. With that thought in mind, let me simply remind us: Wherever God dwells with his people is heaven.

If, for all eternity, God would dwell at Busch Stadium in St. Louis or Kaufman Stadium in Kansas City, where I often go to watch baseball games, that would be heaven. I'm not being flippant; I really believe that. Wherever God dwells with his people, that's going to be heaven.

I don't like to travel alone, but if my wife, Lori, is with me, I find travel enjoyable. Wherever she is, I'm happy. We were happy in a little two-bedroom apartment, and we were happy when we lived in a big house on five acres of land. And we're happy now in a modest home on a corner lot in a nice neighborhood. What made me happy wasn't the geographical location, but the company of someone I love. Wherever heaven is, if you love Jesus, trust me, you'll be happy!

If that's in the sky far away, or if it's right here on a brand-new earth, wherever God is, that's heaven. While it's interesting to conjecture about the geographical location of heaven — and we will do that momentarily — the more important thing we can say with certainty is that where God is, that's heaven. Let's look at some interesting biblical texts about all of this. What else can we say about heaven?

THERE IS AN "INTERMEDIATE HEAVEN" OR "PARADISE"

And he said to him, "Truly, I say to you, today you will be with me in paradise" (Luke 23:43).

So we are always of good courage. We know that while we are at home in the body we are away from the Lord, for we walk by faith, not by sight. Yes, we are of good courage, and we would rather be away from the body and at home with the Lord (2 Cor. 5:6-8).

As Jesus is being crucified, there are two thieves also being crucified with him. One of the thieves says, *"Jesus, remember me when you come into your kingdom."* Jesus then replies, *"Truly, I say to you, today you will be with me in paradise."*

So, what exactly is *paradise*? In what is called the Septuagint (the pre-Christian Greek translation of the Old Testament), the word translated *paradise* designated a garden or a forest, and carries with it the idea of bliss and rest between death and resurrection. In the Talmud (the central text of rabbinic Judaism), *paradise* is mentioned, as well as a place referred to as *Abraham's side*.

These are both seen as places of blessedness where righteous people go when they die. I believe it is heaven in the sense that God is there, but it is an intermediate heaven in the sense that it is not our final place of existence — the new heaven and new earth (Rev. 21-22).

Look at 2 Corinthians 5:6-8:

So we are always of good courage. We know that while we are at home in the body we are away from the Lord, for we walk by faith, not by sight. Yes, we are of good courage, and we would rather be away from the body and at home with the Lord.

What does that mean? It means that once we, as Christians, are away from the body, we're with God. Our spirits, our souls, the essence of our being, go to be with God immediately upon death. That's a spiritual reunion, but our spirits are later reunited with a glorified version of our bodies at the resurrection. When we die, we don't cease to exist. The Bible makes it clear that we who believe in Jesus go to be with him where he is in heaven. But there's more.

HEAVEN, "THE DWELLING OF GOD," WILL BE WITH MAN

Then I saw a new heaven and a new earth, for the first heaven and the first earth had passed away, and the sea was no more. And I saw the holy city, new Jerusalem, coming down out of heaven from God, prepared as a bride adorned for her husband. And I heard a loud voice from the throne saying, "Behold, the dwelling place of God is with man. He will dwell with them, and they will be his people, and God himself will be with them as their God" (Rev. 21:1-3).

Although we may have a wonderful and fulfilling relationship with God while here on Earth prior to death, our relationship with God is even richer, even fuller, as he makes his dwelling with us.

While I wouldn't want to over-emphasize the concept of geography, suffice it to say that Scripture indicates this new Jerusalem, this city of heaven, *comes down.* Well, to what location would it likely come down? Earth! The picture is that of our final place of habitation in this beautifully adorned heaven that God brings down to Earth for us to enjoy. Now, I don't know all the particulars; neither does anyone else. But it appears the Earth is created anew (as the Bible says it will be), and it becomes the place where heaven is ultimately found.

Part of our problem in understanding heaven is our Western baggage. For too many people, the idea of "heaven on Earth" doesn't ring true. The reason is, they've been told by pop culture that heaven is a place where people float on clouds. How many commercials have we seen, depicting heaven with a person (having become an angel in death, which is obviously another big problem) playing the harp, and floating on a cloud? Sadly, a lot of people get more of their theology from television commercials and books *about* heaven than from the Bible.

For example, Maria Shriver (yes, the one related to the late President John F. Kennedy) wrote a book called *What's Heaven?* It's a children's book, and I'm sure it's put together with good intentions. The problem is the content. In the book, Shriver says heaven is:

> ... somewhere you believe in ... It's a beautiful place where you can sit on soft clouds and talk to other people who are there. At night you can sit next to the stars, which are the brightest of anywhere in the universe.... If you're good throughout your life, then you get to go to heaven.... When your life is finished here on earth, God sends angels down to take you up to heaven to be with him.

Then Shriver mentions "Grandma" and says she "Is alive in me.... She is watching over us from up there."[3]

Well, I don't think Grandma is watching over anybody (that sounds insensitive, but I think it's biblical). And I don't believe we're floating on clouds in heaven. Further, being good all your life won't get you into heaven.

The garden of Eden, right here on Earth, before sin entered the world — what was it? It was *paradise*. Why couldn't God make our ultimate *paradise*, our eventual home, a perfected place to inhabit *right here* on Earth? If heaven, at some level, is not connected with

Earth, then why would God go to all the trouble to recreate Earth and make it new?

Isaiah 65 refers to this new heaven and new Earth, and this concept is echoed in the writings of Peter and John (2 Pet. 3; Rev. 21-22). The biggest issue is that heaven is the place God dwells (Rev. 21:3). Now, I know that many of you have perhaps heard this concept previously. Let me simply say the Jehovah's Witnesses are incorrect about more things than space will allow me to mention here. They're in error regarding their views about Jesus' deity, and they're incorrect about the identity of the 144,000 in Revelation. They're sincere, but they're sincerely wrong about a lot of things.

However, as Christian theologian Craig Keener writes, "we should grant that they are right in one sense when they speak of life on the new earth."[4] In some ways, Jehovah's Witnesses seem to have been the only ones making a big deal about how Earth is made new and inhabited by God's people for eternity. The cult (counterfeit Christian organization) has gotten this right, while a lot of Christians, to our shame, have been talking about turning into angels, playing the harp, and floating on clouds!

Western Christianity has inherited an allegorical view of heaven from the Platonism of some early interpreters. Philo and Origen, among other early church leaders, came to embrace an allegorical view of heaven. They rejected the notion of heaven as a physical realm and spiritualized the biblical teaching of resurrected people inhabiting a resurrected Earth.

Plato, the Greek philosopher, believed the body was evil. Therefore, only the spirit, or that which is spiritual (that is without a body), could be good.[5] His followers began to embrace the view that human spirits are better off without bodies and that somehow heaven is a disembodied state.

Clearly, the Bible does not teach this. There is graphic imagery given of a future paradise — a place of reunion, a place of joy, a place of perfection, a place where death no longer invades our space and God has wiped away every tear from our eyes! Look again:

Then I saw a new heaven and a new earth, for the first heaven and the first earth had passed away, and the sea was no more. And I saw the holy city, new Jerusalem, coming down out of heaven from God, prepared as a bride adorned for her husband. And I heard a loud voice from the throne saying, "Behold, the dwelling place of God is with man. He will dwell with them, and they will be his people, and God himself will be with them as their God. He will wipe away every tear from their eyes, and death shall be no more, neither shall there be mourning, nor crying, nor pain anymore, for the former things have passed away" (Rev. 21:1-4).

In discussing Revelation 21, John Newport records:

The destination of the new Jerusalem is earth. God has come to make His eternal dwelling with us. The earth that God called good in the beginning He has now restored and called good again, so good that He is willing to dwell with us here. Our biblical faith is not an escape from the material world. Its final destiny is not an ethereal existence where floating spirits circle a heavenly throne. The Bible's last pictures show God on earth entering into fellowship with a resurrected people who live a bodily, human existence.[6]

I believe the concept of heaven is greater than our imaginations could ever begin to grasp. The greatest features of life on planet Earth are but a feeble symbol of that which is to come. Having said that, I remind you that so much on Earth is beautiful and lovely and enjoyable. Would it not stand to reason that the heaven which is to come will be filled with a reprise of what God has begun here?

THERE IS AN ULTIMATE "HELL" CALLED "THE LAKE OF FIRE"

The apostle John writes:

Then I saw a great white throne and him who was seated on it. From his presence earth and sky fled away, and no place was found for them. And I saw the dead, great and small, standing before the throne, and books were opened. Then another book was opened, which is the book of life. And the dead were judged by what was written in the books, according to what they had done. And the sea gave up the dead who were in it, Death and Hades gave up the dead who were in them, and they were judged, each one of them, according to what they had done. Then Death and Hades were thrown into the lake of fire. This is the second death, the lake of fire. And if anyone's name was not found written in the book of life, he was thrown into the lake of fire (Rev. 20:11-15).

Just as there is an intermediate heaven called "paradise," there is an intermediate "lake of fire." We could spend a lot of ink and paper on this and, in the process, spend hours nuancing the concept. But suffice it to say hades (sometimes wrongly translated "hell") in the New Testament is the realm of the dead. When the Great White Throne Judgment occurs, death and hades give up their dead (the unrighteous), who are cast into the lake of fire. We simply cannot fathom how terrible that will be, but it will be terrible, and it is real.

People often ask, "Do you think hell (and they're really referring to the lake of fire) is literally fire?" And I respond, "Yes, and then some." Just as words are inadequate to represent all the beauty and glory of heaven (streets of gold ... there we walk on what our culture most values here), so words are inadequate to represent all the terror and horror of the lake of fire, the place of eternal punishment.

While I have no problem embracing the view that the fires of hell should be taken literally, I think it's of utmost importance to recognize the larger issue that hell is separation from God. But that doesn't mean I don't believe the fire is *real*. Not surprisingly, many Christian leaders differ on the question of whether the lake of fire is literal or figurative.

Charles Spurgeon, for example preached about hell to his congregation in London:

Thine heart beating high with fever, thy pulse rattling at an enormous rate in agony, thy limbs cracking like the martyrs in the fire and yet unburnt, thyself put in a vessel of hot oil, pained yet coming out undestroyed, all thy veins becoming a road for the hot feet of pain to travel on, every nerve a string on which the devil shall ever play his diabolical tune.[7]

Contrast Spurgeon's thoughts with the words of Billy Graham:

The only thing I could say for sure is that hell means separation from God. We are separated from his light, from his fellowship. That is going to be hell. When it comes to a literal fire, I don't preach it because I'm not sure about it. When the Scripture uses fire concerning hell, that is possibly an illustration of how terrible it's going to be — not fire but something worse, a thirst for God that cannot be quenched.[8]

There are two major views of hell: *conditionalism (annihilationism)* and *traditionalism*.[9] *Conditionalism* is the view that the punishment in hell concludes as people are destroyed in hell; they simply "are no more." The second view is *traditionalism*. This is the idea that the punishment in hell lasts forever.

Those who hold the conditional view argue that the Greek word *aionios*, often translated "eternal," should be rendered "of long duration." On the contrary, as Lewis Sperry Chafer notes, "One passage alone, 'and these shall go away into everlasting punishment: but the righteous into life eternal' (Matt. 25:46) — demonstrates the truth that the word *aionios* means unending condition for one class as much as for the other."[10]

Hell (ultimately the *lake of fire*) is the final destination of those who reject Christ. I believe that eternal bliss lasts forever and eternal punishment lasts forever. *The Baptist Faith & Message 2000* states it this way: "The unrighteous will be consigned to Hell, the place of everlasting punishment. The righteous in their resurrected and glorified bodies will receive their reward and will dwell forever in Heaven with the Lord."[11]

YOU DON'T HAVE TO GO TO HELL; YOU CAN GO TO HEAVEN!

For God did not send his Son into the world to condemn the world, but in order that the world might be saved through him (John 3:17).

So many people who oppose Christianity say, "I wouldn't want to believe in a God who is so vengeful that he sends people to hell." They miss the point. God doesn't send people to hell; people send *themselves* to hell by willingly rejecting Jesus. God has provided a way of escape from his wrath and judgment. God has provided a home in heaven for those who repent of their sin and believe in his Son, Jesus.

Verse 17 makes it abundantly clear. Jesus didn't come to condemn the world but to save the world.

Let's say you're in a burning house, and I walk into that house, extend my hand, invite you take my hand and ask you to let me lead you to safety. If you say, "No thank you," and you perish in the fire, did I choose that ending for you, or did you? If I provide the way of escape, offer to guide you through the process, and even pledge to stay with you the whole way, if you refuse my offer, have I caused your demise or have you?

Listen to me: We're condemned already! We're sinners. We're sinners by *nature* and by *choice*. We're born in sin, and in time we choose to sin. "Sin involves not only evil acts, but also 'fixation on the self ... we are caught fast in the self.'"[12] But God provides a way out for us. Enter Jesus. Jesus, who has always existed, left the home office of heaven, robed up in flesh as a man, lived a perfect sinless life, and on the cross of Calvary laid down his life for humanity. If we don't accept his sacrifice, and we miss heaven and go to hell, did God send us to hell or did we send ourselves?

EVERYONE IS ALREADY BOUND FOR HEAVEN OR HELL

Whoever believes in him is not condemned, but whoever does not believe is condemned already, because he has not believed in the name of the only Son of God (John 3:18).

One major problem our culture faces is that, when it's convenient or self-serving, people act as if they believe, and they act as if everyone else has believed. Not long ago, the first pastor with whom I served, Dale Prince, went to heaven. His daughter, Paula, shared a video of one of his last sermons. Prince preached that sermon on March 1, 2020, just a month before his eighty-sixth birthday, and just nine months before he died. He was talking about how he read the obituaries every day. And he said something I have said so often, "Have you ever noticed everybody that dies goes to heaven? Everybody in the obituaries goes to heaven. I've never read of anybody going to hell. Everybody that dies in our culture, they all go to heaven."[13]

The Bible is clear: Those who believe in Jesus go to heaven; those who don't go to hell. Jesus claims his exclusivity in terms of being the "only way" for people to be made righteous, and thus prepared for heaven. He says in John 14:6, *"I am the way, and the truth, and the life. No one comes to the Father except through me."*

Hollywood royalty Oprah Winfrey disagrees. In fact, she famously said, "There are millions of ways to be a human being and many paths to what you call God. There couldn't possibly be just one way."[14] Oprah and her ilk only believe *part* of the truth. Oprah says that you can believe in Jesus and get to heaven. But she also says Jesus isn't the *only* way to heaven. Well, Jesus said he is. So, who are you going to believe: Oprah or Jesus?

I've heard a lot of people say through the years, "I can't believe there's only one way." My response is, "I can't believe there is even one way! Thank God he made one way available for undeserving people like me to be forgiven!"

John 3:18 makes it abundantly clear: Jesus didn't come to condemn the world; the world was condemned already. To believe in the "name" of Jesus is to trust in him, to trust in his character. Right now, every person who has the mental capacity and cognitive maturity to understand right and wrong and the concept of sin, and who has not believed in Jesus, is bound for hell.

I don't debate according to the rules of debate or philosophize according to the rules of philosophy. The reason I don't is not because I don't respect those disciplines; I do. But the problem is this: a person can be right according to the rules but wrong in his or her conclusions. I learned that the hard way. I could win the debate every time but really get nowhere with people in the process.

But here's what I'm going to tell you: it simply stands to reason that this present life on Earth isn't all there is. The vastness, complexity, order, and beauty of the universe screams to us to get ready; this is all just the prelude. This is only the opening act of the play. To think that all of this was put together for our short stint on Earth, and then after seven or eight decades we go to dust and that's it ... no way!

At some level, this illustrates more than one "elephant in the room." The first one is the fact that we're going to die. Typically, nobody wants to think about that or talk about that much. But the other elephant in the room is what we believe about heaven and hell. We believe there is a place called heaven, where God dwells, and will dwell, with the redeemed of all the ages. And there is a real place called hell, where all who have rejected Jesus spend eternity, separated from God in everlasting punishment.

Further, we believe there's only one way to get to heaven. And the world simply can't tolerate this kind of narrowmindedness. We believe — and orthodox Christianity declares — that only by repentance from sin and faith in Jesus does one go to heaven.

Speaking of Jesus, the Bible says, *"But to all who did receive him, who believed in his name, he gave the right to become children of God"* (John 1:12). It doesn't say be kind to your neighbor and you'll go to heaven. It doesn't say go to church and you'll go to heaven. It doesn't say give away all you have to the poor and you'll go to heaven. It says, *"But to all who did receive him, who believed in his name, he gave the right to become children of God."*

According to Scripture, there is a book that contains the names of all the redeemed. It's called *The Lamb's Book of Life.* Our name isn't in that book because we're good. The only way our name gets in the book, and the only reason we get to go to heaven and avoid hell, is because of what one man did: the God-man, Jesus. Because Jesus died on the cross, he is the propitiation for our sins.

1 John 2:2 says of Jesus, *"He is the propitiation for our sins, and not for ours only but also for the sins of the whole world."* Propitiation means "a sacrifice that bears God's wrath and turns it to favor." That's what Jesus' death on the cross did; he turned God's wrath to favor. So, we experience grace, mercy, forgiveness, and eternity in heaven, all because of what the God-man, Jesus, did.

My dad's name was Kin, just like mine. No, this isn't a typo. He spelled it a little differently than I spell my name. My dad was a good man, but he became a great man after he became a follower of Jesus in his early fifties. My dad died March 13, 2018, at the age of eighty-nine. The Saturday before he died, around 4:45 in the afternoon, my sister, Lindalu, and my wife, Lori, and I were in the living room with him. Dad was sleeping in a hospital bed under hospice care. Now, we had had some really powerful and beautiful moments with him already by that point.

I was sitting on the sofa, which we had placed just to the side of the bed. He had been out of it for quite a while. Dad began to blink his eyes and slowly open them. So Lindalu, Lori, and I stood up at his bedside. I stroked his hair, and his eyes found focus. He looked at me and smiled. My dad was dying and he smiled. We told him we loved him, and he said what he's always emphatically said, "I love all you guys!"

I asked him, "Dad, are you in any pain?" He shook his head. And then my dad smiled. He had a faraway look in his eyes, like he was looking right past us, and he said, "You wouldn't believe it."

I said, "What's that, Dad?"

He said, "This is so beautiful! You wouldn't believe it!" Then he said, "This is paradise! It's gorgeous! It's perfection!"

Now, I had been awake a long, long time at this point. We were all very tired, keeping vigil at my dad's bedside. So, I turned to Lori and asked, "Did he say what I thought he said?"

And she said, "Yes!"

For the record, I believe what the Bible says in Hebrews 9:27a — *"And just as it is appointed for man to die once ..."* I don't think people die, go all the way to heaven or hell and then have a choice to come back to Earth for another round. I think we die and go to heaven or hell, and that's it. But I do believe sometimes God gives dying people a glimpse of what they're about to experience. I believe this is what happened to my dad, and I'm grateful I was there to hear about what he was seeing.

While dying, my dad said, "This is so beautiful! You wouldn't believe it! This is paradise! It's gorgeous! It's perfection!"

I immediately took out my phone and sent myself a text with Dad's exact words. What a gift God gave to my dad, and in so doing, my dad's faith extended a gift to me because I was able to know some of what he was about to experience.

And then he closed his eyes for a moment or two. He opened them, looked at me, smiled and said, "And just think; one man did all this!" It took a minute to sink in. He was talking about Jesus, and he was right. One man did it all; one man made it possible! As Acts 4:12 reminds us, *"And there is salvation in no one else, for there is no other name under heaven given among men by which we must be saved."*

QUESTIONS FOR PERSONAL OR GROUP STUDY

1. What do you say to someone who says he can't believe there could only be one way to be made right with God?
2. What do you believe about heaven and hell?

3. How would you respond if someone asked, "How could a good God send people to hell?"
4. Do you believe heaven and hell are for all eternity? Why or why not?
5. Why do you think the Bible describes an "intermediate state" between physical death and future resurrection?

BURIAL VS. CREMATION

DOES IT MATTER HOW WE CARE FOR A CORPSE?

In 1846, former president John Quincy Adams suffered a stroke. Although he returned to Congress the following year, his health was clearly failing. Daniel Webster described his last meeting with Adams:

> Someone, a friend of his, came in and made particular inquiry of his health. Adams answered, "I inhabit a weak, frail, decayed tenement; battered by the winds and broken in upon by the storms, and from all I can learn, the landlord does not intend to repair."[1]

One of the most poignant stories I've read about death came from a preacher from another era, a giant of the faith named Donald Grey Barnhouse:

> I was driving with my children to my wife's funeral where I was to preach the sermon. As we came into one small town there strode down in front of us a truck that came to stop before a red light. It was the biggest truck I ever saw in my life, and the sun was shining on it at just the right angle that took its shadow and spread it across the snow on the field beside it. As the shadow covered that field, I

said, "Look children at that truck, and look at its shadow. If you had to be run over, which would you rather be run over by? Would you rather be run over by the truck or by the shadow?" My youngest child said, "The shadow couldn't hurt anybody." "That's right," I continued, "and death is a truck, but the shadow is all that ever touches the Christian. The truck ran over the Lord Jesus. Only the shadow is gone over mother."[2]

These thoughts serve as a stark reminder of what each of us inevitably faces. If you're a Christian, you don't believe death is the end. I know death is not a particularly pleasant subject with which to deal, yet there are some things that need to be noted. Particularly, many people wonder, practically speaking, about what to do after someone's death. Should there be a funeral? What's the difference between a "funeral" and a "celebration of life" or a "memorial service"? Is a visitation or a "wake" an outdated concept? Is it helpful toward healing, or is it barbaric, to have people view a dead body? What are the differences between burial and cremation? With the ever-increasing popularity of cremation, many Christians are even wondering, "Is cremation an acceptable option for a believer?" Why hasn't cremation been popular among Christians until recently?

Let me clarify, lest someone jumps to an inaccurate conclusion. I know that families sometimes bury the ashes of their loved ones who've been cremated. That certainly constitutes *burying* someone. When I reference burial in this chapter, however, I'm talking about the process of placing a body in a casket and then putting the body to rest in a grave or an above-ground facility (columbarium, crypt, mausoleum). Whether the casket is placed above ground or in the ground, we typically think of burial as a process that involves embalming, whereby the body is preserved. Each state has laws about these sorts of things; embalming isn't always required.

DOCTRINE VS. PREFERENCE

The apostle Paul writes:

> *For I delivered to you as of first importance what I also received: that Christ died for our sins in accordance with the Scriptures, that he was buried, that he was raised on the third day in accordance with the Scriptures* (1 Cor. 15:3-4).

That text is the gospel. If I had one last opportunity to preach one last sermon, or one last opportunity to write for which I would be remembered, burial vs. cremation wouldn't be my choice. I would like to think my main effort would be on the gospel itself. But once we know the gospel, we still have experiences in life that make us ask some questions: "What about _____?" You can fill in the blank. So, what about burial? What about cremation? Which is right?

It's probably good I don't know when I'll deliver my last sermon or write my last piece of correspondence. If I had one last chance to preach one last sermon, I would preach Christ and him crucified. Now you may say, "Ken, that's the only thing you should ever preach." And in many ways, you're right, but back to the idea of context. If I only preach how to be saved, then the people to whom I preach would know how to be saved but wouldn't have the instruction necessary for how to live once saved.

That's the impetus behind a book like this: we must learn to live as God's people. The whole counsel of God's Word offers a treasure trove of knowledge for how to live. But the most important thing you'll ever hear, and the most important sermon I could ever preach, is quite simply the gospel of Jesus.

The gospel is, in fact, the first-tier doctrine of Christendom. It's a non-negotiable teaching. It's the information that matters most. You see, you can get to heaven without hearing about creation, sexism, gender bending, depression, cremation, and so forth, but you can't get there without hearing the gospel.

So, why take the time to deal with something like burial vs.

cremation? Simple. Because we're not all going to die tomorrow, so we need to know *how to live* as believers. Your kids need to know they're created in the image of God and that God doesn't make mistakes. Their gender, among other things, is one of his good gifts to them. That's true, even if their university professor says otherwise. They need to be armed with the truth. They need to know that the resurrection really happened. And they need to know creation happened in the way Scripture records it.

We also need to be taught the discipline of giving. The church doesn't run on our winsome personalities. It takes money. And if nobody is giving, a whole lot less gets done. As Jason Allen, president of Midwestern Baptist Theological Seminary, often says, "The Bible reminds us that where there is no vision the people perish. But remember, too, where there is no money the vision perishes."

So, all this is to say, burial vs. cremation is a discussion of something other than a first-tier doctrine. In other words, we can't fellowship as brothers and sisters in Christ if you don't believe in Jesus, but we can fellowship as brothers and sisters if you believe in cremation and I don't. I recognize there are different views on this particular ancillary issue, and I'm not looking for a fight; I have a mortgage to pay, after all. But I do sense it's a topic worthy of discussion.

My goal simply is to inform, to offer information via biblical insights. Whether you change your mind after reading this chapter or remain firmly convinced of your position, you can't undo what's been done. And remember, this is a secondary issue, anyway. Whatever you think about it after the fact doesn't change how we should feel about and respect each other.

CARE OF THE BODY IS A CHRISTIAN CONCERN

Or do you not know that your body is a temple of the Holy Spirit within you, whom you have from God? You are not your own, for you were bought with a price. So glorify God in your body (1 Cor. 6:19-20).

If you go back and read 1 Corinthians 6 from verse 12 forward, you recognize Paul is talking about caring for our bodies. He zeroes in on sexual immorality, among other things, and how it's a sin against one's own body. But his closing words in this chapter are vital for us as we consider what to do with our bodies in death. I'm not in any way implying the Holy Spirit stays within a body once death occurs; I don't believe that. But, most certainly, it is the Christian understanding that the body is the temple of the Holy Spirit. Paul makes that clear.

So how we care for the body, the temple, really does matter. And it would make sense that it would matter in death as well as in life. In years past, burial was the norm, although cremation, with growing secularization in our culture, has become more popular in recent years. So, what is burial? Webster's Dictionary defines *burial* as "the act or process of burying."

Burial most often takes place underground, but sometimes people are buried above ground. Until recently in our culture, when we talked of burial, we envisioned a body placed in a casket, then the casket placed in a vault that is in the ground. Cremation, by definition, is "the disposal of a dead person's body by burning it to ashes; the incineration of a dead body." Sometimes the ashes are kept in an urn. Sometimes they're buried. Sometimes they're scattered around a place that held significant meaning for the deceased.

There are many different reasons burial vs. cremation has become more prominently discussed. Certainly, there are religious objections to cremation, as well as religious objections to opulent caskets and funerals. Perhaps the biggest "game-changer" on the American scene with respect to funerals grew out of the 1963 book *The American Way of Death* by Jessica Mitford. The book presented a scathing indictment of the funeral industry, accusing it of exploitation. Mitford asked, among other things, "What is the psychological, sociological, and religious significance of embalming in American rituals of death?"[3]

The book had a significant nationwide impact and caused many to look at their local funeral homes and funeral directors differently.

Was an embalmed body necessary? Was a funeral service even necessary? These and other questions began swirling. How a culture deals with the body of a deceased person is tied to a lot of cultural mores. Christians don't necessarily feel compelled to run from our culture's traditions, yet we see Scripture as the more important influencer over our practices.

In Philippians 1:20, the apostle Paul says he wants to magnify Christ *"in my body, whether by life or by death."* The point is that we realize God owns this temple; we belong to him, and we want to exercise care related to our body in life *and* in death. Our culture still recognizes this to a degree. Most certainly, combat veterans understand this. Why is it that men and women risk their lives to retrieve the body of a dead comrade in the midst of the horror of artillery fire and hand grenades? Because they recognize a sacredness of the body. The flesh and blood *matter.*

In Romans 8:11, Paul writes:

> *If the Spirit of him who raised Jesus from the dead dwells in you, he who raised Christ Jesus from the dead will also give life to your mortal bodies through his Spirit who dwells in you.*

At the very least, we see this as an incentive to take extra care of the body, even in death. Perhaps Christians have gone too far in this direction, embracing materialism as we honor the dead.

In 1950, Douglas Parker (no relation to this author) published an article in the *Michigan Christian Advocate* entitled, "How Pagan Are Our Funerals?" In the article, Parker wrote:

> I once heard a minister decrying the use of expensive caskets. His righteous indignation was considerably weakened, however, by the fact that he took great pride in encasing his own corpulent body in a new Buick for his work and pleasure. Expensive caskets and more expensive automobiles are simply a sign of our gadget-studded and materially dependent culture. Families take pride in caskets. Granted that is the wrong emphasis, but so is our whole culture.

When all Christians agree to take the chrome and luxuries off their automobiles, then we shall have a right to plead for simpler caskets.[4]

Perhaps with the growing trend of cremation, the pendulum swings in the opposite direction. Does cremation indicate too much of a dismissive attitude toward death and the body? Cremation involves the burning of the human body. Bear in mind, this is a second-tier issue for believers. The Bible does not say, "You shall not cremate," just as it doesn't say, "You shall embalm, purchase a casket, and bury." I do have to note, however, in every situation with which I'm familiar in Scripture, in order to honorably dispose of the dead, the individual was buried. That's at least worth a pause.

For example, Deuteronomy 34:5-6 recounts the death of Moses:

So Moses the servant of the LORD died there in the land of Moab, according to the word of the LORD, and he buried him in the valley in the land of Moab opposite Beth-peor; but no one knows the place of his burial to this day.

The context indicates that God is the one who buries Moses. Please don't miss this: *burial* is how God disposes of the body. Burial is, in fact, highlighted often in the Bible, and I think we do well to take note of that. In fact, the body of Moses is such a big deal that Jude makes mention of Michael the archangel contending with the devil in a dispute over it (Jude 9).

A whole chapter of the Bible is dedicated to the burial of the body of Sarah, Abraham's wife. Jacob's death and burial takes the space of a half chapter in the Bible. So even though we might say, when talking about our death, "It doesn't matter to me; I'll be gone," that's a bit of avoidance. If for no other reason, we need to think through these things so that those who are left to pick up the pieces once we're gone have a clear understanding of what we thought and what they might deem best.

SYMBOLISM RELATED TO THE HUMAN BODY ABOUNDS

Let's look at a couple of biblical texts related to death and burial:

And what you sow is not the body that is to be, but a bare kernel, perhaps of wheat or of some other grain (1 Cor. 15:37).

So it is with the resurrection of the dead. What is sown is perishable; what is raised is imperishable. It is sown in dishonor; it is raised in glory. It is sown in weakness; it is raised in power. It is sown a natural body; it is raised a spiritual body (1 Cor. 15:42-44).

Burial is heavy with symbolism. Paul speaks of burial as a picture of being sown in the ground. When resurrection occurs at the return of Christ, what is sown in the ground (the body) comes out with far grander beauty. Burial, sowing the seed of the body, is a biblical picture of belief in resurrection. At the risk of sounding offensive, many would say cremation tends to weaken that biblical imagery.

Now, let me address something important that you might be questioning. I want to be clear in saying that God puts back together whatever needs to be put back together in the end. Terrible accidents, world wars, and events like the tragedy of 9/11 won't keep those who perished from experiencing the same glorified resurrection body as those who are buried in a casket.

Unlike those whose bodies are destroyed in death, what we're talking about here has to do with a choice most of us have. The biblical record reflects death and laying a body to rest in terms of *sleeping*. In other words, while the soul of a believer goes to be with God at death, the body of that person awaits the day of resurrection.

Paul writes in 1 Thessalonians 4:15, "*We who are alive, who are left until the coming of the Lord, will not precede those who have fallen asleep.*" Sleep is a biblical euphemism for death. The imagery of a dead body is reminiscent of sleep. That imagery is lost in cremation. According to Timothy George, early Christian gravesites were called *coemeteria* (cemeteries), which literally means "sleeping places," reflecting belief in a future resurrection.[5]

So, there's beautiful symbolism in Scripture and in Christian practice related to our care of the body in death. For example, we know the dead don't need clothes. Yet, not only is there dignity in burying someone fully dressed, but it symbolizes our belief they will live yet again!

Several scriptural thoughts lead us away from the idea of *burning* and turn our thoughts toward *burying*. One is that the body is always viewed as important, both now and in the life to come; we've seen this already. The other thought is related to fire and what it means both now and in the life to come.

In the Bible, using fire to consume the body on earth was a contemptible practice. It was viewed as scornful treatment. Again, let me say, I recognize for those of you who have had a loved one cremated, that has not been the case for your family. But burning bodies as we read in the Scripture, at some level, is related to judgment. In Joshua 7:24-25, the family of Achan is stoned to death, and their bodies are burned in what is clearly connected to judgment. Amos 2:1 records the sin of Moab in burning to lime the bones of the king of Edom.

Further, biblically, we see that after death, fire is a picture of punishment — specifically, a picture of hell. According to Jesus in Matthew 5:22, hell is a place of fire that is meant for the resurrected bodies and souls of unregenerate persons to experience.

So, the picture the Bible gives is favorable toward burial. It captures more of the symbolism that comforts us related to death. A body being sown back into the ground, and the imagery of the dead person at rest, offer more comforting symbolism than cremation.

In his book *Rest in Peace*, about the modern-day funeral industry, Gary Laderman speaks candidly about the importance of the comfort that a well-preserved body may offer grieving families. He writes of the body, "It is the final memory picture which remains with family and friends as long as they live, that can be a comfort to them or a source of horror."[6]

I can say from personal experience what a comfort it was to see the way my parents' bodies looked, just prior to burial, compared to the way they looked in their final days. They had both experienced severe illness, and their faces and bodies bore the marks of such. But in death, thanks to the great care given them by those preparing their bodies for the funeral, our family was given a positive visual memory because we were able to see, in many ways, how they *used* to look ... before sickness ravaged their bodies. Unfortunately, cremation doesn't offer that opportunity, and much of the spiritual symbolism related to the body is lost in the absence of burial.

MAKE INFORMED CHOICES

Regardless of your leanings, either toward burial or cremation, it's important to know all the facts before you're in the position to make such an important decision. If we're honest, cremation is a soft way to describe the practice. At least when we say *burial*, the word denotes what's actually taking place. The word *cremation*, meanwhile, somewhat softens the reality. Before you die, or before your loved one dies, long before you're faced with making a choice, read about the practice of cremation and the practice of burial. I believe that will help you make an informed choice.

Suffice it to say, some history of cremation is attached to more secular thinking than spiritual thinking. According to Timothy George, the first cremation in America took place in 1876.[7] Readings from Charles Darwin and the Hindu scriptures accompanied the service. For many years, the church rejected cremation as an option, not viewing it as an acceptable alternative to burial.

One of the more compelling arguments for cremation is economic feasibility; that is, it's simply less expensive. I know that to be true, and I'm not sitting in judgment of any family that has made the choice to cremate based on a financial situation. I know from personal experience that burial in any form is expensive. I would simply say that if economics is a significant factor in your decision, figure out how to avoid that being the deciding factor.

Let me close this chapter with John Piper's words on the subject:

I am encouraging churches to cultivate a Christian counter-culture where people expect simple, less expensive funerals and burials, and where we all pitch in so that a Christian burial is not a financial hardship on anyone. And because of the biblical pointers [about this] I am arguing that God-centered, gospel-rooted burial is preferable to cremation. Preferable. Not commanded, but rich with Christian truth that will become a clearer and clearer witness as our society becomes less and less Christian."[8]

As I finish this chapter, it's an overcast Kansas City day, and this is a really dark subject. So, let me leave you with some good news. Whatever is left, or if nothing is left, of a Christian's "earthly tent" (body) in the end ... I am confident God will transform it into a glorious, imperishable, resurrection body!

QUESTIONS FOR PERSONAL OR GROUP STUDY

1. What types of symbolism related to burial does Scripture utilize?
2. Given that he had all the options in the universe at his disposal, does the fact that God buried Moses (Deut. 34:5-6) influence your view about burial vs. cremation?
3. How does the growing trend toward cremation due to cost factors influence the way you view the practice?
4. On matters where Scripture is not definitive, how do you determine the so-called best practice?
5. How might the church help a family in need if the family's desire is burial for their loved one, but they can only afford cremation?

NOTES

CHAPTER 1 — WHY TRUST THE BIBLE?

1. W. A. Criswell, *Why I Preach that the Bible is Literally True* (Nashville, TN: Broadman & Holman Publishers, 1995), 17.
2. Criswell, 36.
3. Criswell, 22.
4. J. Scott Duvall and J. Daniel Hays, *Grasping God's Word* (Grand Rapids, MI: Zondervan, 2012), 25.
5. These names and dates come from a wide variety of commonly available sources such as "The Biographical Test Updated," *Christian Research Journal*, Vol. 35, No. 03 (2012); *The New Evidence that Demands a Verdict*, Josh McDowell; and *How We Got the Bible*, Neil R. Lightfoot.
6. Duvall and Hays, 34.
7. Norman L. Geisler and Frank Turek, *I Don't Have Enough Faith to Be an Atheist* (Wheaton, IL: Crossway, 2004), 228.
8. Criswell, 135.

CHAPTER 2 — CREATION VS. EVOLUTION

1. *Resource*, July/August, 1990.
2. John MacArthur, *The Battle for the Beginning* (Nashville, TN: Thomas Nelson Publishing, 2005), 25.
3. William W. Klein, Craig L. Blomberg, and Robert L. Hubbard, *Introduction to Biblical Interpretation* (Dallas, TX: Word Publishing, 1993), 21-51.
4. MacArthur, 12.
5. "Age of the Earth," https://nationalgeographic.org/topics/resource-library-age-earth/?q=&page=1&per_page=25.
6. MacArthur, 20-23.
7. *Treatises on Various Subjects*, The Fathers of the Church, Vol. 16 (ed. CUA Press, 2010).
8. Ps. 8:1-9.
9. MacArthur, 11.
10. Richard Dawkins, *A Devil's Chaplain* (London: Weidenfeld & Nicolson, 2003), 81.
11. MacArthur, 11.
12. MacArthur, 14.
13. Stephen Jay Gould, *Ever Since Darwin* (New York, NY: Norton, 1977), 26.
14. MacArthur, 33.
15. MacArthur, 77.
16. John M. Frame, *No Other God*, (Phillipsburg, NJ: P & R Publishing, 2001), 15-24.

CHAPTER 3 — SOCIAL MEDIA AND HOW WE SPEAK

1. Robert Robinson, *Come, Thou Fount of Every Blessing*, The Baptist Hymnal, No. 15, (Nashville, TN: Convention Press, 1991).
2. Dan Graves, "Did Robert Robinson Wander as He

Feared?" https://www.christianity.com/church/church-history/timeline/1701-1800/did-robert-robinson-wander-as-he-feared-11630313.html.

CHAPTER 4 — SAME-SEX ATTRACTION

1. https://www.healthline.com/health/different-genders#2.
2. See *The Baptist Faith & Message 2000*, Article III.
3. https://healthresearchfunding.org/15-notable-ambiguous-genitalia-statistics/.
4. Karen Mason, *Preventing Suicide: A Handbook for Pastors, Chaplains and Pastoral Counselors* (Downers Grove, IL: InterVarsity Press, 2014), 36.
5. Mason, 38.
6. Owen Strachan, *Reenchanting Humanity: A Theology of Mankind* (Geanies House, Fearn, Ross-shire, Great Britain, 2019), 140.
7. https://stmuhistorymedia.org/ancient-greek-pederasty-education-or-exploitation/.
8. J. Alan Branch, *Born This Way? Homosexuality, Science, and the Scriptures* (Wooster, OH: Weaver Book Company, 2016) 17-29.
9. Branch, 20.
10. Branch, 21.
11. Branch. 29.
12. Branch, 37.
13. https://www.cbsnews.com/news/president-obama-says-sasha-and-malia-influenced-his-stance-on-same-sex-marriage/.
14. http://www.renewamerica.com/columns/fischer/101126.
15. https://www.cdc.gov/msmhealth/STD.htm.
16. https://academic.oup.com/ije/article/30/6/1499/651821.
17. https://repository.sbts.edu/bitstream/handle/10392/2393/2004-04-20.pdf?sequence=1&isAllowed=y.

CHAPTER 5 — RACISM AND SEXISM

1. Danny Akin, Richard Caldwell, H. B. Charles, Jr., Christian George, Jim Hamilton, Carl Hargrove, Juan Sanchez, and Owen Strachan, *A Biblical Answer for Racial Unity* (The Woodlands, TX: Kress Biblical Resources, 2017), 100.
2. *Ibid.*
3. Akin et. al., 101.
4. *The Baptist Faith & Message 2000*, Article XVII (Nashville, TN: LifeWay Christian Resources, 2000), 21.
5. Akin et. al., 100.
6. *Our Daily Bread*, March 6, 1994 (Grand Rapids, MI: Our Daily Bread Ministries).
7. Owen Strachan, "Divine Order in a Chaotic Age: On Women Preaching," https://www.patheos.com/blogs/thoughtlife/2019/05/divine-order-in-a-chaotic-age-on-women-preaching/, May 17, 2019.
8. Abraham Kuyper, *Stone Lectures* at Princeton (1898).
9. Mary Kassian, "Complementarianism for Dummies," https://www.thegospelcoalition.org/article/complementarianism-for-dummies/, Sept. 4, 2012.

CHAPTER 6 — ALCOHOL AND MARIJUANA

1. https://www.dea.gov/drug-scheduling.
2. *Ibid.*
3. Peter Masters, *Should Christians Drink? The Case for Total Abstinence* (London: The Wakeman Trust, 2001), 76.
4. Masters, 41.
5. Masters, 19.
6. Masters, 20.
7. Masters, 21.
8. *Ibid.*
9. ESV Study Bible, 2411.
10. Masters, 7.

CHAPTER 7 — WHAT'S WRONG WITH GAMBLING?

1. Samantha Gluck, *Phases of a Gambling Addiction*, https://www.healthyplace.com/addictions/gambling-addiction/phases-of-a-gambling-addiction, April 23, 2019.
2. Martha C. Shaw, Kelsie T. Forbush, Jessica Schlinder, Eugene Rosenman, and Donald W. Black, *The Effect of Pathological Gambling on Families, Marriages, and Children*, https://www.cambridge.org/core/journals/cns-spectrums/article/effect-of-pathological-gambling-on-families-marriages-and-children/58D1EF6DE18E978872B1B97F1A8C8E6D, Aug. 2007.
3. Dylan Matthews, *Studies: Casinos Bring Jobs, but also Crime, Bankruptcy, and Even Suicide*, https://www.washingtonpost.com/news/ wonk/wp/2012/10/30/studies-casinos-bring-jobs-but-also-crime-bankruptcy-and-even-suicide/, Oct. 30, 2012.
4. Jan Hogan, *Treating Gambling Addiction as an Illness in Las Vegas*, https://www.reviewjournal.com/life/treating-gambling-addiction-as-an-illness-in-las-vegas/, Sept. 23, 2015.
5. *USA Gambling Statistics*, https://nogamblingaddiction.com/ addiction-statistics.htm.
6. Brainy Quote, https://brainyquote.com/ quotes/joseph_conrad_136254.

CHAPTER 8 — DEPRESSION HURTS

1. Irwin G. Sarason and Barbara R. Sarason, *Abnormal Psychology: The Problem of Maladaptive Behavior* (Upper Saddle River, NJ: Pearson Prentice Hall, 2005), 331-371.
2. Sarason and Sarason, 336.
3. Sarason and Sarason, 344.
4. Sarason and Sarason, 334.

5. W. Sibley Towner, "The Book of Ecclesiastes," *The New Interpreter's Bible* (Nashville, TN: Abingdon Press, 1997), 271-272.

6. Towner, 272.

7. Sarason and Sarason, 337-341.

8. Sarason and Sarason, 337.

9. Sarason and Sarason, 339.

10. Sarason and Sarason, 337-341.

11. Sarason and Sarason, 334-336.

12. Jonathan D. Holmes, *Counsel for Couples: A Biblical and Practical Guide for Marriage Counseling* (Grand Rapids, MI: Zondervan, 2019), 44.

13. Zach Eswine, *Spurgeon's Sorrows: Realistic Hope for those who Suffer from Depression* (Fearn, Ross-shire, Scotland, UK: Christian Focus Publications, 2014), 68-69.

14. Eswine, 69.

15. Robert W. Kellemen, *Gospel-Centered Counseling* (Grand Rapids, MI: Zondervan, 2014), 203.

16. Eswine, 112.

17. Eswine, 112.

CHAPTER 9 — THE SANCTITY OF LIFE

1. https://www.azquotes.com/author/14530-Mother_Teresa/tag/abortion.

2. http://www.pagadiandiocese.org/2016/04/25/very-surprising-quotes-from-abortion-doctors-make-it-clear-abortion-is-wrong/.

3. https://www.sbc.net/resource/library/resolutions/on-the-sanctity-of-human-life/.

4. John J. Davis, *Abortion and the Christian* (Phillipsburg, NJ: Presbyterian & Reformed Publishing, 1984), 43.

5. Randy Alcorn, *ProLife Answers to ProChoice Arguments* (Sisters, OR: Multnomah Publishers, 1992), 65-66.

6. Alcorn, 230.
7. https://time.com/4384947/dolly-sheep-cloning-history/.
8. https://www.ncbi.nlm.nih.gov/pmc/articles/PMC1174766/.
9. *Ibid.*
10. https://www.theatlantic.com/ideas/archive/2019/06/noa-pothoven-and-dutch-euthanasia-system/591262/.
11. https://www.westernjournal.com/toddlers-can-killed-shocking-new-euthanasia-law-proposal/.

CHAPTER 10 — MARRIAGE

1. Andreas Köstenberger, *Marriage and the Family: Biblical Essentials* (Wheaton, IL: Crossway, 2012), 9.
2. Köstenberger, 12.
3. Alistair Begg, *Lasting Love: How to Avoid Marital Failure* (Chicago, IL: Moody Publishers, 1997), 93.
4. Köstenberger, 38.
5. Köstenberger, 39-44.
6. John R. W. Stott, "Marriage and Divorce," in *Involvement*, vol. 2 (Old Tappan, NJ, Revell, 1984), 163.
7. Köstenberger, 39-40.
8. Köstenberger, 40.
9. Gary Chapman, *Covenant Marriage* (Nashville, TN: Broadman, 2003), 8-10.
10. J. D. Douglas and Merrill C. Tenney, ed., "Covenant," *The New International Dictionary of the Bible* (Grand Rapids, MI: Zondervan Publishing House, 1987), 237.
11. Gary Smalley and John Trent, *Love is a Decision: Proven Techniques to Keep Your Marriage Alive and Lively* (Nashville, TN: Thomas Nelson, 1989), 35-40.

CHAPTER 11 — DIVORCE, REMARRIAGE, AND COHABITATION

1. CSB Study Bible (Nashville, TN: Holman Bible Publishers), 1820.
2. *Ibid.*
3. https://www.baptistpress.com/resource-library/news/facebook-considers-whether-gateway-is-hate-group/.
4. *Ibid.*
5. https://www.umc.org/en/content/ask-the-umc-what-happened-at-general-conference.
6. https://www.umc.org/en/content/homosexuality-full-book-of-discipline-statements.
7. https://theologythinktank.com/the-call-to-be-hated/.
8. J. Carl Laney, William A. Heth, Thomas R. Edgar, and Larry Richards; H. Wayne House, ed., *Divorce and Remarriage: Four Christian Views* (Downers Grove, IL: InterVarsity Press, 1990), 186-192.
9. Daryl Wingerd, Jim Eliff, Jim Chrisman, and Steve Burchett, *Divorce and Remarriage: A Permanence View* (Kansas City, MO: Christian Communicators Worldwide, 2009), 61.
10. Andreas Köstenberger, David W. Jones, *Marriage and the Family* (Wheaton, IL: Crossway Books, 2012), 142.
11. David Instone-Brewer, *Divorce and Remarriage in the Church* (Downers Grove, IL: InterVarsity Press, 2003), 107.
12. Instone-Brewer, 109.
13. Instone-Brewer, 110.
14. ESV Study Bible (Wheaton, IL: Crossway Books, 2008), 2201.
15. https://www.thespruce.com/cohabitation-facts-and-statistics-2302236.
16. *Ibid*.
17. Stephanie Pappas, "Marry or Move In Together? Brain

Knows the Difference," https://livescience.com, Feb. 14, 2014. Source: Moreland and Muehlhoff, *The God Conversation: Using Stories and Illustrations to Explain Your Faith* (Downers Grove, IL: InterVarsity Press, 2017), 152.

18. Dr. Brown, a broadcaster, seminary professor, author, and founder and president of Key Life Network, has said this on many broadcasts, and in many sermons.

CHAPTER 12 — THE PLAGUE OF PORNOGRAPHY

1. Jonathan D. Holmes, *Counsel for Couples: A Biblical and Practical Guide for Marriage Counseling* (Grand Rapids, MI: Zondervan, 2019), 138-139.

2. Patrick Carnes, *Out of the Shadows: Understanding Sexual Addiction* (Center City, MN: Hazelden, 2001), 82.

3. Sebastien Malo, "Is the Super Bowl Really the U.S.'s Biggest Sex Trafficking Magnet?" https://reuters.com/article/us-football-nfl-superbowl-trafficking-an-idUSKBN1FL6A1.

4. Carnes, 35.

5. Carnes, 14.

6. William Struthers, PhD, "The Effects of Porn on the Male Brain," https://equip.org/article/the-effects-of-porn-on-the-male-brain-3/.

7. Struthers.

8. Adam Whithnall, "Pornography Addiction Leads to Same Brain Activity as Alcoholism or Drug Abuse, Study Shows," https://independent.co.uk/life-style/health-and-families/health-news/pornography-addiction-leads-same-brain-activity-alcoholism-or-drug-abuse-study-shows-8832708.html.

9. Jim Cress, "Modern-Day Sexual Craze and Chaos: The Facts," *Christian Counseling Today*, Vol. 22, No. 1, p 35.

10. Cress, 35.

11. *Ibid.*

CHAPTER 13 — HEAVEN AND HELL

1. Anthony C. Thiselton, *Life after Death: A New Approach to Last Things* (Grand Rapids, MI/Cambridge, U.K.: William B. Eerdmans Publishing Company, 2012), 149.
2. https://thefederalist.com/2018/01/22/new-harvard-research-says-u-s-christianity-not-shrinking-growing-stronger/.
3. Quoted in N. T. Wright, *Surprised by Hope: Rethinking Heaven, the Resurrection, and the Mission of the Church* (New York, NY: HarperOne, 2008), 17.
4. Craig S. Keener, *The NIV Application Commentary: Revelation* (Grand Rapids, MI: Zondervan Publishing House, 2000), 502.
5. Randy Alcorn, *Heaven* (Wheaton, IL: Tyndale House, 2004), 52.
6. John P. Newport, *The Lion and the Lamb* (Nashville, TN: Broadman Press, 1986), 310.
7. Edward William Fudge and Robert A. Peterson, *Two Views of Hell: A Biblical & Theological Dialogue* (Downers Grove, IL: InterVarsity Press, 2000), 20.
8. *Ibid.*
9. Fudge and Peterson, 11.
10. Fudge and Peterson, 126.
11. *The Baptist Faith & Message 2000*, Article X.
12. Thiselton, 183.
13. Dale C. Prince, sermon — "The Christian's Highest Ambition," preached at Forest Hill Baptist Church, Germantown, Tenn., March 1, 2020.
14. https://www.boundless.org/faith/can-we-still-say-jesus-is-the-only-way/.

CHAPTER 14 — BURIAL VS. CREMATION

1. Gary Laderman, *Rest in Peace: A Cultural History of Death*

and the Funeral Home in Twentieth-Century America (New York, NY: Oxford University Press, 2003), xxi-xxii.

2. I've struggled to pinpoint the source, but this story often has been repeated in books such as *Tony Evans' Book of Illustrations* (Chicago: Moody Press, 2009), 72.

3. Laderman, xxii.

4. J. Douglas Parker, "How Pagan Are Our Funerals?" *Michigan Christian Advocate,* August 31, 1950, 8.

5. Timothy George, "Cremation Confusion," *Christianity Today,* May 23, 2002, 66.

6. Laderman, 23.

7. Randy Alcorn, "Thoughts on Cremation vs. Burial, and the Resurrection Question," Dec. 9, 2013, http://epm.org/blog/2013/Dec/9/cremation-burial-resurrection.

8. John Piper, "Should Christians Cremate Their Loved Ones? A Modest Proposal," April 26, 2016, http:desiringgod.org/articles/should-christians-cremate-their-loved-ones?

ABOUT KEN PARKER

 Dr. Ken Parker became the senior pastor at First Baptist Church of Kearney, Missouri, in January of 2006. Prior to coming to Kearney, he served as the founding pastor of Southpointe Family Church (SBC) in Fort Smith, Arkansas. He also served as pastor of Fianna Hills Baptist Church in Fort Smith and First Baptist Church in Union, Missouri. Before becoming a senior pastor, Ken served churches in his home state of Illinois, and in Missouri as an associate pastor with responsibilities in worship and student ministry.

He is a graduate of Missouri Baptist University (B.A. - Church Music & Vocal Performance), and a three-time graduate of Midwestern Baptist Theological Seminary (M.A. – Counseling, M.Div., and D.Min.). Parker was a trustee for ten years at Missouri Baptist University and ten years at Midwestern Seminary, where he now serves as Professor of Pastoral Ministry & Counseling. He has been a Midwestern adjunct professor since 2008.

Parker has served his denomination (the Southern Baptist Convention) on various boards and was twice elected first vice-president and twice elected president of the Missouri Baptist Convention (MBC). He currently serves as chairman of the Board of Trustees of Baptist Homes & Healthcare Ministries, an MBC-affiliated ministry headquartered in Jefferson City, Missouri.

Parker and his wife, Lori, have two adult sons; Zach (married to Chloe) and Luke, and three grandchildren: Ryann Kay, Hudson James, and Jack Andrew.